The Raven's Gift

ALSO BY JON TURK

In the Wake of the Jomon:
Stone Age Mariners and a Voyage Across the Pacific

Cold Oceans:
Adventures in Kayak, Rowboat, and Dogsled

Janice —
Because we might not
save the world
after all

Jon T

The Raven's Gift

A Scientist,

a Shaman, *and*

Their Remarkable Journey

Through *the*

Siberian Wilderness

JON TURK

St. Martin's Griffin
New York

THE RAVEN'S GIFT. Copyright © 2009 by Jon Turk. All rights reserved. Printed in the United States of America. For information, address St. Martin's Press, 175 Fifth Avenue, New York, N.Y. 10010.

www.stmartins.com

The Library of Congress has cataloged the hardcover edition as follows:

Turk, Jonathan.
    The raven's gift : a scientist, a shaman, and their remarkable journey through the Siberian wilderness / Jon Turk.—1st ed.
        p. cm.
    ISBN 978-0-312-54021-0
    1. Siberia (Russia)—Description and travel. 2. Wilderness areas—Russia—Siberia. 3. Siberia (Russia)—Social life and customs. 4. Koryaks—Russia—Siberia—Social life and customs. 5. Turk, Jonathan—Travel—Russia—Siberia. 6. Scientists—United States—Biography. 7. Moolynaut. 8. Women shamans—Russia—Siberia—Biography. 9. Women healers—Russia—Siberia—Biography. 10. Koryaks—Russia—Siberia—Biography. I. Title.
    DK756.2.T87 2010
    915'.704860922—dc22

                                                                2009033518

ISBN 978-0-312-61177-4 (trade paperback)

10 9 8 7 6 5 4 3

To Moolynaut, who summoned me back to Vyvenka

and introduced me to ancient wisdoms

Contents

Acknowledgments

Nearly ten years elapsed between the day I first met Moolynaut and the moment when *The Raven's Gift* was released. During that decade, my Siberian adventures and the project of writing this book became an integral part of my life. I wrote for a while, realized that the act of writing changed me, then either returned to Siberia or wrote some more.

First of all, I must thank Moolynaut and Kutcha, who healed me and chose me as their messenger.

Moolynaut never used words as her primary form of communication and much of her message was clarified by the Koryak people I met on this forgotten and frozen tundra: Lydia, Oleg, Sergei, Nikolai, Marina, the babushka (whose name I never learned), and Alexei.

A special thanks to Misha Petrov, who paddled across the Pacific Ocean with me, became my blood brother, and journeyed with me on this voyage of self-discovery.

Chris Seashore was my wife and best friend for twenty-four years, eleven months.

Another special thanks to Richard Parks, my agent for nearly twenty years, who has patiently guided my career, and to Michael Flamini, at St. Martin's Press, who saw vision in this manuscript.

A great many close friends and relatives helped nurture the manuscript and the spiritual awakening that was growing inside me. Early in the process, Chris; her sister, Karen Seashore; my father, Amos Turk, and siblings Janet Wittes and Dan Turk were instrumental.

When I bumbled into a seemingly insurmountable writer's block, The Banff Centre in Alberta offered me two generous fellowships to hone my writing, where I worked under the expert guidance of Marni Jackson, Tony Whittome, Ian Pearson, and Moira Farr. Special thanks to Marni for contributing the title, *The Raven's Gift.*

In the past few years, Marion Mackay, Julia Pyatt, Heather Kerr, Fern Marriott, and Rachel Mann have all helped immensely by reading segments of my manuscript and by discussing the themes I was trying to develop.

Finally, I want to thank Nina Maclean, who has shared her life with me, become my ski buddy and wife, and is the most careful, patient, and insightful editor I have ever worked with.

Part 1

To Vyvenka by Kayak

I have seen that in any great undertaking it is not enough for a man to depend simply upon himself.

—Lone Man, Teton Sioux

A Walk with My Dog: Spring 1970

Forty years ago, I was a research chemist, working at night, in the absence of sunlight, buffered against all vagaries of weather by a precise climate control system. In an effort to probe into the nature of the chemical bond, that much studied but still mysterious collection of forces that holds all matter together, I blasted molecules apart with a beam of high-energy electrons and then accelerated the resultant fragments into a powerful magnetic field.

It was intense, stressful work, and one sunny weekend day, in the spring of 1970, I went for a walk with my dog across an alpine meadow in the Colorado Rockies. A few patches of crusty snow lingered in shady and north-facing aspects, but the open spaces were dominated by young, green grasses, the lifesaving nutrition for elk and deer after a long, hungry winter. The earth was moist and spongy underfoot and I knelt down to smell a glacier lily that had opened its petals to the warm, spring sun. My dog suddenly raced off at sprint speed for about fifty yards, leapt into the air like a fox, with his front paws spinning, and landed, digging furiously, clods of sod flying into the air. I felt certain that he was chasing a ground squirrel, futilely trying to dig faster than the rodent could run through its tunnel, the way dogs chase prey, as sport, because they know that a bowl of kibble awaits them back home and failure holds no penalties.

I sauntered over, but by the time I arrived, my dog had abandoned that hole, sprinted another fifty yards, and repeated this same odd behavior. There was no evidence of any burrow in the vicinity of the first hole, nor at his second, or his third, or fourth. Had he gone mad? I watched him more closely. Each time, after breaking through the protective sod, he shoved his nose into the earth and sniffed, then dug, and sniffed again. What did he smell down there? I squatted on my hands and knees and tentatively stuck my nose into one of his holes. Even my human senses could detect the sweet aroma of decay as mites and bacteria woke from their winter somnolence and began to munch and crunch, as only mites and bacteria know how, to convert bits of roots and old leaves into soil.

I assumed that my dog, with his animal instinct, was rejoicing in the process of spring, in the primordial smell of rebirth and renewed growth, a smell that originated when organisms first ventured onto the naked rock of the continents. By the time I reached the fifth hole, my nose and cheeks were smudged with dirt and bits of moist soil lodged onto the hairs of my nostrils, so the earth was inside me, as if we had just made a lifelong pact of togetherness. I lay on the grass, sandwiched between the chill spring dampness on my stomach and the warm sun beating against my back.

The next morning, I returned to the lab, as usual, but something inside me had changed. Although the dog caper, by itself, didn't create an instant epiphany; it was the tipping point. Over the next few weeks, I realized that I couldn't spend my whole life down there in that room, which suddenly felt like a dungeon, manipulating particles that I could never see, under the flicker of fluorescent lights, in a world permeated forever with the smell of acetone and benzene. A year later, I finished my thesis, stuffed my Ph.D. diploma in the glove box of a battered Ford Fairlane, lashed a canoe on top, and headed into the Arctic.

Since that time, my entire adult life has been a balancing act between science on one hand and the smell of the earth that became so seminal that spring day in the Rockies on the other. I have made the bulk of my living writing college-level textbooks on geology, environmental science, chemistry, physics, and astronomy. At the same time, I moved to a ski town and became involved in high-intensity rock climbing, skiing, kayaking, and later mountain biking. Climbing a vertical granite wall in a remote region of the Canadian Arctic—vulnerable to gales from the North Pole—involves a different level of intensity than smelling the spring earth. But the relationship between the two is stronger than most people would suspect. During expeditions, the often razor-thin margin between life and death depends on a tactile, sensory awareness of the environment that incorporates but also transcends logic. My first introduction to that awareness occurred on a spring day when I was walking in a meadow with my dog.

Over the decades, these two aspects of my dichotomous personality have forged a comfortable symbiosis. I have grown to enjoy the exhilaration and toil of arduous expeditions to remote, dangerous, and beautiful places, and at the same time I am always happy to return home, sit in a comfortable office chair, and distill complex scientific concepts into sentences that a college student can understand and appreciate.

But if I thought I understood my relationship with these two disparate worlds, nothing had prepared me for the day when I stood naked on one leg before Moolynaut, a one-hundred-year old Siberian shaman and healer, with my right hand behind my back and my left arm pointed straight in front of me. When I stabilized my balance, she chanted herself into a trance and asked Kutcha, the Raven God, to heal my overused and battered body.

My First Visit to Vyvenka: July 10, 2000

Misha and I paddled our kayaks toward shore and then paused when we felt the waves steepen as they touched the seafloor. Dense, saucer-shaped clouds raced across the Arctic sky, piling up against one another as if there weren't enough room to dissipate across the vast tundra. Wind drove spume and rain in horizontal sheets until you couldn't distinguish the boundary be-tween air and sea, but I needed to ignore the mayhem and "collect my forces," as Misha would say. Tantalizingly close, we could clearly see the town of Vyvenka, a ramshackle collection of tar-paper shacks, rusted machinery, and the roofless gutted skeletons of old Soviet apartment buildings, perched precariously on a sand spit, nine time zones from Moscow. But refuge was still two hundred yards away—just beyond the surf. From our vantage on the backs of the waves, we couldn't see the break, but we could hear the roar as waves dropped onto the beach, churning sand and rocks in their turbulence.

Misha looked at me, smiled to reveal his prominent gold tooth, and re-peated his boyhood Soviet slogan, "Labor and Defend."

Weeks before, I had charged into the surf yelling Crazy Horse's battle cry, "It is a good day to die!" But Misha objected, so now we rallied behind "Labor and Defend."

"Da, conyeshna [yes, of course]," I replied in Russian. Then I pointed my paddle like a lance. "Labor and Defend."

I paddled toward shore, turned to watch the wave patterns behind me, calculated my timing, and took a few hard strokes. My kayak balanced on the tip of a breaking wave until the liquid mountain collapsed into a dark, ominous tube, and I dropped into its maw. Water cascaded over me, block-ing out the daylight. Inside the wave, I reached out with my paddle, like a blind man, to find a pillow of upwelling water that would support me, as firmly as if I were leaning against solid ground. At the same time, I cocked my hips to drive the chine of my kayak, like a ski edge, into the wave. In a few moments, my head rose out of the gray-green darkness, even as my shoulders continued to be massaged by churning foam. Then the boat hit the sand and bounced onto the beach. I stumbled out of the cockpit and fell when I tried to stand.

Eleven hours earlier I had stuffed my torso into the cramped kayak and then I had paddled steadily, chilled by the subarctic seawater that constantly rolled across the deck. Now I was stiff and my pelvis was letting me know in no uncertain terms that it didn't want to support my weight. I had ripped my pelvis apart in an avalanche a few years previously, and the screws and bolts that held me together didn't do nearly as good a job as the original equipment that I was born with. Another wave rolled up the sand, enveloping me in its Arctic iciness. With my paddle in one hand, I crawled through the sandy foam as the swash threatened to pull my kayak back to sea. A skinny, shirtless boy in wet, baggy underwear appeared out of nowhere and held my bow steady.

Using my paddle as a cane, I struggled to my feet and slowly regained my balance as my joints painfully rearranged themselves toward verticality, as if I were the first ape coming down out of the trees. I looked back out to sea and waved jauntily to signal Misha that everything was fine; even though it wasn't, because the surf was steep and dangerous.

Now Misha accelerated and dropped into the surf. But he had inadvertently chosen an extraordinarily steep wave and he capsized, swimming to the beach alongside his overturned and waterlogged kayak.

After I helped him to his feet, he smiled sheepishly and then regained his composure and proudly repeated, "Labor and Defend."

We laughed together, retrieved his boat, and spilled the water out of the cockpit. A woman approached across the wet sand. She was Koryak, a member of one of the indigenous Siberian tribes that have traditionally lived in northeast Siberia. Even though it was mid-July, she was dressed in an ankle-length woolen Russian peasant coat and a bulky dog-fur cap. Her large, round cheeks and high cheekbones stood out from the fur, overshadowing her almond eyes and small, O-shaped mouth. She spoke in faltering, grammatically tortured but carefully enunciated English.

"Welcome. I am good to see you. My name is Lydia. I am wait to you because I am knowing that you are to come at this place. Maybe that our great-grandmother—how do you say this?—has made it to be that this storm did brung you to our village."

I turned and watched the surf pounding the beach. A wave hissed to its apogee, curled, and collapsed, expelling the air in its bowels with a *woomph*. Foam raced down the face of the wave, like so many sea serpents, and white, violent swash slid up the beach, dissipating into tendrils that swirled around our boots. A gust of wind spun kelp and sand into tight circles that joined waterspouts and the horizontal spume blowing in from the sea.

I turned back to face Lydia and pick up the tangled thread of our conversation. At first, I couldn't understand what she had said, so I sorted through the words and rearranged the syntax. Then I looked at her again to see if I could discern any hidden guile. Lydia smiled serenely.

"Why would the great-grandmother make a storm to bring us here?" I asked.

"I do not know."

I felt that it was my turn to speak, but I didn't have anything intelligent to say, so I asked lamely, "And what is the great-grandmother's name?"

"Moolynaut." And then Lydia fell silent with an expression that discouraged any further questioning.

Overhead, the dark clouds twisted into knots as they raced across the ocean to vent their fury over Vyvenka. Should I be thankful that Moolynaut had granted us safe passage through this storm? Or angry that she had caused such a commotion in the first place?

Lydia spoke again: "I now go at the house. You and Misha must to be hungry. I will take for us some food."

Then, in Russian, she instructed Misha to find her husband, Oleg, and his sidekick, Sergei.

Misha strolled off into the wind, Lydia retreated toward the houses, and I sat down to wait on the cowling of my kayak.

A little over a year ago, Franz Helfenstein and I set out to sail and paddle three thousand miles across the Arctic rim of the North Pacific, from Japan to Alaska. Government bureaucrats insisted that we hire a Russian "guide," but our liaison functionary got scared and quit after a week. We continued for several months, dodging and cajoling our way past the feared Russian Pogranichniki, the elite shock-troop border guards. But when we arrived in the port city of Petropavlovsk-Kamchatskiy (PK), we could no longer ignore the law. We couldn't find anyone with kayaking experience, but then Misha came to visit, dressed in a well-pressed business suit. Even though he had never been in a kayak before, he wanted to paddle across the North Pacific with me, because, as he explained, "I am making too many papers at home," and, "I must see the Wild Nature." He had a warm smile and an easy grace, and despite the madness of it all, for some reason I trusted him. It was late in the season, so Franz and I returned to North America for the winter. Franz had other obligations, and in late May of the second year, Misha, my wife, Chris, and I set out to paddle along the northeast coast of Siberia. After six hundred miles, Chris developed tendonitis and flew back to PK and Misha and I continued.

A kayak is the smallest oceangoing craft and the North Pacific is one of the most tempestuous seas in the world. For the past seven weeks, Misha and I had paddled every day until we were exhausted, intent on reaching Alaska before autumn storms turned our expedition suicidal. I looked out to sea again and imagined myself floating not so much on the water as within it. It seemed improbable that we had survived such power and chaos, but the smell of sea in my sinuses assured me that we had.

I was born a few weeks after the end of World War II, grew up sheltered and mildly prosperous, went to Andover and Brown, and then to graduate school for organic chemistry at the University of Colorado. My professors told me that I was headed toward a comfortable career in academia, but at the age of twenty-six, hounded by restless spirits, already with a failed marriage behind me, I followed a mysterious internal voice into the Arctic.

Now, after many years at sea in small boats, I had become a bit of a mystic. No matter how seaworthy my craft or how skillful I believe I am, there comes a time when the boat feels too small and vulnerable to survive the vast and primordial ocean. And in that moment, it seems as if something else has kept me alive. And even if I didn't really believe that some guiding hand had plucked me to safety when my skill and luck ran out, the sea had gently reached into my brain to turn some switches off and others on, leaving me to trust my life to an intuition so much more reliable than the left-brain thought patterns I had so carefully nourished in the chemistry lab.

Yet on the one hand, I didn't believe that some old Koryak shaman had conjured up a storm that forced us to land at this desolate, windswept village on the Eastern edge of the eastern world. On the other hand, I've been an adventurer for decades, often wandering alone, vulnerable, and hungry, dependent on the kindness of strangers. In Russia, people called me a *puteshevstinek*, a traveler who told stories, entertained, and carried the news. There is no space in my traveling lexicon for cynicism, criticism, and doubt. Instead, I've learned to listen, accept, and record.

A few hours earlier, a storm had arisen suddenly and unexpectedly. There had been no falling barometer, no warning from high-flying cirrus clouds or menacing lenticulars. Just an abrupt, intense wind. But none of that mattered anymore. Misha and I were safely onshore, and I had little interest in the cosmic or magical underpinnings that controlled our fate. Soon Lydia would invite us into her home, with a warm hearth and, I hoped, fresh bread baking in the oven. Yes, I could see smoke rising from the chimneys of storm-battered homes.

Misha and two strangers approached along the beach. Misha was tall, solid, and blond, with disarming blue eyes—a Scandinavian Russian and a descendant of the marauding Vikings who spread terror throughout Europe a thousand years ago. One of the strangers was a powerfully built, barrel-chested man who walked with a bowlegged gait, derived from standing on the decks of small ships on stormy seas. The other was short and wiry, with a cocky stride, looking like a teenager racing off to drink beer with his friends. While Misha wore a bright orange paddling jacket I had given him, the two Koryak men were dressed in ragtag bundles of tattered, earth-colored canvas clothes, with fur hats and worn, patched rubber boots. The wind swirled sand and spume into a haze around the three men, so they looked like ghost warriors emerging from the shadows of their ancestors.

Misha and I had been paddling together for 750 miles and seven weeks, sharing danger, hunger, and exhilaration. Even though he managed to remain incongruously tidy in this violent land, the determination and steadfastness in his eyes could be scary if you didn't know him, trust him, and love him as well as I did. The barrel-chested stranger, Oleg, was of mixed ancestry, part Koryak, with a bronzed tint inherited from a Cossack sable trapper from the Black Sea or the Caucasus Mountains. The wiry man, Sergei, was purebred Koryak, lean and angular, with high cheekbones and a cigarette dangling out of his mouth as if it were permanently impaled on a lower canine. His face was weather-wrinkled and his eyes squinted into the storm. In his face I could see Stone Age ancestors shouldering their spears as they migrated from Central Asia into the high Arctic and then across the Bering Land Bridge to North America.

I thought about my own lineage. Centuries ago, my distant relatives had escaped Jerusalem ahead of Roman soldiers; then they had settled in Spain, only to flee the Inquisition—toward the temporary safety of northeastern Europe—which degenerated into pogroms—followed by the Nazi Holocaust—leading my family to a placid existence in suburban Connecticut.

On the beach, Misha, Oleg, and Sergei joined me and we gathered in a tight circle, as if Moolynaut had gathered this disparate group in her whirlwind, like the columns of airborne kelp that spun along the beach.

Visiting Moolynaut

Misha, Oleg, Sergei, and I walked above the beach, past Lydia's brave, storm-battered garden of potatoes, carrots, radishes, and lettuce, to a small duplex patched together from an eclectic assortment of concrete, salvaged lumber, tar paper, and driftwood. Lydia met us at the doorway, reached up to my wool hat, and deftly pinched off a thread. Misha's hat was made of nylon, so she unzipped his anorak and grasped a thread from his jacket. She told us to wait, disappeared into the house, and reappeared with a small shovel full of burning embers. She dropped the two threads onto the red-hot embers and chanted a few verses in the old, guttural Koryak tongue—to incinerate any *cherney*, or dark spirits that we may have imported from the fearsome, alien, and predatory outside world.

When I stepped inside, a blast of warm air hit with the abruptness of a rogue wave at sea, except that this wave enveloped me with peaceful comfort.

It didn't matter—not one tiny bit—that torn wallpaper drooped, a bare light-bulb hung by frayed wire, or the lone window was half-obscured by a greasy film of seal fat and coal dust. A tiny, rickety table stood against the window and a few stools were scattered about, but from my perspective, the only significant and salient piece of furniture was a massive brick coal-burning stove, a *petchka*. Shimmering lines of heated air rose from its cast-iron top.

Lydia explained that this home belonged to a man named Goshe. After his wife died a year ago, her ghost frequented the apartment, so he kept a fire in the *petchka* to keep her warm. Sometimes he visited during the day, but he slept at his mother's house. Goshe was working now and we were welcome to stay here until the storm subsided. Lydia assured us that Goshe's wife's ghost was lonely but not evil and she wouldn't bother us. Then Lydia giggled, holding her hand across her mouth,

"Oh, I am so sorry. I have losing my politenesses. Do you have hot dresses to cloth yourself in?"

When we nodded, she continued, "Look at you. You are also very much wet. Please, make himself happy. I will take back soon with many foods."

Lydia raced off to the adjoining apartment, where she lived with her husband, Oleg. After she departed, Misha and I stripped off layers of soggy, wet Polartec and basked, naked, in front of the stove, silently comfortable with an intense friendship cemented by shared danger and unity of purpose. Then we put on our wondrously dry—and only mildly smelly—shore clothes.

Lydia, Oleg, and Sergei returned an hour later with fresh bread, slathered with thick layers of red caviar, and plates piled high with baked salmon and boiled potatoes from Lydia's garden. Our new friends asked about our expedition and Misha chronicled our journey. We talked into the night about the sea, the salmon run, and sea mammals we had seen, with Misha faithfully translating when I lost the thread of the conversation. Then, fed, warm, safe, and dry, we rolled our pads and sleeping bags out on Goshe's musty, threadbare rug and fell asleep.

I awoke the following morning confused and disoriented. I couldn't hear the surf. The wind. The sound of flapping nylon. After living in a tent for seven weeks, I couldn't understand why I was suddenly surrounded by faded green wallpaper with a faint hint of dead flowers. Oh yes, I was indoors, in Vyvenka, in Goshe's house. I sat up. Misha was sleeping next to me, so I dressed quietly and stepped outside. Gale-force wind eddied around the protected doorway, the air was hazy with flying spume, and a heavy rain was falling. I pulled my hood over my head and walked to the beach. Even though it would be suicide to kayak today, I analyzed the surf with the intimacy that I shared with this sea—friend and foe, enemy and lover. Soon I heard footsteps in the sand behind me and Sergei approached.

We stood silently for a few moments and then he said, "*Plocha* [bad]."

Beads of rain poured off his hat, landed on his nose, and then dropped to the water-soaked sand, but he seemed inured to the wetness. I nodded and replied in pidgin Russian, "If we go sea today, we die."

Sergei stooped down, picked up an imaginary paddle, faced north, and pantomimed that he was paddling across the storm-tossed sea, fighting the waves, and rocking his body with the turbulence. Then he smiled devilishly and spoke. I missed half of what he said, but caught the words, "You. . . . strong men . . . You go . . . Alaska . . . today."

I laughed at the joke and said, "*Da, conyeshna* [yes, of course]."

And then we stood there, a fisherman and a kayaker, lost in our private memories of the sea.

After a few moments, Sergei tapped me on the elbow and we walked back to the house. Misha was awake and soon Lydia entered with hot tea and another aromatic loaf of fresh bread. I sat to eat and we chatted briefly about the storm and the impossibility of continuing until the weather improved.

Then Lydia announced, "Today we will go through the river to look at Moolynaut. This time also, Moolynaut must look at you."

In all the confusion of a strange place, in a foreign culture, with new friends who spoke a language I only half-understood, I had completely forgotten about Moolynaut. I thought back to the previous afternoon and remembered the conversation with Lydia on the beach. Oh yes, Moolynaut was the woman who had conjured up this storm. But the facts, the implications, and the innuendo were hazy. Had I missed something in the language gap? After all those days of living in wet clothes, I was finally dry and the phrase "through the river" sounded suspiciously wet. Couldn't I just sit in this womblike room, near this radiant *petchka*, eating hot bread, drinking horrible, bitter Russian tea, and feeling my muscles heal—fiber by fiber, cell by cell, molecule by molecule?

"Who is Moolynaut?" I asked.

"She is the grandmother of all people in Vyvenka. She is a very strong woman with many powers. She is old, maybe ninety-six, but she do not know exactly. She want to see you."

Oleg started talking in rapid-fire Russian and Misha stopped translating. From the few snippets of Russian that I understood and from people's actions, I could tell that we were preparing for an imminent journey, with or without my consent. Misha dressed as if we were going to sea, so I reluctantly followed suit. Then we all filed out of the building and walked down the muddy, potholed street of downtown Vyvenka.

Beneath a pregnant sky, howling wind, and incessant rain, we passed small tar-paper-covered houses, piles of driftwood and coal, sleds in assorted states of disrepair, and gardens with northern-latitude vegetables. There were a few plastic-covered greenhouses full of cucumbers and tomatoes. Sleepy, motley, tethered sled dogs looked up from their summer slumber while loose dogs gamboled about and fought short, vicious battles.

The town was a hundred yards wide, built on a sand spit, bounded on one side by the ocean and on the other by a low, steep hill. The storm had lifted the sea up the beach, and I imagined that during the stronger gales of autumn the swash would inundate the town and wash all the dog shit and loose trash into the Pacific.

Lydia explained, "The hill is the back of a sleeping whale. Now the whale is sleeping. Someday many mice will come to Vyvenka. These are the whale's wives. Then the whale will swim away."

Misha asked, "Will the village sink into the sea when the whale swims away?"

Lydia responded, "Of course. The village is here for only some time."

I searched her eyes for some sign of concern about impending catastrophe, but there was none. Any geologist will tell you that sand spits are temporary features on the landscape, so her legend accurately predicts the future.

People pushed rickety wheelbarrows or pulled broken-down wagons with wobbly wheels toward or away from the town well. A generation-old Soviet motorcycle with a sidecar roared through the rain-soaked street, splashing everyone. Past the houses, a row of crumbling Soviet-style apartment buildings extended northward, with siding, walls, and roofs removed, as if the Russian army had bombed them in an attempt to subdue a ragtag band of terrorists.

A century ago, one long lifetime, when Moolynaut was a little girl, the Koryak people were nomadic, following domestic reindeer herds and living in skin tents, called *yurangas*. But Stalin was a ruthless sociopath who had no tolerance for cultural or intellectual expression, and as a result, he wantonly imprisoned, tortured, and shot millions to create and enforce his evil and distorted vision of Soviet society. From the slave-labor mines, belching smelters, and sprawling factories of central Siberia he dispatched murderous armies, followed by clanking bulldozers, across the greatest empire the world has ever known, from Europe to the Pacific Ocean, from the taiga forests of Lake Baikal to the high Arctic. With rifles, disease, and machinery, the Russians eviscerated cultures, leveled tundra and forest, and built endless rows of dank, dark, musty concrete apartment buildings, equipped with electricity and central heating. Then they shot anyone who attempted to live a traditional lifestyle in their beloved *yurangas*.

Vyvenka lies next to one of the richest salmon rivers in the world, and the tundra west of the village is an ideal pasture for domestic reindeer. The Soviets modernized and collectivized both of these industries. Soon the sound of diesel-powered fishing boats, trucks, and shore-based freezers rent the previously still air. Every autumn, ships brought coal for the heating plant, diesel fuel for the generators, and food, clothing, and other commodities for the stores—and returned to PK and Vladivostok with fish and meat. You can argue the pros and cons of Soviet policy, but life was predictable during this time. People who followed the rules were guaranteed a warm house, food, medical attention, schools, and a one-week-a-year vacation so they could fly south and lounge in a spa with hot springs and daily massages.

After perestroika in 1988 the system sputtered along for a few years on confusion and inertia, but in the early 1990s freezer ships and fuel tankers failed to show up. Business mafia from Moscow and PK cajoled, threatened, and bribed big-city bureaucrats into issuing exclusive permits so the locals couldn't harvest their own fish. Russians from nearby villages poached the domestic reindeer from clanking, tracked, armored personnel carriers called *visdichots*. Corrupt officials invented illegal and unreasonable taxes—and when the people ran out of money, the officials took their tithe in meat.

In 1995 the electric generator in Vyvenka consumed its last drops of diesel, the pistons coasted into silence, and the town snuggled deep into the darkness of subarctic winter. A year later, the village ran out of coal for its heating plant, even though there was an active coal mine fifteen miles north of the village. Steam pipes froze and cracked, and huge frost crystals grew on the inside walls, ceilings, and floors of people's homes. The Russian engineers, teachers, doctors, and service workers returned home to Moscow, abandoning the Koryak residents to their own ingenuity. Almost immediately, the locals dismantled most of the hated apartments with axes and crowbars, until wind blew through hollow skeletons of the ravaged buildings, adding an eerie Mad Max road warrior look to the village. Residents used salvageable lumber to build smaller houses and tossed the scraps and splinters into their *petchkas*.

Oleg, Sergei, Lydia, Misha, and I turned left off the main street, onto a footpath that led over the hill. As soon as we left town, the scenery and conversation became more relaxed. We crested the windy ridge and looked down at the broad Vyvenka River Valley, clothed in tundra, vast and as inscrutable as the ocean, except that it felt so comfortable, safe, and secure because it was dry land. The Vyvenka River formed a thin blue line that snaked through the mixed landscape of willow, grass, and sedge. Rain diminished, but the wind still formed steep whitecaps in the estuary.

Lydia commented nonchalantly, "The name Moolynaut means 'She Who Gives Blood for the People.'"

I waited in case Lydia had more to add, then questioned, "And why does she have that name?"

"Because when people have ill, Moolynaut can make them to be not ill."

"Where did she get that power? How long has she had it?"

"She was born with this strong. Her mother had this strong and her grandmother even long before. Her grandmother had very strong. Very very strong. More strong even than Moolynaut or the mother of Moolynaut. Moolynaut had her strong even when she was a small girl. She is born with this."

Lydia descended the hill and I followed on the narrow trail, digesting this recent information and adding it to the report that Moolynaut had conjured up the storm. Then I shrugged it off. Expeditions simplify life. There is food or starvation. Rest or fatigue. Safety or mortal danger. Right now, I was batting a thousand: fed, rested, and safe—and nothing else mattered. Lydia's stories became part of the mysterious landscape, indistinguishable from delicate sea stacks to the east or the flocks of puffins that wheeled overhead. After a few moments, we reached Oleg's aluminum speedboat that was pulled up on the beach. Oleg was the proud owner of a brand-new 35-horsepower Yamaha outboard, the first get-up-and-go internal combustion engine I had seen since Misha and I left PK.

Someone forgot something and raced off, so we sat down to wait and chat. Misha told Oleg that I had been a commercial salmon fisherman in Alaska for four years. Oleg wordlessly raised his eyebrows to show interest, and we discussed prices and markets. I learned that in the bandito-cowboy capitalism of modern Russia, local fishermen earned about five cents on the dollar, while the predatory businessmen and crooked bureaucrats stole the rest. Oleg muttered quietly, "If they only robbed three-quarters of our money, they'd still be rich and we would have enough for a decent life, but they take ninety-five percent and life is hard."

Yet Oleg's motor was proof that he had outfoxed the foxes. We pushed the boat into the water and Sergei, dressed in hip waders, held it bow to the beach while Oleg pulled the starter cord. The motor sparked to life with a warm purr and Oleg looked at me with a proud smile across his broad, hardened face. I nodded and gave him a thumbs-up. I wanted to ask how he had managed to purchase the motor in this impoverished land, but I was almost certain that the answer involved some underhanded and illegal skullduggery—and I'd learned long ago not to interrogate a friend who just might be a low-level bandit.

Lydia climbed aboard first and sat on an overturned plastic crate in the lee of the windshield. As the honored American guest, I got the second crate. Misha squatted on a reindeer hide, also within the protection of the wind-shield. Oleg and Sergei stood in the rear, exposed to wind, rain, and spray. Wolfchuck, Oleg's dog, jumped onto his accustomed perch on the narrow, slippery front deck. We accelerated to planing speed and skipped along from whitecap to whitecap. Wolfchuck rocked unsteadily on the deck, des-perately trying to dig his claws into the aluminum to maintain traction. Spray streamed over the windshield, dousing Oleg and Sergei until their cot-ton parkas were soaked. The red glow on the tip of Sergei's cigarette fizzled into a wet ash, but he showed no signs of discomfort.

We sped upstream into protected waters, the rain stopped, and the sun poked through scudding clouds. Oleg opened the throttle full bore and slalomed adroitly past unseen sandbars. People on both banks were setting nets and cleaning salmon. Commercial fishing was conducted in the ocean, but locals fished for subsistence along the riverbanks. After half an hour, we veered toward the left bank where a man in a wooden rowboat was picking fish out of a gill net. Onshore, a small, wrinkled old woman was squatting on the tundra, cleaning fish. She was dressed in brown canvas trousers and a blue felted overcoat, with a bright red scarf tied on her head. She wielded a long, thin, razor-sharp filleting knife, slicing the iridescent red meat with deft, sure strokes.

Nearby hills blocked the wind, and the land absorbed the Arctic sun's summer heat. My skin tingled to welcome the unfamiliar warmth. When we stepped out of the boat, Moolynaut stood with slow determination, as if charging each creaky joint to straighten. When she was almost vertical, she balanced herself on a worn cane. Maybe she had been five feet tall in her youth, but now she was bent over with age and her head was no higher than the middle of my chest. Her face was deeply wrinkled, but her eyes were alert and she welcomed us with a warm, confident smile.

Lydia addressed her in the old tongue and at the end of every sentence she replied, "Ah . . . ah . . . ah," in a throaty, raspy yet sonorous voice to indicate that she understood.

Then Moolynaut looked directly at me. "You are American?" she asked in Russian.

I said, "*Da*," and she continued, "Welcome back. It is a long time since the Americans came here. They came every year to trade. Before the Bolsheviks. I was a little girl, but I remember this. They brought beautiful horses. White horses. And then when hard times came, they brought rifles. Winchester rifles. Have you heard of Winchester rifles?"

I nodded and she repeated, "Ah . . . ah . . . ah," several times, as if she was thinking about the past. Then she looked toward the river and we both watched the lazy current.

"And cartridges," she continued. "Rifles are no good without the cartridges."

Now Moolynaut looked intently into my eyes. After what seemed like several minutes, she spoke softly: "But that was a long time ago." Then, abruptly, she sat back down on the tundra, picked up her knife, and resumed cleaning fish.

Lydia ushered us into the tiny shack that was Moolynaut's summer home. After my eyes adjusted to the darkness, Lydia told me to sit on a narrow sleeping platform positioned next to a small plank table that was nailed into the wall. We couldn't all fit around the table, so Sergei unceremoniously ripped it out of the wall, splintering the brittle gray wood. Oleg darted outside and returned with a driftwood log. Then the two men moved the table into the middle of the room and balanced the loose end on the log. Lydia started a fire in the sheet metal stove and stoked it until the shack was nearing sauna temperatures, yet my hosts didn't take off their heavy storm clothes. I stripped down as much as was polite but still yearned for the fresh air and sunlight of the tundra. Lydia prepared soup with fish, potatoes, and tundra herbs. Because I was the guest, she served me the fish head, with white eyeballs staring from its death mask. Then she stepped outside to call Moolynaut in for lunch.

Moolynaut ate her soup with loud slurping noises. When she was finished, the two women talked in Koryak and Lydia turned to me. "Jon. Now you are to ask the great-grandmother your questions."

My mind raced. My questions? I didn't conjure up a storm to summon her. She summoned me. She should be the one with the questions.

Everyone watched me, waiting. What I really wanted to ask was, "OK, who's going crazy? You or me?" But I couldn't say that. How about, "Did you really conjure up the storm? And if so, why?" That didn't sound right, either. I saw before me an old woman who had been cleaning fish and was now eating lunch. If what Lydia told me was correct, she was one of the last indigenous Siberian shamans and carried the history of a century within her, interpreted through a reality that I only vaguely understood. I had so many questions, but I had to come up with something simple and plausible. The grizzly bear is the most powerful and dangerous terrestrial animal in this landscape and the animistic Koryak religion honors bears with special reverence, so I tried, "Tell me a story about grizzly bears."

Moolynaut looked up, as if she searched deep into time and space; then she started in Russian. Misha translated.

"Once, a long time ago, when I was a little girl, I was picking berries with my mother. I walked over the top of a hill and suddenly I saw a bear. The bear stood up and it was very big. Very, very big. I was frightened and ran away. But the bear didn't eat me."

Then she dipped her wet soupspoon into the communal sugar bowl, ate a heaping spoonful of sugar, and walked back into the sunshine to clean fish. Everyone seemed satisfied that my questions were answered. We drank tea and chatted until Oleg announced that it was time to return home.

As we walked back into the bright sunshine, Moolynaut stood and slung a heavy load of sliced salmon across her back. She dropped her cane, and even though she walked with a shuffle and a stoop, she adroitly crossed a bouncy, rickety plank that bridged a small ravine. There was a drying rack across the ravine and she was curing rows of salmon in the hot summer sun. Misha and I walked across the plank to say good-bye.

I told her that I was honored to meet her. She nodded, held me with her eyes, and replied in Russian, "Yes, please come back. It will be good for you."

Then Moolynaut chanted in the old tongue, offering a prayer for our safe passage.

After we returned to town, Lydia reiterated the invitation. She enjoined us to return for the spring festival, when people gathered to celebrate the end of the long winter with foot and dogsled races, wrestling matches, dances, music, and feasting.

Sergei enthusiastically joined in, "You and Misha are travelers. Oleg and I are travelers, too. We can travel together across the tundra. You guys have money for gas?"

When I nodded, he suggested that the four of us should journey to the Holy Stone, repeating Moolynaut's enjoinder: "It will be good for you."

"What is the Holy Stone?" I asked.

"The Holy Stone is the center of our power and our magic."

Oleg chimed in, "But when you visit the Holy Stone, you must not take any pictures. The last person who took pictures of the Holy Stone . . . he fell in the river and drowned three days later."

Sergei added, "And everybody who traveled with him . . . they died, too. Within a month. Mysteriously. Just died."

Lydia added, "And when you pass the Holy Stone, you must to left a special thing. Not a big thing, maybe just a small thing of big love. One time, when I was a little girl, I passed the Holy Stone. I had some special sweet, but I did not want to put it to the stone. I wanted to eat it by himself." Lydia held her hand to her mouth, giggled like a schoolgirl, and then continued, "I was riding a horse. An hour after we were crossed a river. The horse jumped into the air. Just jump. No why. I fell and broke my leg. This way you must all time put a gift to the Holy Stone."

I wanted to say, "Hey, guys, why all the commotion? Who says I'm coming back?" But somehow it seemed like a done deal, so I smiled and agreed, "I won't take any pictures of the Holy Stone and I'll bring something special to leave there."

Leaving Town

The gale subsided two days later, so Misha and I loaded our kayaks and carried them back to the beach. Oleg gave us a detailed description of currents and prevailing winds between Vyvenka and the next prominent landmark, Govena Point.

"And beyond that?" I asked.

Oleg shrugged. "I have never been farther north."

Sergei grinned, shifted his cigarette from one canine to the other, and commented, "You are kayakers. Like my great-grandfather in the old days, before the Soviets. You will understand the seas when you get there. They will speak to you."

Lydia promised that she would return home immediately, dip a piece of hare skin in butter, throw it in the fire, and say, "Spirit of the hare, follow these men. Give them good luck and help them travel quickly."

After blasting through the surf, Misha and I bobbed on the residual storm swell and settled into the silent, mantric repetition of paddling. The three-day visit in Vyvenka had been full of mystery, but we were midway through an arduous and dangerous expedition and now we needed to concentrate again on the open sea.

We plotted a course across Govena Bay, with Vyvenka receding in our wakes and a storm-tossed coastline stretching out before us. After several hours, I stopped to stretch tired shoulders. Misha coasted up and suggested, "Maybe we eat a little?"

I nodded and grabbed the rim of his cockpit so our boats banged softly against each other. Misha reached under his spray skirt for a chunk of *sala* (raw pickled pork fat). He held up two greasy packages wrapped in tattered plastic. Back home, I wouldn't touch the stuff, but we were in Kamchatka, paddling across the North Pacific.

"With garlic or no garlic?" he asked.

"Garlic would be good today."

As Misha carefully cut two equal chunks, I asked, "What do you think about that whole business with Moolynaut?"

"What do you say? 'Whole business'?"

"Sorry, that is American slang. I forget sometimes. Do you think Moolynaut made a magic storm to bring us to Vyvenka?"

"Yes, I, too, am think about this things. I do not know. I hear many stories about special people who live on the tundra. People with great strong. How do you name them in English?"

"Shamans."

"Yes, shamans. Very good. We have the same word in Russian. I hear many stories about shamans. But I am a Russian, not a Koryak. I work all day at a computer. Like you. You and me, we cannot know about this things."

Misha chewed his *sala*, lost in thought. Then he continued, "A storm came and we landed in Vyvenka. That is really. Maybe Moolynaut made this storm. Maybe Lydia only thought that Moolynaut made it. But Lydia was not making a joke to us. She was telling what she thinks is really. This is really."

I noted that Misha didn't go so far as to say he didn't believe. It all seemed crazy to me, but no matter. Right now I just needed to find the strength to paddle one thousand more miles to Alaska before we were beset by autumn storms. I turned my *sala* over in my hand and considered tossing it into the sea but reminded myself that I needed calories to survive this journey. I could worry about hardened arteries after I reached Alaska.

I had one more question. "Misha? Do you think that Moolynaut really wants us to come back?"

Misha replied slowly, "I am think on this things also. I do not know. I have said this at you before. I am a Russian, not a Koryak. Every people have a way of saying. Maybe that was her way to say 'good-bye.' Maybe she want us to come back. Maybe she does not want that we come back. Maybe she does not matter—yes or no."

The far shore was still several hours away, so we finished our lunch and resumed paddling. Our boats drifted apart and I felt relaxed, quietly enjoying my own thoughts, buoyed by the waves, with the Govena Peninsula a thin line of green ahead and the Vyvenka coast a thin line of green behind. On the other hand, my left elbow tendon throbbed after only a few hours of paddling. I was fifty-five and age, distances, and old injuries had left their toll.

I thought back to past expeditions and a flood of memories returned: storms at sea, windy ridges, swirling snow, thirst, hunger, frozen fingers, the exhilaration of the summit, the close companionship of expedition partners huddled against a storm, and the glory of returning sunshine. If I could complete this crossing of the North Pacific, it would be my most significant adventure ever.

Significant? What does that mean? I hadn't discovered any new spice islands or foreign lands to conquer, and nobody in the outside world gave a hoot whether I succeeded or not. Yet my expeditions were important to me, and wasn't that enough?

I felt content with my life: goals accomplished, pinnacles not reached. Yet, in all the decades of adventure, I had so frequently passed through people's lives with a casual glance and then moved onward toward some dot on my map, which I had arbitrarily highlighted boldly in red. Now I thought about the hundreds of people in huts, tents, yurts, *yurangas*, and villages throughout the world who had shared their food with me and given me shelter—and then invited me to return. Always I had smiled and said something friendly like, "Time is long and you never know what will happen." But I had never returned.

Many years ago, I was driving across Arizona and picked up a young Navajo hitchhiker. We chatted, I bought him lunch, and he asked me if I would walk across the desert with him to join his elders in a peyote ceremony. For some reason—something about deadlines and commitments—I declined. Now, Oleg, Sergei, Lydia, and Moolynaut had given me a second opportunity to look into a similar window. I felt that if I turned this down, I might never get a third chance.

I didn't need to follow a teacher or a shaman—and certainly didn't believe that Moolynaut had swirled the heavens and seas so Misha and I would spend three days in town. So what was pulling me back?

The people in Vyvenka live in poverty and hardship, ravaged by foreign armies and predatory businessmen, perched on a sand spit that will someday swim away and carry their village into the sea. Yet life goes on with laughter and love and few complaints.

Both Moolynaut and Sergei had told me that a journey to the Holy Stone would "be good for you."

For many years, I had repeated a Kurt Vonnegut quote as a mantra: "Unusual travel suggestions are dancing lessons from God."

Wasn't that enough? Was there anything in life more important than following blind curiosity?

I thought about the questions I wanted to ask Moolynaut, the mystery behind our original conversation. The ocean adventure before me suddenly seemed tame beside a different kind of adventure that was simultaneously offered and obscured by an old woman who told me a simple story about a girlhood encounter with a bear. In an instant, even as I had little premonition of the enormity of my decision, I steered close to Misha and asked, "*Tak* [so]. Would you like to go to the Holy Stone?"

Without slowing his cadence, Misha replied, "Why not?"

A few strokes later he added: "But first we must paddle to Alaska by our own hands." And then he set his paddle down and held up both hands, in case I didn't understand.

Part 2

Wingtip to Wingtip

For the Lakota, there was no wilderness,
because nature was not dangerous, but hospitable,
not forbidding, but friendly.

—Chief Luther Standing Bear, Oglala Sioux

Broken

After Misha and I left Vyvenka, we paddled north and completed our passage to Alaska by mid-September. During the entire four-month expedition, my muscles had routinely and insistently sent urgent missives to the brain, screaming that they were tired, spent, done, overburdened with lactic acid, and disintegrating—fiber by fiber, molecule by molecule—from overuse. But the brain had insisted that this body was not a democracy and the muscles had no right to express dissent or to demand habeas corpus when sentenced to the gulag. Finally, when the journey was over, the rabble overran the castle, the dictatorship toppled, and I returned home to Montana to rest and heal.

I lived in a small house in the forest with Chris Seashore, my wife, lover, ski buddy, best friend, and frequent expedition partner. Chris was a short, square-shouldered Scandinavian, a tuned athlete and superb skier. On skis, Chris rarely jumped over an obstacle; instead she always found the path of least resistance around it. She approached life with the same fluidity and grace, planted solidly on the Earth. We met when Chris was thirty-one, but even at that young age her fair skin had wrinkled in the harsh mountain sunlight so that crow's-feet wrinkles radiated from the corners of her eyes. I tried moisturizing the skin by frequently kissing the wrinkles, but the crow's-feet continued to deepen because time, wind, and high-altitude sun were stronger than my kisses. Many times when we lay beside each other in bed, sat across the supper table, or stood on snowy windswept ridges, I noticed that her cheekbones were anomalously prominent—but I never asked her about it. I wonder if one of Chris's distant ancestors had married a Sami reindeer herder, mixing indigenous genes with Viking blood. It's just a thought, but it might also explain her imperviousness to cold and her deep-seated love of wild northern landscapes.

Chris had joined Misha and me on the kayak expedition in 2000 but suffered severe tendonitis in her forearms and wrists and flew home from the village of Ossora, a week's passage south of Vyvenka. When I told her about Vyvenka and Moolynaut's invitation, she eagerly embraced the idea.

"How could we not go to the spring festival and the Holy Stone?"

Furthermore, as long as we were in Vyvenka, Chris suggested that we travel inland to find and visit reindeer-herding nomads.

Arctic tundra consists of a thin veneer of soil lying on top of a thick foundation of ice. The ice is impermeable, so when the snow melts in June water is trapped on the surface, creating an immense circumpolar bog. Zillions of mosquitoes breed in the standing water, so summer travel across the tundra consists of slogging across an infinity of muck while the biting scourge drains your blood. Early spring is the best time for travel, because the temperature remains mostly below freezing but well above winter extremes, days are long, sun-drenched snow covers the ground, and there are no bugs. As a consequence, we made plans to return to Kamchatka in April.

After I graduated from the university in 1971, I ran a chain saw for a brief period, cutting ski trails, then learned carpentry and framed houses in Colorado, Connecticut, California, and finally Montana. At the same time, with the environmental movement just beginning to be heard, I joined my father, sister, and brother-in-law to write the first college-level environmental science textbook in the country. As time passed, I quit carpentry and earned a comfortable living writing a sequence of texts. I married twice and had three children, Nathan, Reeva, and Noey.

By 1980 I was single again and living in Telluride, a resort town in western Colorado. I dislocated a shoulder in a ski wreck, and while I was waiting for the swelling to subside so I could have an operation I hitchhiked north to Bozeman, Montana, where I met Chris Seashore through some old friends. After a few introductory chats, I asked her if she would like to float rivers and hike in the Utah desert with me. It was an audacious invitation to a first date and she later told me that she almost declined, but the landscape, not me, won her over.

We made love in the moon shadows of a gnarled juniper and then zipped our sleeping bags together to enjoy our new intimacy. A few weeks later, when it was time for Chris to return home and start her summer's work as a timber cruiser for the U.S. Forest Service, I tried to separate the bags, but the zipper jammed. As I fiddled with a recalcitrant slider, Chris stepped back, observing my frustration. I looked up. She was tanned from the hot sun, wearing a dirty T-shirt and her signature baseball cap, slightly askew, not in an orchestrated statement of style, but simply because she hadn't put it on straight.

Casually she remarked, "Well, if you can't separate the bags, I guess I'll take them both and you'll have to move in with me."

I smiled, tried to emulate her nonchalance, and responded, "I need directions to your house."

Chris lived in an old ghost town that had been resettled by a small ragtag bunch of hippies and ski bums and two aged Finnish miners who had done their time in the hard-rock gold and copper mines of Butte. A few weeks later, after closing up some business in Telluride, I drove north, turned off the paved road, and downshifted to ascend the hill, following the directions that Chris had scribbled on a piece of scrap paper, back in the desert. It was early July, and heavy, wet snowflakes settled on the fresh leaves that had emerged from their protective buds. I passed the weathered, skeletal remains of an old ore crusher and a boardinghouse, from the days when this mountainside was buzzing with the clank of steam engines and the calls of men.

Chris's small cabin was nestled into the hillside and sided with brown cedar shakes that were half-enveloped by hops vines. I pulled to the side of the road, turned off the engine, set the brake, and momentarily slumped against the steering wheel, exhausted after my thirty-hour drive from southern Colorado. I knew that Chris was still at work and would be home in an hour or so, so I stepped into the snowstorm and slid down the grassy bank toward her front door.

A deep, angry voice from above shattered the stillness: "Hey! What hell kind of guy you think you are, 'nooping around Wanapekea's house?"

A fat old man, waving a cane over his head like a saber, scurried down the hillside, with amazing speed and agility for someone who looked like he should be enjoying his final days on the rocking chair, perched between the fireplace and a diminishing bottle of vodka.

I didn't want to grab the rusty shovel that was leaning against the house and do battle with this gnome who was guarding the princess's castle, so I found words to avoid armed conflict. By the time Chris came home, I was in Jussi's kitchen, drinking horrible coffee and eating sugary cinnamon buns from the day-old counter at the closest supermarket in Anaconda.

The next fall, Chris and I moved to Bozeman, where she was finishing her degree in soil science at Montana State University. A few years later, we moved to Alaska, where I worked as a commercial fisherman and Chris got a job doing minerals exploration for Anaconda Corporation. In late August of 1984, flush with cash from productive summers, we met in Anchorage and decided to drive back to Montana, buy a house, and get married. For a few years we tried the laid-back-in-the-woods lifestyle but were repeatedly drawn toward bigger mountains, steeper ski lines, and deeper snowpack.

We bought an apartment in Fernie, British Columbia, in 1994, six years before my first visit to Vyvenka. Three years later, on a subzero January day in 1997, Chris and I climbed a ridge with several friends to seek fresh powder. Chris and two others skied down in a cloud of fluff that reflected rainbows in the morning sunshine. I climbed a little higher to take a slightly steeper and more committing line.

In retrospect, I should have been more observant. I should have recalled the precise behavior of the snow beneath our feet during the past two days. I should have dug down and searched for almost microscopic signs of crystalline weakness in the snowpack. But my friends and I were talking about this and that, joking, thinking about the past, the future, or some other place. I forgot the most fundamental survival axiom in the mountains: live in the moment.

The first four turns were glorious, dancing with gravity as sparkling crystals washed across my face and over my head. Then, even as I was floating downslope, I felt an eerie motion-within-a-motion as my skis dropped—probably less than an inch—not toward the bottom of the mountain, but toward the earth itself. No! It hadn't happened. No! I was just imagining. Cracks radiated rapidly from the tips of my skis; then the entire slope segmented into a terrifying maze of jagged lines.

I've read stories about people who have outrun an avalanche, as if it were a discrete object like a charging grizzly bear. But when you are the trigger that sets the slide in motion, shock waves race through the snowpack at approximately 200 miles an hour and the entire hillside fails virtually simultaneously, so that the avalanche is above you, below you, and on either side, churning, roiling, with an eerie silence that belies the power unleashed.

I was swept off my feet and for a brief moment rode downslope in the bright sunshine, on a block of moving snow, feeling magically invulnerable, as if I would slide gracefully to the bottom, stand up, and walk away. But the block fractured, I fell into a gaping crack, and then the snow snapped shut, engulfing me in an impenetrable dark grave. The snow began churning like an ocean wave and I was catapulting, somersaulting downslope.

Above me there was light, air, sky, life. Below me there was death by suffocation. The line was thin—five inches, ten, twenty, I don't know—thin and absolute. I whispered to myself, "You are too puny to fight the snow, so use its power to your advantage." I sped down the mountain at perhaps 50 miles per hour, flopping like a rag doll.

With a clarity I will never forget, I told myself, "The avalanche is like a river. You are like a kayaker. Think like a kayaker. Keep track of your body position. The avalanche is flowing downhill, but inside the main current there are swirls and eddies. Use the swirls to your advantage. Swim when buoyed upward by the current. Rest when the swirling snow pushes you downward."

Light, no light. Light. A tiny, imperceptible dot of light. Life.

My survival hinged on one simple imperative: "Keep track of your body position."

My head is up, toward life-giving air. That spot of light. Life. Now I'm upside down. Whoops. Head up. Head down. Whoops. My left arm just ripped out of its socket. Small matter. I had more important things on my mind right now. "Keep track of your body position. Head up. Head down."

I slowed and felt a sharp pain rip through my abdomen as I was compressed beneath the decelerating snow. A new pain. I would deal with that one, too, at some other time. Meanwhile, a mental map of the mountain raced through my brain. I must be at the bench, where the slope levels off, two-thirds of the way down. The snow and I would speed up in a moment as the slope below became steeper. Calm calculation morphed into hope. Like a judo master using the strength of his opponent for his own advantage, I could harness this change of speed, coupled with the motion of the snowy wave, to lift me to the surface.

I waited an agonizing split second until my head was pointing uphill, my back pillowed by the snowy wave.

"Now!" I thought. "This is the moment that will concentrate all other moments past and future. This is the moment when I choose to live or die."

I backstroked furiously with my good arm and the forearm of my dislocated shoulder. The wave pushed against my back, gently lifting me, while snow passed underneath. Yes! I was moving slower than the avalanche itself! That tiny spot of light was growing bigger. I was rising! I was breathing. Air. Blue sky.

When I came to a halt, I was lying on my back on the surface of the snow, in the bright winter sunshine. Even before I caught my breath, I recognized familiar spruce and fir beneath uplifted limestone crags. I wanted to jump to my feet, wave my arms, and shout to my friends below, "I'm OK!"

But I couldn't stand. I couldn't move my legs.

"Oh, my God. I'm paralyzed!"

I lay on the snow, imagining with horror that I would spend the rest of my life in a wheelchair.

But a hopeful voice inside me spoke out of the abyss: "You're OK, Jon. You're badly hurt, but not paralyzed."

Then another voice argued back, "You're just lying. False hope is worse than no hope."

"No, I'm not paralyzed."

"Prove it to me."

"OK, I'll wiggle my toes. If I can wiggle my toes, I'm not paralyzed."

I paused. Was this the beginning of my healing, or the end of my life as I had known it for fifty-one years?

I built up my courage and then shouted a command through my nervous system, moving electrical impulses across mysterious synapses: "Toes! You guys down there! Listen up! I'm talking to you. Wiggle!"

My toes bumped reassuringly against the inside of my ski boots.

A few hours later the doctors in the local hospital told me that I had separated my pelvis and ripped my adductor muscles off the bone. Internal bleeding was life threatening. An emergency response team flew me to Calgary in a helicopter and surgeons bolted me back together with a titanium plate and four large screws. After surgery, I spent ten days in the hospital and six weeks in bed. Then, surrounded by the abundant paraphernalia of a physical therapy clinic, I hobbled back onto my feet, balancing precariously on crutches.

For the first few days I was thankful that I could go to the bathroom by myself. Three weeks later, Chris took me to ski the bunny slope of a local ski area near Darby. After one pathetically off-balance run, I cried and told her, "If this is all I get, it's so much better than a hospital bed. I will be content." But by evening I reasoned, irrationally, "If I can ski a bunny slope, I should be able to ski steep slopes in the high mountains." Chris shook her head worriedly.

I spent four hours every day in the gym and on July 5th, five months and nine days after the accident, Chris and I climbed to a rocky pass in the Canadian Rockies, beneath imposing limestone walls and high peaks. We ate lunch at the col, leaning against each other gently. Then, I took a deep breath, ignored the voices of sanity inside me, stepped into my skis, and stared down a steep snow patch above a small cliff. I had to make three quick turns and then cut hard right to avoid toppling over the rocks. I hadn't made an aggressive turn since before the accident.

Chris looked at me as if suddenly comprehending the situation. "Are you sure this is a good idea, Jon?"

I grinned and dropped into the fall line, beyond the realm of conversation or caution. My edges chattered on hard snow, carrying me through awkward and unpracticed turns. Skiing had been my life—and then it had almost taken life away from me. Now my skis were bringing me back, out of the abyss, into the glorious compression of a turn, the freedom of unfettered motion.

That day, I proved that I could still ski. But I never healed completely and in the ensuing years I suffered episodic intense pain. On good days, I continued my active, outdoor lifestyle, but on bad days, I could barely walk. Yet, partly out of innate optimism, or maybe obstinate denial, I decided to follow through with prior plans to kayak across the North Pacific. If you accuse me of being a fool, I'll smile sheepishly and shrug. Adventuring had been the focus of my existence for nearly thirty years. I knew how to cope with pain but couldn't imagine becoming sedentary.

I met Moolynaut on the second year of that passage and now, in the spring of 2001, four years after the accident, I wanted to return to Vyvenka and travel to the Holy Stone. Chris and I bought a video camera to shoot footage of nomadic reindeer cultures—assuming we could find reindeer people in the devastated landscape. We never discussed the ramifications of traveling across a harsh and remote land with a half-damaged body.

A month before we left, as I was breaking trail up a steep slope, I felt a sudden and particularly intense pain in my injured and bolted-together pelvis. I stopped and leaned on my ski poles. What physical damage was triggering those rapid electrical impulses in my nerve endings? On the one hand, it was late afternoon and we had enjoyed superb skiing all day. There would be no shame in going home. But on the other hand, the sun still shone above the western peaks. I could push through the pain. I said nothing to my friends, shifted my weight back onto my feet, and continued upward, toward the ridge marked by a familiar dead spar that uplifted my spirit because its white branches arced like a dancer's arms.

I spent that evening on the couch and went to bed early. When I had to pee in the middle of the night, my pelvis hurt so much that I crawled to the bathroom.

My local doctor, Ron Clark, took an X-ray and observed that the plate holding my pelvis together had broken and the screws were loose. The symphysis pubis junction that had separated during the accident had mended together with a hodgepodge of bone and scar tissue, but then my body's repair job had fractured. Ron explained that, in a healthy person, the pelvic junction flexes slightly, but the combination of hardware and scar tissue permitted no motion. I had repeatedly stressed this system by skiing too aggressively and eventually everything had broken, just as a paper clip will break if you bend it back and forth many times.

"So what's holding me together now?" I asked.

"Maybe nothing," he replied with a slight chuckle.

"And what's causing the pain?"

"Well, it's a complex system; it could be any of a number of things."

I made an appointment with Dr. Schutte, a sports-orthopedic surgeon in Missoula, Montana. He was busy and couldn't see me until the day before our scheduled departure for Siberia.

Chris and I considered abandoning the expedition, but the pain was episodic and usually I felt fine. Our tickets were nonrefundable, so we decided to pack anyway and make the final decision at the last minute.

Dr. Schutte's a hardworking man who has maintained an enigmatic whimsy despite his serious profession. He took several X-rays and confirmed that the plate was broken, the screws were loose, and there was, in the words of the radiologist, "a linear lucency through the bony bridge that could be due to refracturing."

Repeating the question I had posed to Dr. Clark, I asked, "So, what, exactly, is causing the pain?"

"I'm not sure. Your pelvis was displaced considerably during the avalanche. . . . There's been a lot of trauma and soft tissue damage. . . ."

I thought, "If no one knows what's causing the pain, how can we find a cure?" I waited for him to continue.

Dr. Schutte concluded, "I'm a knee and shoulder specialist. I don't operate on the pelvis. You'd better go see a specialist. I suppose he could remove the plate. But bone has grown around the edges of the metal, so removal would be painful and the rehabilitation might be six months. At your age, maybe it would be a year before you regained full athletic performance. There's significant risk involved and I'm not quite sure that the operation would solve the problem."

He waited for the information to sink in. "Do you want to make an appointment with a hip and pelvis specialist?"

I thought back to the hospital in Calgary. When I woke up from the anesthesia, immediately after the accident, nine tubes were transporting liquids or gases into or out of my body. In frustration, I shook the oxygen mask free, let it fall to the floor, and then felt dizzy, so I meekly pushed the call button and asked the nurse to replace my mask. But that was just the beginning. After I left the hospital and returned to our apartment in Fernie, Chris rented a hydraulic crane from the home-care agency. Every morning she hoisted me out of bed and wheeled me to the toilet seat. When I was done, she lifted me into a recliner. In the afternoon she transported me from the recliner back to bed. I remembered the eventful day when Chris lowered me into a wheelchair and I decided to roll down into the hallway for exercise and entertainment. But because my injured left arm was weaker than my right, I repeatedly veered off course and banged into the wall. The window at the end of the hallway was positioned in the stairwell, below my line of sight, so when I reached the zenith of my pitiful expedition I couldn't even look outdoors. Frustrated, I turned the wheelchair around, stared down the tunnel of pastel green walls, rolled to the apartment, and asked Chris to transfer me back into the recliner.

I had agreed to the first operation because I couldn't move my legs, stand, or walk. Now I walked most of the time and even skied on good days. I wasn't eager to chance another operation, especially when it might do more harm than good.

Dr. Schutte waited for an answer.

It was easy to decide against another operation but scary to commit to an expedition on the remote Siberian tundra. Images swirled in my brain, overlapped, and intermingled.

"No, I don't want an appointment. We have tickets to Siberia."

Dr. Schutte looked surprised. "When do you leave?"

"Tomorrow."

He smiled, asked me about the expedition, and listened carefully to my story. Then he turned to the light box mounted on the wall and studied the eerie black-and-white images of my pelvis with its ruptured steel and bent screws. With his back to me, he asked, "Do you run or jog anymore?"

"No, not too much. Not since the accident."

He nodded slowly. "I didn't think so." He abruptly snapped the X-rays off the light box and slipped them into a manila folder. Then he faced me, extended his hand, and spoke in a soft voice, like that of a friend: "Good luck in Siberia. Don't run. Come back if the problem persists."

Return to Vyvenka

Because there are no convenient flights to the Russian Far East, Chris and I flew three-quarters of the way around the world, through New York and Moscow, to PK, a city of a quarter of a million, home to the Russian Bering Sea fishing fleet and the nuclear attack submarines that once—and may still—lurk off the coast of California. On the afternoon of March 30th, Misha met us at the airport, with a big smile and a bouquet of roses for Chris. We were zombielike after crossing nineteen time zones, sleeping two nights on an Aeroflot seat, and breathing that curious concoction of gases that constitutes airplane air, but Misha blithely announced that we had arrived in time for the weeklong annual geology party.

At the time, Misha was forty years old. As a young man, he had graduated from the prestigious geology and mining institute in St. Petersburg. During Soviet times, young scientists received better pay and early retirement if they volunteered to work in the Siberian wilderness. Intrigued by the adventure and the benefits, Misha signed on as a hydrogeologist to map water reserves on the Kamchatka Peninsula. There he married Nina, another hydrogeologist, and they settled into a small apartment in the town of Termalny (Hot Springs), located about a half an hour's drive from PK.

When I was in grade school, I learned that Soviet collectives formed a hated structure that ruled people's lives with an iron fist. But that image is an Americanized, propaganda-oriented oversimplification. I don't know how people felt elsewhere, but in Kamchatka, during the 1980s, members of the hydrogeology collective spent their summers in the wild landscapes around them. The autocratic, repressive government in Moscow was far away, while their comrades were close, sharing camps, poor food, marauding bears, and homemade vodka that they distilled over forest campfires. The geologists became lifelong friends and the collective was their professional society and social structure. When Communism collapsed starting in 1988, these men and women found themselves collectively out of work, so they created a company, Aquarius, that was a capitalistic collective. In the massive confusion following the collapse of the Soviet Empire, Aquarius privatized four valuable natural resources: a hot springs spa, an artesian well of pure drinking water, another well that supplied mineral water, and a third well that tapped into underground carbon dioxide. I've never understood exactly how the process of privatization worked, or didn't work, but in the madcap days following the economic restructuring of the Soviet Empire, called perestroika, clever people provided for themselves, and those who were less clever, or less aggressive, lost out. Misha is clever. Aquarius entered a joint venture with a large fishing company, bought modern automated bottling equipment from Switzerland, and sold soft drinks, mineral water, and industrial carbon dioxide gas. When Chris and I arrived in the early spring of 2001, Aquarius was a thriving venture with a 25 percent annual growth rate. But at the same time, Misha had forfeited the healthy, invigorating, scientifically challenging outdoor life of a field geologist for the paper-shuffling, bureaucrat-bribing, money-counting life of a Russian businessman.

Regardless, the men and women of Aquarius still lived in communal apartment blocks in Termalny. And they still partied together. We drank vodka, danced, and ate. Grossly out of tune, but with arms waving like Frank Sinatra at the opera, I drunkenly belted out "Yesterday," by the Beatles—to thunderous applause.

A trim, beautiful woman with heavy makeup, abundant cheap perfume, and excellent English asked me to dance, and as we glided around the room she said, "There are governments and there are people. Our governments have been at war. But we are the people—Russian and American—and there has never been a war between us. Welcome to Russia." She pressed her breasts against my chest, and through the haze of jet lag and vodka I marveled at the madness of the Cold War that had caused so much fear, hatred, and expense.

Misha and Nina have two daughters, Anastasia, who was twelve at the time, and Maria, who was ten. The family lived in a drab concrete Soviet-era apartment, three flights up a dingy, poorly lit stairwell. The plumbing worked sporadically. But Nina had decorated the place with new carpets, frilly curtains, abundant houseplants, and other accoutrements of a happy home. Every Sunday, on her day off, Nina vacuumed, mopped, and scrubbed, and the small apartment was always filled with love.

For a few days, Misha dashed about frantically to tie up loose ends at the office; then, on April 6th, Chris, Misha, and I threaded our way between the knees of people straddling bundles of dried fish and bags of onions to claim the last three empty seats for the Yak-40 flight to the twin towns Korpf/Tillichiki, 775 miles north of PK. There was no road between Korpf/Tillichiki and Vyvenka, 25 miles to the south, but Misha had arranged for Oleg and Sergei to pick us up with their snow machines.

As the turboprop circled downward, a strong wind buffeted the aircraft and blew serpentine wisps of snow across the runway. The Russian woman next to me was carrying an immense bouquet of red roses. The plane coasted to a stop, the high-pitched whir of the engine receded into silence, the door opened, and the passengers stood to exit the tunnel-like cocoon of the aircraft. A blast of frigid air jostled the hairs inside my nose and settled into my sinus, announcing, "See, those protective layers of clothing are nothing to me. In two seconds, I penetrated the armor and burrowed inside. Think of what I can do in a day, a week, or a month."

The woman behind me let out a small cry of alarm and I turned to watch the wind tearing petals off the roses and swirling the incongruous red fragments in ascending whirlwinds around the silver fuselage of the plane, as if we were being welcomed to a Hawaiian flower ceremony.

A crowd of Russians in Western clothing waited on the edge of the tarmac to greet passengers while three Koryak men, dressed in deerskin shirts, sealskin mukluks (boots), and patches of worn Russian army fatigues, stood on the other side of the fence. Their hats, made of fur and covered with decorative beadwork, rose over the men's heads with lobes that reminded me of a wolf's ears decorated for the circus. Each man wore a long knife strapped obliquely across his pelvis. Their dun-colored furs and splotchy forest green camouflage looked out of place against the wispy rose petals that now spun overhead and blended with the blowing snow.

Oleg, corpulent and solid, looking like a sumo wrestler, greeted us with a massive bear hug. Sergei stepped forward with his gaunt, bouncy stride and smiled toothlessly while Simon, Vyvenka's mayor, shook hands with the familiarity and grace of a wilderness politician. Three snow machines were parked in the street—two ancient double-tracked Russian Burans and Oleg's shiny green Yamaha. We lashed our gear onto the handmade birch sleds for the ride to Vyvenka.

As we were tying down our loads, I was jolted upright by a loud clanking sound as a monstrous, armored, terrestrial warship clanked down the street, on steel tracks, as if racing to the front at the battle of Leningrad. Chris and I were the only people who seemed alarmed, and when I asked what the commotion was all about Misha casually replied that this was a *visdichot*, as if the name could explain its existence. But over the years, I learned that these beasts, the pinnacle of World War II technology, are the SUVs and pickup trucks in this harsh land.

When everything was lashed securely, the men pulled the starter cords and the two tired Burans coughed and sputtered to life while the Yamaha purred. Oleg told Chris to ride stylishly on the comfortable backseat of his machine, while Misha and I straddled the loaded sleds and hung on like bull riders as we bounced over the rutted, frozen city streets. Sparks flew out from beneath the snow-machine skis as we skidded over the bare road and the spinning tracks hurtled gravel at our faces.

The economy of Korpf/Tillichiki is based on a rich salmon fishery and the second-largest platinum mine in the world, located fifty miles inland. But despite the great resource wealth, the town was seemingly about to disintegrate and blow away with the wind, like the rose petals. Unpainted, faded, weather-beaten siding hung loosely on tired nails while rusted metal roofing flapped loudly against the skeletons of abandoned, ravaged, and cannibalized structures. Trash scudded across the road like tumbleweed. A few drunks stumbled past, followed by a young mother pulling a bundled baby in a plastic sled. Oleg took a sharp right turn down an alley decorated with frozen laundry and then suddenly, as if we had driven through some magical door, we burst out of town and onto the tundra. I turned my head back to be sure that Korpf/Tillichiki wasn't just a temporary chimera and then looked forward at the primordial Arctic wilderness that spread out before us, as far as the eye or the imagination could conceive. As the snow machines skidded onto the smooth ice of a lagoon, the sled careened wildly in the gusting winds and tentacles of snow drifted across the ice like a choreographed troop of dancing snakes. Within a few minutes, frostbite bit into my exposed chin and cheeks. Misha, who was behind me, muttered something in Russian and then laughed loudly.

After about five minutes, we reached the end of the lagoon and the machines slowed as they bounced through soft snow onto hummocky tundra. After a few bounces, a mechanical clanking sound screeched above the normal engine whine and we slid off the packed trail, auguring into bushes. Sergei lit a cigarette while Oleg walked over and surveyed the situation. The drive track had slid off the guide rollers. Oleg muttered softly, *"Paiyette,"* which means roughly "no big deal. That's the way it goes. That's life."

Misha, Chris, and I dug the machine out while Sergei beat worn and reluctant parts into their intended positions with a heavy hammer. With the windchill reduced and some vigorous exercise, my blood again pumped warmth throughout my body. After two more breakdowns, we reached a pass overlooking the Vyvenka River and stopped for a break.

Without preamble, Oleg launched into a story:

"Many years ago, a strong young man and a beautiful maiden fell in love. But the boy was poor, so the girl's father would not consent to marriage. Saddened, the maiden sat outside on a summer night, combing her long, shiny hair. She was so beautiful that the moon fell in love with her and asked her to escape with him into the heavens. The girl refused and instead eloped with her human lover. The father pursued the young couple. The moon, angry at the rejection, threw huge stones at the unfortunate youths. The boy and girl realized that they couldn't escape both the father and the moon, so they jumped off a cliff to their deaths. The impact of their landing made a huge hole in the ground. The water that gushed up from the hole formed the Vyvenka River. The hills on either side of the river are the stones tossed down by the vengeful moon. Ever since that time, the Vyvenka River has been the economic lifeblood of my people. Thus the lovers' sacrifice ensured health and prosperity for future generations."

Abruptly Oleg pulled the starter cord on his machine, signaling that the story was over and it was time to go. Misha and I climbed back onto the toboggan behind Sergei's sled, and he started cautiously down the steep hill. Almost immediately the toboggan slid faster than the snow machine, threatening to overrun it. I was sure that we were all about to tumble through the bushes in a giant tangle of people and machinery, but Sergei stood on the running boards, looked back at us with a devilish grin, and gunned the throttle. The machine pulled ahead of the toboggan, but the acceleration sent us bouncing and flying through the alders, just like Calvin and Hobbes on their toy sled, until we finally reached the river and glided onto smooth ice. Close to town, a dozen people were spread out across the lagoon, ice-fishing. The river veered left and we followed the well-worn trail over a low hill toward the ocean, and town.

Lydia stepped outside as soon as she heard the snow machines. Following her accustomed ritual, she held a small shovel heaped with glowing coals. She pulled pieces of wool from our hats and dropped them into the embers. The wool shriveled and burned as she chanted an incantation. Once she exorcised any evil spirits that might have hitchhiked into her isolated sanctuary, she laid the shovel in the snow, hugged each one of us, with an especially warm embrace for Chris, and beckoned us into Goshe's apartment.

The Village of Vyvenka

In medieval times, Russia was a European nation, lying west of the Ural Mountains. Then in 1552, Russians started expanding eastward—conquering, killing, taxing, and enslaving the indigenous people who had lived across an unimaginably vast swath of Siberian taiga and tundra since Paleolithic times. The fierce Koryak and their neighbors, the Chukchi, lived farthest from Moscow and were the last people to be subdued. The first Russian soldiers reached the northeastern shore of Asia in 1697 but were repulsed by Koryak warriors wearing bone-plated seal-hide armor and walrus-skin helmets. Even after Russian reinforcements poured into the land, attacked isolated villages, and took hostages, the determined warriors kept fighting. But like the brave Apache and Sioux in North America, the Koryak couldn't hold out forever. After sixty years of warfare and devastation from European diseases—after their population had been reduced from thirteen thousand to five thousand—the surviving Koryak capitulated.

That was a long time ago, and in my five visits to Vyvenka no one has ever discussed the Russian conquest. The Koryak people don't talk about hardships and bad times. You live through bad times and go on. In a land of constant bad times, it is the only way.

Kamchatka is a narrow peninsula, the size of Italy, but with one two-hundredth the population, that protrudes like an elephant's trunk from the east coast of Siberia. Vyvenka lies on the northeast coast of this peninsula, at sixty degrees north, 375 miles due south of the Arctic Circle, about the same latitude as Anchorage, Alaska. While huge forests flourish at that latitude in North America, Vyvenka is surrounded by subarctic tundra. Grasses, mosses, and sedge cover exposed ridgetops and plateaus, while low bushes and even a few hardy trees grow in hollows protected from the harsh winter wind.

The World Heritage Centre of UNESCO has recognized Kamchatka's unique geology and ecology by designating six world heritage sites throughout the peninsula. These designations were based on the observations that Kamchatka has the highest density of active volcanoes in the world, the greatest diversity of salmon, trout, and char, an estimated 12,500 Kamchatka brown bears (grizzly bears), over half of the planet's Steller's sea eagles, and hundreds of species of endemic arctic and subarctic plants that are found nowhere else in the world.

During Soviet times, two thousand people lived in Vyvenka, including Russian doctors, lawyers, teachers, engineers, and other government employees. But when perestroika hit and the economic structure evaporated overnight, almost all the Russians left. In 2007, 350 people lived in the village.

To understand Vyvenka, you have to stretch and perhaps redefine your concepts of isolation and poverty. Vyvenka is nine time zones from Moscow—more than a third of the way around the world and three times as far as New York is from San Francisco.

When the Russians conquered Siberia and extended their empire to the

Pacific in the eighteenth century, they didn't build roads across the new land in the same way that North American conquerors assimilated their Pacific coast. Maybe Siberia is just too harsh, or maybe the only explanation is that, as Winston Churchill famously said, "Russia is a riddle, wrapped in a mystery, inside an enigma." But whatever the reason, the first all-season east-west road across Siberia, navigable by ordinary two-wheel-drive, low-clearance automobiles, was completed in 2003. This road snakes its way across the southern border of Russia to Vladivostok eighteen hundred air miles to the south of Vyvenka, with no north-south spurs connecting Vladivostok with anyplace in Kamchatka. If you harnessed up a dog team and traveled due west from Vyvenka, you might bump into a road suitable for two-wheel-drive automobiles somewhere near the Ural Mountains, but the journey would be likely to take a year or more, depending on your skill, logistics, weather, and luck. When Vitus Bering set out from Moscow in the 1720s, he traveled three years before he reached the Pacific Ocean. If, instead, you chose to travel by reindeer sled and follow the compass arrow northward, you would cross uninhabited tundra until reaching the Arctic Ocean seven hundred miles away. The Pacific Ocean guards the town's eastern flank.

Some maps show a few roads crisscrossing the line of sixty degrees north latitude in the Siberian tundra. I've seen those maps, but I've also traveled across this landscape, by ski and snow machine, and I've talked to hunters around smoky campfires and propped my map against the rusted hulk of a *visdichot* and asked the driver to tell me about lands that I haven't visited. From all these experiences, I've come to understand that the roads drawn on maps are often a chimera. As Nikolai, from the reindeer camp, once told me, his gnarled finger pointing to one of those enigmatic red lines on a well-worn map: "I don't know why anyone thinks that there is a road here. Maybe someone drove a snow machine across the tundra one day to look for his lost dog and the next day a mapmaker from America flew overhead in a helicopter and saw the snow-machine track and said, 'Oh this must be a road.' So now there is a road on the map."

In most parts of the world, a road is a horizontal structure built by engineers and construction crews who move dirt and rock to create a firm bed, install culverts to improve drainage, and erect bridges across rivers. But no one in the Russian Far North has the money or the inclination to build such a road for the sparse traffic that it might bear. Instead road building—such as it is—comes free when winter ice freezes everything solid and creates a firm, smooth pavement over rivers, swamps, and mountain passes. When the ice melts in spring, the road disappears, but that's no reason to worry; if you wait five or six months, another crude road, navigable by *visdichots* and six-wheel-drive military trucks, will rebuild itself—once again, free of charge. You learn patience in the North. As Oleg would say, "There is no other way."

Supplies reach Kamchatka by ship, and the telephones work sometimes, but people are poor and in the mayhem of modern Russia transportation and communication are unreliable. As a consequence, according to our North American perspective, the villages of the Russian Far East are hell-holes with deteriorating infrastructure, intermittent electricity, poor food, crumbling buildings, and nearly nonexistent communication. But if you interpret people's lives through the lens of North American opulence, don't bother traveling among the impoverished people of the world. When Misha and I landed in Vyvenka on our kayak expedition in 2000—hungry, cold, wet, and scared—we found shelter, warmth, and food. Later, when we returned four more times, Moolynaut, Lydia, Oleg, and Sergei became close friends, so Vyvenka also represented extended family.

On the kayak expedition, Misha and I needed to buy food. Beneath a cracked glass display case on the counter of the dark, cavernous store, with its filthy, nearly opaque windows, lay two-year-old American Valentine's Day chocolate, wrapped in a red heart-shaped box with a gaudy ribbon, French nail polish, and valve springs to some nameless engine designed by an engineer in a faraway land. But Oleg told me that it was virtually impossible to buy a new spark plug for his snow machine, and he looked at me with interest and a shade of disbelief when I told him that in America you could order any part for any machine and it would generally be delivered within twenty-four hours. At that time, Misha and I had no use for snow-machine parts, but we were hungry, so we bought white rice, cooking oil, sugar, tea, and a bag of stale cookies—and worried that we would starve to death on such inadequate food. But Oleg contributed dried fish and a huge jar of rich, fatty salmon caviar. Lydia offered us some precious jam, a few radishes, and freshly dug potatoes. As we paddled north in our kayaks, we set a net almost every night and feasted on fresh salmon.

So, yes, Vyvenka is a dilapidated, decrepit collection of tar-paper shacks, perched so close to the ocean that storm waves routinely batter against the houses, but to my friends it is home, and during the years that I have visited this remote outpost my belly has always been full and my sleeping bag has remained dry.

One day, on my third visit to Vyvenka, after I felt comfortable enough to probe deeper into people's lives, I asked Lydia what people did when they got sick. She told me that people often went to see Moolynaut first because she was a powerful healer. And if that didn't work, there was a nurse in town.

"And if neither Moolynaut nor the nurse can cure them?" I asked.

Lydia explained that there was a hospital and an evacuation helicopter in Korpf. Then she added, "If the helicopter is working, if the weather is good, if there is fuel, if the pilot is sober, and if there is money, then the helicopter will take people to the hospital. If the helicopter does not come, then sometimes we can bring people to Korpf by snow machine or speedboat. But if there is no snow or if the weather is too bad for the speedboat, then people just die." She looked up and smiled warmly, as if challenging me gently with her equanimity.

Moolynaut

After Chris, Misha, and I arrived in Vyvenka and were cleansed by fire, Lydia ushered us through a curtain of warmth into Goshe's kitchen—exchanging the harsh, uplifting infinity of the open tundra for the secure, confining enclosure of a house. Nine months ago Misha and I had kayaked through the surf to land in this isolated but embracing village, and for some inexplicable reason we had returned. Once we were inside, and even before I had removed my coat, Lydia poked a finger at splotches of frostbite that had formed on my face during the snow-machine ride and remarked, "Ah, you are a white man, but you look like a hunter."

Then Lydia asked why Chris's face wasn't nipped by the cold and Sergei replied that she was smart enough to wear a face mask, while I was strong but stupid. Everyone laughed good-naturedly and the barren, ramshackle room filled with the joy of reunion.

After tea, Lydia told us to wait while she brought Moolynaut to visit. We sat on rickety stools by the small table, warmed by the massive brick *petchka*. Moolynaut entered, dressed in a faded floral cotton dress and red wool leggings, with a red kerchief over her head. She greeted us warmly, speaking in a hoarse but melodious voice, like a feminine version of Louis Armstrong: "I am happy that you came back. I told you this before; I am happy to see Americans again." I told her that I was glad to be back in Vyvenka. We exchanged small talk about the fishing season, the intensity of winter, and the welcomed return of the spring sun.

Then the conversation paused. I reminded myself that Moolynaut was a shaman, highly respected by her tribe. Her name, in Koryak, translated as "She Who Gives Blood for the People." I had to establish a foundation before I could probe the mystery behind this woman. This was going to take time and patience. As a starting point, I asked Moolynaut to tell me the story of her life.

Moolynaut spoke in Russian, waving her arms animatedly and looking skyward at pleasant memories. Misha translated.

Moolynaut was born in a *yuranga* on the Kamchatka tundra, near the Vyvenka River, just north of Man with the Fast Shoes Mountain. She thinks she was born around 1904 but isn't certain and doesn't particularly care about the date. One of Moolynaut's grandfathers was an American. He arrived on a ship that traded with the Koryak, but he was so ill that the captain left him behind, under the care of a woman named Arnaut, a local shaman and healer. The young sailor grew strong on reindeer meat and chants and eventually married Arnaut. But despite his powerful and respected young wife, new home, and growing family, the sailor stood by the sea for many hours every day, staring across the ocean, wishing to return to his homeland. Finally, one day another Yankee trading ship arrived and he left Kamchatka and his family forever.

A Koryak *yuranga* is roughly circular, with four-foot vertical sides and a domed roof with a smoke hole in the center, similar to the yurts of Tibet and the *gers* of Mongolia. But the northeast Siberian *yuranga* is larger than similar structures in Central Asia and is subdivided into small skin-walled family sleeping quarters located along the perimeter. An open hearth, communal kitchen, and dining area are located in the center. Six families lived in Moolynaut's *yuranga*.

Moolynaut stopped in her narrative, smiled, held her arms skyward, and explained, "On a spring day, like today, sunlight filtered through the skins, casting a soft, warm glow all around you, not like it is in a house, with solid walls and roof, an electric lightbulb, and one small window."

Before the Soviets conquered eastern Siberia, there were few towns in the Russian Arctic. Vyvenka didn't exist, but there was a small village in Tillichiki. Only poor people, who didn't own reindeer, lived in town. Reindeer herders called the villagers mouse-eating people because they were often so hungry that they ate rodents.

Moolynaut explained that her father, Yuuka, owned two thousand reindeer and three thousand white horses. I imagined this huge herd of white horses running across the tundra, leaping across bogs, manes flying. But I didn't believe the image, so I queried, "Three thousand horses? Are you sure? Why did he need that many horses? And why were they all white?"

The room fell silent. Lydia looked away, avoiding eye contact with me. Oleg standing to the side, near the *petchka*, arms folded across his massive chest, raised his eyebrows, indicating surprise and alarm at my indiscretion. Only Moolynaut held my gaze. "Yes," she repeated steadily. "My father, Yuuka, owned two thousand reindeer and three thousand white horses. And my uncle owned five thousand reindeer. Together we had seven thousand reindeer and three thousand white horses. My father was a rich man. The horses were very beautiful. When I was seven or eight he gave me a white horse and we galloped across the tundra together. My father sold the horses to other clan leaders because everyone wanted to own beautiful white horses, like my father."

I never questioned another story again. During my five visits to Vyvenka I heard many stories. Some seemed totally preposterous to my Western mind, while others were believable, and many seemed halfway in between. But after that day, I simply recorded, never questioning or doubting, and throughout this book I tell tales exactly as people told them to me.

After a silence, Moolynaut continued her story. She explained that even though her people owned a lot of livestock, they had few material possessions from the white man's world. They had little contact with the Russians at that time, but the Americans sailed into Gecka Bay every year and her father bartered deer meat, skins, and walrus ivory for flour, sugar, tea, clothing, and some metal tools, weapons, and kettles.

Far away, Czar Nicholas II held tenaciously to power while intellectuals and anarchists met in dank cellars to plot a revolution. Soon, news of war filtered across the tundra to Kamchatka. Sometime between 1920 and 1924, victorious Red armies moved into the land. Moolynaut's clan retreated with their deer and established a system of lookouts to monitor hostile troop movements. Initially they eluded their pursuers, but it's hard to hide on open tundra with families, small children, and ten thousand animals. Finally, the Koryak engaged and defeated a small Red Army detachment near Heart Mountain. When the Soviets dispatched a larger force, the Koryak held a council at the Holy Stone and decided that if the Russians planned to kill the clan leaders because they were rich capitalists, then they would all fight to the death. But if the Soviets only took their deer and asked the people to change their lives, they would surrender.

At this point Moolynaut suddenly stopped talking, and after a moment of silence Lydia continued in English, "The Soviets agreed. They knew that we had rifles and that we were brave and strong. They knew that the Russian armies would have difficulty surviving in this harsh land and that we would fight. So they didn't kill us and imprison our people in the gulags."

Then she looked at me intently, pointed at my notebook, and asked, "You will write what I say in your book when you return to America?"

"Yes," I replied. "If you want me to."

"Then write this: The Soviets forced our people to move into the villages and become 'mouse eaters.' Moolynaut's mother and father had no other way. When my father died and my mother was left alone to raise four children, she had no other way. People with small children did what the Soviets said so their children would live. But the older people, if their children were already grown and could care for themselves . . ."

Lydia stopped for a moment. "Some of the older people . . . walked into the tundra to die."

Misha translated into Russian, and Oleg nodded stoically. Moolynaut suddenly announced that she was tired. She quickly gathered her coat and walked out the door without looking back or saying good-bye.

Moolynaut told me the remaining story of her life in bits and pieces, spread out over a total of five and a half years and five visits. Sometimes she would tell only the skeleton of a story and flesh out the details a year later, picking up the narrative as if no time had passed. Often the tale would take abrupt jumps forward or backward by decades.

While Moolynaut was very precise about some details, especially in describing her childhood, at other times she left me hopelessly confused. For example, on two different occasions Moolynaut told me that she had four husbands, and at two other times she told me that she had two husbands. At various times she reported that she had two, three, five, and seven children. To this day, I'm not sure whether the information gap was generated by Moolynaut's memory loss or an unwillingness to drag out all the complexities of a long and tragedy-filled life.

The last time I saw Moolynaut, in November 2005, I resolved to get my facts straight, so pen and notebook in hand, I asked her directly, "How many children did you have?"

We were close enough friends by this time that she had invited us into her house. She was sitting on the floor, on a thin threadbare rug, in a room with no furniture but a south-facing window. Warm sunlight filtered through the window, so that the windblown snow outside seemed distant and abstract. Her right leg was tucked under her left knee, and her left leg was stretched straight in front of her. Moolynaut reached forward and touched her toes, then remained silent, stretching. She considered my question for several moments and then sat upright, looked directly at me, and replied, "*Mnoga* [many]."

At the risk of being insulting, I asked again.

She chanted for about five minutes in the old tongue, rocking back and forth, singing in a low, throaty, whisper, and answered, "They are all dead now."

Then she continued softly, "*Mnoga. Mnoga* children, *mnoga* grandchildren, *mnoga* great-grandchildren. *Eideen* [one] great-great-grandchild. Most are dead now. After my husband died—the Russian husband, the best one— I thought that I couldn't live anymore. But eventually I realized that I must continue because they are all still living within me."

I didn't ask about her family history again.

On several occasions, Moolynaut explained that when she was eighteen or nineteen the Soviets took her father's livestock and ordered Yuuka and Moolynaut to work on a fishing boat. They assigned the two of them to a massive barge called a *kongass*, about sixty to seventy feet long, with no motor or sail. She described in detail that it was built of three-inch-thick planks laid up over even thicker ribs that were joined to a keel sawn from a single massive tree harvested from a distant forest near Vladivostok.

The Koryak people in Kamchatka catch herring and salmon in huge traps. A trap consists of a half-mile-long net made of fine mesh, anchored on one end to the beach and running out to sea at right angles to the shore. The fish aren't caught by this net but diverted into the trap, which is a mazelike enclosure, also made of fine mesh. The *kongass* is anchored to this trap. When the trap fills up, the crew lowers a fine-meshed net, called a seine, to scoop up all the fish.

One day I explained to Moolynaut that I worked for four years as a fisherman in the North Bering Sea and recalled vividly that even though we had hydraulic winches, we cut our hands handling heavy nets, and that cuts and blisters often festered because they were constantly immersed in cold salt water. With that introduction, I asked her if she found the work on the *kongass* difficult. She nodded and said simply that she worked alongside the men and that it was very hard because she was small, but she was young and strong. Then she explained proudly that despite the hardships her brigade usually caught two or three times their quota.

I tried to imagine Moolynaut as a young woman, barely five feet tall and probably no more than a hundred pounds. But before I could complete my reverie, she said simply, "I wanted to work with deer. My father wanted to work with deer. We knew how to herd deer and didn't know much about fishing. But we did what the Soviets told us to do."

One spring day, when she was thirty years old, a violent storm pounded the coast. The heavy *kongass* chafed against its old, worn mooring lines until the ropes snapped and the wind drove the barge into the surf. Moolynaut, Yuuka, and the rest of the crew jumped into the icy Arctic water. Dragged down by heavy skin clothing, Moolynaut watched daylight fading above her and was on the verge of accepting death when she felt a hand grasp the back of her jacket and her father wrenched her back to the surface. Her father had tied himself to a float made from an inflated walrus stomach, and when they surfaced they started paddling to shore, clinging to the float. The water was frigidly cold, and when they began to lose their strength her father told her that they would live if she turned her head so her eyes, ears, and nose were exposed to the sun. Once they reached shore, they stripped naked to shed their heavy wet clothing, rubbed their bodies vigorously to stimulate blood flow, and raced several miles down the beach to the warmth of a shack.

After the shipwreck, Moolynaut was reassigned to the *kaholtz* (collective) Lenina, where she herded deer. The tribe was nomadic, moving with the herd. The Soviets built a string of small wooden houses along the deer's migration route and she lived alternately in these houses and in *yurangas*. But outside of these barest details, she never talked much about her life.

One day, I asked Moolynaut to explain where her healing power came from. Instead of answering my question, she told me that the old man

Danielich's wife, Nrooly, was a great healer. She could change the weather or make a wave in the sea. One day the hunters carried in a man with a broken femur. The bone was protruding through the skin and he was in great pain. Nrooly sang a song to put the man to sleep, and when he awoke the next morning he was well again.

Listening to Moolynaut tell her story, I realized that she didn't think of her life as a day-to-day, hour-after-hour chronology as most of us in North America would. Events that occurred in the Real World intermingle with experiences in the Other World, and through silence and omission I learned that the most important narrative is the cycle of seasons and the flow of time on the tundra.

Spring Festival

When Moolynaut was a young girl, the spring festival was held on the tundra, either at the Holy Stone west of Vyvenka or at another Holy Stone farther south. At that time, people lived in nomadic family bands and migrated continuously to find fresh forage in a frozen land where plants and animals clung tenaciously to life. The Koryak couldn't afford to congregate in large groups, because their animals would overgraze the range, so most of the time families were isolated. However, twice a year, at the spring and autumn festivals, disparate bands coalesced to have a party, visit relatives, establish alliances, and exchange the news. These meetings were also a time when young people could meet youths their own age and choose marriage partners from outside their immediate families.

In one conversation, Moolynaut told me, "Even enemies came to the festival because this was a time of peace. No one was allowed to fight at the Holy Stone. Sometimes when the festival was over the warriors went away and then became enemies again. But sometimes enemy warriors decided to marry a woman from another clan or they decided that it was too much work to be enemies anymore, so they became friends. Things happened that way."

Moolynaut also explained that people often traveled for many weeks to gather at the festivals. However, travel in those days was different from today. Nomads lived in tents and traveled constantly, so it was no big deal to wander toward the Holy Stone as the festival approached, rather than toward some other direction. And if an adventurous and horny youth decided to strike out across the land without tribe and herd, in search of a good party and, he hoped, a beautiful woman, he traveled by foot, dog team, or reindeer sled, hunting and foraging along the way. Since dogs, people, and deer had to eat anyway, there was little added expense to travel. Paradoxically, in modern times the introduction of the internal combustion engine reduced, rather than increased, the range and frequency of travel. As I explained previously, summer travel by machine is impossible because there are no roads. But even in winter, a person needs gasoline, which is prohibitively expensive. Moreover, since there is no infrastructure en route, travelers need to carry all their fuel and spare parts, which seriously limits their range.

Today the spring festival in Vyvenka is held on the outskirts of town and is a local affair, with few visitors from adjacent villages. The morning of the big event was cold and raw, with a moist wind blowing in from the sea and hard, crunchy snow underfoot. Many people were dressed in traditional beaded reindeer-skin *kuchlankas* (parkas), while others were bundled up in Western clothes. Volvo, Oleg and Lydia's ten-year-old, was puffed up with pride because he was planning to race in the dogsled competition. He left early with Oleg to join the men. Angela, Oleg and Lydia's six-year-old daughter, started with us but quickly ran off to join her friends. In a small village where everyone knows everyone else, with no violent crime or dangerous automobile traffic, children appear and disappear at random. Lydia was carrying her *boubin*, a traditional handheld disk drum, resembling a two-and-one-half-foot-diameter tambourine. Instead of cymbals, light chains jingled from the back. Lydia talked to us in English and then chanted in the old tongue while beating the drum with a fur-covered dog's foot.

We walked over a low pass to the festival grounds on the tundra. Lydia reminded us that the hill to the north was a sleeping whale and the pass was the whale's neck. Then she smiled her signature innocent, enigmatic smile and instructed us to walk softly, so as not to awaken the giant.

As we crossed the pass, the windblown, crusty snow sounded hollow underfoot, reverberating like Lydia's ceremonial drum. I tapped my toe gently against the crust. Westward from the whale's neck, the tundra stretched to the horizon, covered by windblown snow, with occasional willows and gnarled, ground-hugging elfin cedar peaking out from their winter cloak. Polar hunters, who watch the seasons change, ice come and go, and animals migrate across the land, never speak of terra firma. It's not a term used by mountaineers or skiers, who routinely witness landslides and avalanches, or by river runners, who float with moving currents that grab trees and chunks of dirt and carry them toward the sea. I had somersaulted down a mountain in the maw of roiling snow. Nothing *firma* about the earth's winter skin. One day a big storm or a tsunami will wash the sand spit and the town of Vyvenka out to sea. Nothing *firma* about that, either.

"Terra firma" is an urban, Roman term. I playfully imagined that it was coined by a wordsmith who lived in downtown Rome, drank water out of lead pipes, and debauched at orgies, eating peeled grapes and roasted hummingbird tongues. Maybe he was a real estate developer trying to sell condos in Pompeii, with a large picture window view of Mount Vesuvius.

As if sensing that I was thinking too much, Lydia picked up the pace of her drumbeat, to bring me back to the spring festival, here in Vyvenka where the Siberian tundra meets the Bering Sea. In the frozen valley below us, Moolynaut and several other old women were in a tight group, all dressed in festively decorated reindeer-skin *kuchlankas*, drumming, chanting, and dancing with surprising agility for elders in their eighties and nineties. We approached and said hello. Moolynaut gave us each a brief hug and smile, then returned to her music. Misha explained that all the old women had eaten hallucinogenic mushrooms and were dancing in a trance, along the road to the Other World.

But the scene was incomplete and I tried to imagine skin *yurangas* stretching across the tundra plain, reindeer, smoky fires, young warriors from distant lands, and the smell of roasting meat.

Numerous dog teams were staked out on the hillside waiting for the big race. A century ago, Roald Amundsen chose northeast Siberian dogs for his successful expedition to the South Pole because these animals were bred to pull heavy loads in extreme cold, with frequent starvation. Today the teams in Siberia have an easy but boring life, because people use them for short hunting and fishing forays, but almost no one makes long journeys across the tundra anymore. Danielich was the only person who used his dogs regularly for transport, because he lived alone, twenty miles out of town.

Suddenly Sergei appeared, as if he had materialized stealthily out of the ether. He didn't say "hello" or "good morning," just started out abruptly, "A trained racing deer can run at eighty kilometers per hour for the first five hundred meters," followed by his signature toothless grin, with the proverbial cigarette impaled on his lower canine.

Misha translated.

I was a little confused. "Are there any reindeer here today? Will there be reindeer races?"

"No, not anymore. No reindeer . . . We had reindeer races in 1998 for the last time. But they were old, slow, and not well trained. It was sad to see them limping along like that."

To make sure we understood, he pantomimed a sick old deer hobbling through the snow. Despite the implication of tragedy, we all laughed, and Sergei continued, "Not like in the old days. I had a fast team. No one could beat me.

"I herded deer for the collective from the time I was seventeen until I was thirty-four. If I kept the wolves away and the deer fat, then every year the brigade leader gave me the oldest, smartest deer and a young, strong one. That was my salary. I would hitch the two together and the old deer would teach the young one how to run. Once the young deer learned and got strong, I would hitch it alone to the sled. Then we would fly. Nobody could beat me. I was the fastest."

"Sergei," I asked, "are there any deer in Vyvenka today?"

Sergei shook his head sadly. "Nyet. In 1985 there were five reindeer-herding brigades in Vyvenka. Each had two thousand deer, so we had a total of ten thousand deer. By 1998 there were only one hundred and fifty deer left. Then they all stampeded during a blizzard. Maybe wolves chased them. No one knows. Eighty ran off a cliff and fell to their deaths. The other seventy disappeared into the blowing snow. We are called the Koryak, 'people of the deer.' But now there are no deer."

When Misha and I traveled along this coastline in 2000, we had seen only five reindeer in four months. In comparison, when I had traveled in the Alaskan and Canadian Arctic thousands to tens of thousands of caribou (close cousins of the reindeer) migrated in fluid waves across the tundra. One ecosystem was alive and complete; the other was missing a critical, living, link.

I needed to understand the forces that railed against these people and drove them into such turmoil that they lost their reindeer, which provided food, clothing, and shelter and formed the foundation of their culture. But we were at a party and this wasn't the time and place to probe too deeply into their collective tragedy.

"Sergei," I asked, "are there any people who are still herding reindeer? We would like to find reindeer and reindeer people. You and Oleg talked about taking us to the Holy Stone. Could we just keep going and search for reindeer people on the tundra?"

Sergei listened and then turned to face the tundra. "I have lived here all my life," he answered. "I herded reindeer. I was in the army. One time I worked on a ship and sailed to Vladivostok. I have been everywhere. But I have never traveled far from here, across the tundra." He was silent for a while. "You buy the gas?"

"Of course I'll buy the gas."

"And oil, too?"

"Conyeshna [of course]."

"Yes, we can do that." And then Sergei abruptly walked away.

Below us, the dancing, drum-beating, mushroom-eating, reindeer-fur-clad old women suddenly set their drums down and trudged back across the whale's neck, toward town. Lydia came by to explain that the first festival event, the old ladies' footrace, was about to start. We followed toward two flagpoles thrust into the snow, about fifty to seventy-five yards apart. When the women reached the closest pole, they began swinging their legs and jogging slowly in place, loosening up like Olympic sprinters preparing for the gold-medal event. People gathered. A young girl was assigned to escort each of the racers, to keep them on track and to prevent falls, collisions, and injuries. The race consisted of a sprint to the far pole, followed by a quick 180-degree turn and a return to the starting line. The old women toed a line in the snow, jostling, giggling, and elbowing one another for position. Moolynaut was hunched over, wrinkled, and frail looking, clutching her cane in one hand and Angela, her escort, in the other. Someone yelled, "GO!"

Cane waving, feet shuffling, head forward, shoulders straightening, Moolynaut pulled into an early lead. She reached the pole ahead of the pack, planted her cane like a slalom racer rounding the next gate, and skidded through an about-face so quickly that Angela lagged behind and then lost her footing. For a brief moment Moolynaut dragged Angela through the snow. The pursuing racers collided in the turn and tangled into a pulsating knot of pushing, shoving, swearing, laughing stoned old women. Angela couldn't regain her footing to keep up with Moolynaut, so the old shaman dropped the six-year-old's hands and accelerated into the home stretch, raising her cane in a victory flash as she crossed the finish line well ahead of the competition.

As the sun began to droop in the sky and the afternoon chill descended, we all returned to town to watch a troop of professional dancers from Korpf/ Tillichiki perform on a temporary stage positioned in front of the faded green wood walls of the town hall. Dozens of Koryak townspeople, with cameras of all types and vintages, jostled and jockeyed for the best photo angles. Sergei brought me a chair so I could stand above the crowd and shoot some footage over people's heads. But after a few moments a rowdy teenager with his mother's camera tried to climb on the chair with me, using my camera arm as a handhold. I pushed, argued, and then gave up.

The spring festival wasn't intended to be a spectator event. I imagined that a hundred years ago, when people traveled for months to shed their incredible isolation for a few short days, the dancing would have been a wild, ecstatic event, with elders mixing with youngsters who would soon fall into each other's arms, embraced by the intermingled smells of musty reindeer skin and sweaty bodies. I hadn't flown three-quarters of the way around the world to record a backwoods professional dance troupe via a few minutes of amateur camera work. In my heart, it was time to start our journey across the tundra, to the Holy Stone, and beyond. The music stopped, the crowd began to disperse, and Misha, Chris, Lydia, and I turned toward home and dinner.

Svetia

Three women broke out of the crowd and hurried to catch up with us. One of the women seemed familiar, but I couldn't remember her name or where we had met. She obviously remembered Chris and me, however, because she gave us each a warm hug. She was a petite young Koryak with a small mouth, impish smile, and lean, angular face. Her two front teeth were symmetrically crooked to form a distinctive V in the top of her mouth. Bright red lipstick, purple eye shadow, and sparkling nail polish seemed out of place in Vyvenka, but the colors complemented her dark complexion beautifully.

"Jon, Chris, it's so good to see you again. It's been a long time. So much has happened."

Misha translated. I remembered her face from somewhere but momentarily drew a blank.

The woman realized that we didn't recognize her, so she said, "Don't you remember me? I'm Svetia, Dimitri's wife."

I felt embarrassed. "Of course. I remember now."

In December 1999, when Misha, Chris, and I were planning our kayak expedition, I received an e-mail from a stranger named Dimitri, who explained that he heard about me and wanted to make contact because we were kindred spirits. Dimitri was planning to walk, alone, from central Kamchatka to Pevek, a city on the Arctic coast, a journey that would cover one thousand miles of sparsely settled tundra. His inland route would roughly parallel the coastal route we were following in our kayaks. He wrote that he was broke and would appreciate it if I could bring him some boots and camping gear. I said that I'd do what I could.

When Chris and I traveled to Kamchatka in 2000 to start our kayak expedition, we met Dimitri and he invited us to his humble apartment and introduced us to Svetia, his wife. They made a stunning couple: a broad-shouldered blond Russian and a small, lean, brown-skinned Koryak.

Svetia had grown up in Vyvenka. Her mother cooked lunches in the school and Svetia's father was a fisherman. Her father died at sea when she was nine, leaving Svetia, her mother, and two sisters in poverty. Dimitri was a Russian reindeer biologist who traveled to Vyvenka to study the diminishing herds. They fell in love, married, had a son, and moved to a suburb of PK. Life was good. Dimitri drew a comfortable salary as a field biologist, and Svetia augmented their income by "preparing things" in the laboratory. They had a big garden and there was always enough to eat.

But Dimitri had wanderlust. He left work to go on long walks that lasted all summer. Svetia accompanied him once but couldn't keep up. As she explained to me, "Dimitri is like a bear; I am only a ptarmigan."

When Chris and I visited, Svetia fixed us tea and laid out a platter of cookies. Dimitri was a whirlwind, showing us photos of past trips and maps of future plans. He opened a closet and dragged out his gear. He had fashioned a pair of skis by cutting plastic sewer pipe in half. Old rubber tire tube served as bindings and he attached pieces of sealskin on the bottoms to give him friction when he wanted to climb uphill. His reindeer sleeping bag and cotton tent were five times the weight of modern Western camping gear.

He was planning to leave a few weeks after we set out. Svetia agreed to stay behind to tend their garden and raise their son. I gave Dimitri a pair of boots. He explained that since he had stopped working, they were poor. Could I give him five hundred dollars?

Five hundred dollars is a lot of money anywhere, but especially in Russia.

I smiled and reached into my wallet. "Here's fifty dollars. Good luck, Godspeed. Be careful."

Now Svetia and her two sisters stood before us. They were drunk. "It's so good to see you. I am glad that you completed your journey to Alaska. It was so dangerous. I was worried about you."

Then, impulsively, she pulled a large amber ring off her finger and faced Chris. "Here, take this."

Chris tried to refuse, but Svetia grasped Chris's hand, pulled off her glove, and slipped the ring on her finger. "You take it, please. You are a brave woman. Not like me. I am just a ptarmigan."

Svetia linked her arm in mine and I steadied her as we walked down the frozen street. Her sisters followed, unsteadily. Slowly, choosing slurred words, she told us her story:

Dimitri left home in early June of 2000, explaining that he wouldn't send any news until he reached Pevek. He claimed that it brought bad luck to communicate with one's family. He must remain alone, in the wilderness, focused totally on the expedition. That was ten months ago. Winter had come and gone and Svetia was worried about her wild Russian husband. Then she heard a rumor that a traveling man had bought food from geologists. One of the geologists took a photo of this man, but for some reason he wouldn't make a copy of the photo and mail it to her. Svetia left her son with friends at home and hitched a ride north on a ship to Manily, where the geologists were based. The photo wasn't of Dimitri. She clung to the belief that Dimitri was alive somewhere out there in the wilderness and that he would show up someday. But I could see in her eyes that she was beginning to lose hope.

Svetia hitchhiked on snow machines and *visdichots* to Tillichiki and then down to Vyvenka to visit her homeland and family for the first time in ten years. Now she planned to wait here for a tanker or a cargo ship and hitch a ride back to PK.

We reached the duplex with Goshe's and Oleg and Lydia's home and stood awkwardly in a small knot at the gate. Oleg and Lydia seemed uncomfortable with the three women and I thought that I understood why. There's a dark side of Vyvenka: despair, drunkenness, poverty, sloth, suicide—the bane of northern towns all across the circumpolar Arctic. Oleg and Lydia knew that I was a writer and they assiduously steered me away from unsavory components. They wanted me to portray their village in shining light.

I'm not blind. When Misha and I visited Vyvenka the first time, a man had gotten drunk, fallen out of his boat, and drowned. This time I heard muted talk of teenage suicide. We saw drunks on the street all the time. In the past, I've written about villages in Canada and Greenland, but I've skipped lightly over the dark side. After I've accepted people's generosity and friendship, I don't feel right exposing their sordid struggles to the world.

Oleg and Lydia saw three drunken women, but I saw a friend and fellow adventurer's wife and her sisters. Lydia pulled me by the arm to lead me inside. She clearly didn't invite Svetia and her sisters. But Svetia gently grasped me by the other elbow, indicating that she didn't want me to go.

I turned to Lydia. "Let me talk for a minute." Chris hesitated, as if she wanted to remain outside with me, but I wanted to deal with this alone. "It's OK, dear; I'll be right in."

Everyone else went inside, leaving me with Svetia and her sisters, with only rudimentary language to bridge the gap between us.

In pidgin Russian and sign language, Svetia asked me to come to her place. Obviously, on the one hand, I couldn't and didn't want to go. My wife and best friends were waiting for me nearby. But, on the other hand, Svetia had been hospitable to me and she was in the midst of tragedy. I wanted to be compassionate, but even compassion has its limits.

Svetia tugged at my elbow.

"No, thank you," I replied, and then indicated that I had to go into the house.

"*Nyet, nyet!* Dimitri is gone for many months. Come to my place. You buy vodka, you take me."

She pressed her body close to mine, put one hand around my waist, and rubbed me erotically with the other, repeating, "Take me. Dimitri is gone for many months. Do you understand? Money, money. You buy vodka, you take me."

She smiled, ran her tongue provocatively across her upper lip, and pursed her lip into a kiss.

"You're drunk," I said in English. "Please go home and sleep it off." Then I stepped back and gently removed her hand.

"Maybe you want my sister?" She lifted my hand and placed it squarely on her sister's breast.

She giggled and held my hand tightly when I tried to pull it away.

"Nyet, nyet! This is a bad idea."

Svetia was undeterred, "One bottle of vodka, one woman. Or better. Two bottles of vodka and three women. Yes, that is much better. All together."

Still clutching my hand to her breast, Svetia's sister reiterated the offer, "Three women, one man, one bed, two bottles of vodka, all together."

All three sisters giggled and smiled in agreement. I pulled my hand free.

It was cold and my nose was running. Svetia took her hand out of her mitten, wiped my nose with her thumb and forefinger as if I were her baby, wiped the snot off on my pants, and said something tender in Russian that I didn't understand.

Lydia stepped out of the house and called, "Jon, please come. It is time to eat. We have a special meal for the festival. It is ready now."

"Just a minute."

Lydia disappeared. Inside the warm house, my wife and my friends were waiting. But I felt an inexplicable bond with this tragic woman, most probably widowed by the adventure lust of her husband. I thought back to my avalanche and hoped that strangers would be kind to Chris if I died in the mountains.

I touched Svetia gently on the hip and beckoned: "Come with me." We walked together past the house, onto the beach, brushing against each other on the narrow path. An old bulldozer was parked on the sand and we slipped behind it to be out of sight. I pulled a five-hundred-ruble note out of my wallet (about twenty dollars) and handed it to her. She grasped my whole hand, not just the money, and cupped the hand firmly around one breast. Then with her free hand she gently lifted the note from my fingers and slipped it into her pocket. With the money safely stowed, she reached down and massaged my penis again.

"*Nyet.*" I gently pushed her away. "Just take the money. You'll need it to get home. Don't spend it all on vodka. I wish I could help. I wish I could find Dimitri for you. I wish he could be here and we could all be friends."

Svetia didn't comprehend the English, but she understood well enough. She nodded and looked at me so plaintively that I placed my hands around her delicate waist. Then she leaned back until I had to hold her hips tightly to support her. The surf pounded against the beach, grinding icebergs into the sand, while the sky shimmered sunset red, reminding me of the vast spaces Dimiti had traveled across. Svetia's makeup and the vodka on her breath mixed with the odors of sea salt and stale machine grease from the bulldozer. She straightened, snuggled up against me, and looked up. We kissed, and her tongue ran softly across my lips, as if we were old lovers. Her shoulders started shaking and I realized that she was crying.

I wanted to cry, too. Even though no one yet knew Dimitri's fate and Svetia believed—or hoped—that he would reappear, I feared the worst. Mistakes happen. I have too many friends who have died on snowy peaks or in stormy seas. Then I remembered the horror of my avalanche. One bad decision in twenty-five years of backcountry skiing. Just a little screwup. I could easily have died but got away "lucky" with six weeks in the crane and a gimp pelvis.

I caressed her shoulders, ran my hands down the small of her back, and said softly in Russian, "It will be OK, little ptarmigan. Somehow it will all be OK."

She looked up and smiled. We could forget that she had just tried to sell her body to me for a bottle of vodka. We could remember this moment. We kissed again in the twilight, listening to the ocean. When she finally pulled away, I kissed the tears that were rolling down her cheeks.

"*Shasliva* [good luck], little ptarmigan."

Svetia nodded and walked slowly toward her sisters, shoulders hunched, still crying.

Lydia

I returned to Goshe's apartment and joined my friends who were gathered in the living room. This room was furnished with a worn, ugly green over-stuffed, sagging Brezhnev-era couch, a threadbare, musty red rug, and hideous faded Brezhnev-era floral wallpaper. In northeast Siberia, the eighteen years of Brezhnev's rule was the only period in all of history when material possessions were readily available. In the late nineteenth century, the Koryak lived mostly in the Stone Age, with a few metal trade items and a rifle or two. After that came the Bolshevik Revolution, World War II, and Stalin, all in quick succession. Then came Brezhnev, who presided over favorable economic times, from 1964 to 1982. That's when people bought their furniture, carpets, and wallpaper. After that, the Soviet economy collapsed. People had money, but it was useless because there was nothing to buy. With perestroika came capitalism, and the system changed. In theory, people could buy anything, but no one had any money. It's different in Moscow—where more people own Rolls-Royces than in any other city in the world. And then there's Oleg's outboard motor and shiny new snow machine, but the fact remains that most of the furniture in northeast Siberia comes from Brezhnev's time.

Lydia announced that it was time to eat, so we gathered in the kitchen. After a feast that consisted of fried fish, boiled potatoes, shredded cabbage, and fresh bread, I realized that if I wanted to understand Moolynaut, I had to learn as much as possible about all the people who lived in the village, so I asked Lydia to tell me the story of her life.

Lydia was born in 1956 and grew up under generally good times, mostly during Brezhnev's regime. Therefore, she didn't have as many terrors to suppress as Moolynaut had. In Lydia's words, "Moolynaut saw too many changes, too much death. Yes? You understand? Sometimes it is not so good to talk about the bad times. This is why Moolynaut does not tell you the whole story of her life."

Lydia continued by suggesting that if I could weave the story of her life with the fragments of Moolynaut's story I might be able to piece together a composite of recent Koryak history.

"My grandfather was born around 1856 or 1857. When he grew up, he had twelve thousand domestic reindeer. Today people become rich because they learn to bribe government officials, talk to banker men, and things like that. But those days were different. If the deer didn't like you, they would run away and go to another man's herd. To keep twelve thousand reindeer, you had to be gentle so the deer wanted to stay with you. You also had to work very hard so all those deer would be fat and happy. Only gentle, hardworking men, like my grandfather, became rich.

"Men came every year from America in big ships. They bought deer meat and gave the people flour, sugar, Winchester rifles, teapots, and many other things. The Americans had good things. Better than the Russian things. They brought big blocks of very white sugar. People talked about this sugar even after the Bolsheviks chased the Americans away. The Americans were always good to us, but they had to go away.

"My grandfather's clan consisted of four families with six to twelve children in a family. It took that many people to manage all those deer. The people lived in *yurangas* in the summer and traveled with the deer. In the winter, sometimes they lived in *zimlankas* [permanent half-underground houses dug into glacial moraines].

"One year a young man drove south from Chukotka with a beautiful well-disciplined dog team and came to our spring festival at the Holy Stone. He was a Chukchi, not a Koryak. The Chukchi and Koryak are like cousins. I don't know exactly when this happened, but it was before the Soviets collectivized us and before life changed. My grandfather killed a deer and gave meat to this man as a sign of friendship."

Lydia interrupted the flow of the story: "If you kill a deer near the Holy Stone, you must only kill a deer with white legs. Otherwise bad things will happen. Do you understand?"

I nodded.

"This man fell in love with my grandfather's daughter and asked to marry her. But my grandfather was a rich man and did not give his daughter away cheaply. This was the way of our people. Not now. Now is different; young people marry the way they want, but in that time a rich man did not give his daughter away cheaply. My grandfather said, 'You must work for me for three years. You must work hard. If you lie with my daughter during that time, I will kill you.'

"That was the way it was during that time.

"After the three years passed, they had a marriage ceremony. All the women in the tribe joined in a circle, with the bride and the bridegroom in the middle. Then the bride started to run away. Her suitor chased her and all the women tried to stop him. They hit him with sticks, kicked him, and tried to trip him. If the young man was fast and strong, he could run past all those women and catch his bride. When he caught her and grasped her breast, then she was his wife. If he did not catch her, then too bad, he was not good enough to marry the woman. He would have to go back home and he wouldn't receive any pay for all the work he did. Every once in a while the women in a tribe killed a slow, weak suitor with their sticks. That's the way people did things in those days.

"Of course, this woman was my mother and this man became my father. After my mother and father married, the Soviets came and took almost all my grandfather's reindeer. They left him with a small herd of one thousand deer. I think that my grandfather could have accepted the loss of the reindeer. But the Soviets did many other bad things. They killed all the sled dogs and the trained sled deer, and burned all of our beautiful birch sleds. When they did these bad things they said, 'It is a new age and the Koryak people must become a part of modern Russia. Now you will have tractors, so you don't need to travel in the old way.'

"I think that my grandfather could have accepted these losses also. But then the Soviets took the children away. They put the children in special schools where they would learn to become Russians. For nine months a year, the children were not allowed to visit their families, talk in the Koryak language, or practice any of the old ways. This started when the children were six years old.

"My grandfather's brother ran away into the tundra to hide. He took his deer, his family, a Winchester rifle, and many cartridges. But the Soviets found him and shot him. My grandfather didn't want to run away. He didn't want to fight. He was sad about losing all his deer. And his grandchildren. He was seventy-eight or seventy-nine years old. He had lived a good life, so he just died.

"This was sometime in the 1930s, maybe 1934 or 1935. I don't remember exactly when. I wasn't alive then, so I can't remember. My mother was born in 1918, so she was about seventeen when collectivization came and my grandfather died.

"The Soviets divided the people into brigades. Each brigade was a collective. In a way, the brigades were not that different from the original clans. Except that life wasn't as much fun anymore because the children were in the Soviet schools and not on the tundra with their families.

"My father became the leader of a brigade. He started with five hundred deer. Or maybe one thousand. I wasn't alive then, so I can't remember. Over the years he built the herd into five thousand. My mother and father had four children before me. One died when it was a small baby, so there were only three left. Then I came in 1956.

"Do you want to hear the story of how I came into the world?"

Lydia relaxed from the concentration of speaking so much English. She smiled, stood, lifted the teapot from the *petchka*, and poured another cup of tea. I encouraged her to continue.

"It was in the early spring, like now, and snow was on the ground. We were living in a *zimlanka* then, an underground house, and my mother was gathering firewood. She felt the birth coming very suddenly, so she dropped the wood and ran to the house. My father opened the door and heard a baby cry.

"'What is that cry?' he asked. 'Where is the baby?'

"'I don't know,' my mother answered. 'It just fell out.'

"My mother and father looked all around. At first they couldn't find me. 'Where is the baby?' my father cried. I was in my mother's boot. I was wet and slippery, so I slid down my mother's pants into her boot. I was crying."

Lydia shook with mirth, and we all joined her in a good laugh.

"My mother brought me to her breast and said, 'We will call our daughter Naventacrov, Woman Who Brings Girls from the Mountains. My mother could see into the future. She knew, right then, that I would have three daughters and only one son.

"My father died when I was four. He had an ill in his stomach."

Lydia pressed against the lower right side of her abdominal cavity.

"An ill right here in a part of the insides."

"Appendicitis?" I asked.

After some discussion we all agreed that it was appendicitis and Lydia continued her story.

"My father died when he was about fifty years old. My mother had children to raise, so she moved from the tundra, into Vyvenka."

Lydia smiled again, "We became 'mouse-eating people,' but you must understand; there was no other way. When I was six, I went to the Russian school with all the other children. That was a very bad time. On the first day, the Russian teacher asked me, 'What is your name?'

I said, 'My name is Naventacrov, Woman Who Brings Girls from the Mountains.'

"The Russian teacher said, 'No, that is not your name anymore. Now you are a Russian. Now your name is Lydia.'

"I cried all day. I cried every day. I was young and I wanted to go home. I did not want to sleep in that schoolhouse with all the other children and no mothers.

"Those were bad times. It is not good to talk about bad times. When you have many bad times in your life, you learn not to talk about these things. You learn to talk about the good times."

"When I came home from this terrible school, my mother told me, 'You can have a bad life, but you must never be unhappy. If you are unhappy you will become hard in the head and then you will be ill.'"

Lydia paused, poured more tea, and continued, "Let me tell you about a good time. My older brother was a doctor for the deer. He traveled in the tundra in the summer and he would take me with him. That was a good time because I was in the tundra, traveling with my brother, working with the deer. Then, later, I went to school in PK to learn English. English is a good language, so I wanted to learn it."

I nodded. Even though her syntax was somewhat tortured in places, her pronunciation was amazingly clear and her vocabulary was excellent.

Lydia sighed. "Then we lost all our reindeer. Sergei has told you about this. We ate our last deer meat in 1998. It was very sad to eat the last deer. It was a sad time. No electricity. No heat. Houses crashed. People were hungry. By December 1998, there were no deer left."

Of course, I wanted to ask, "What happened to all those deer?" and I think that Lydia knew that. But she had already deflected my question with her enjoinder "it is not good to talk about bad times."

A silence hung between us.

If I had come here only three years ago, I would have seen deer grazing on the hills above town. When we think about vanishing cultures, we often assume that seminal events occurred decades or generations ago. Not three years. If I stayed in this room and listened long enough, eventually Lydia might fill in the details. But she was right; her story was sad enough. We didn't need to dwell on the last tragic loss that severed ties with her ancient culture.

Lydia must have read my thoughts. "I have a good life now. I have Oleg and he cares for me. Our oldest daughter is in Khabarovsk, at the university, learning to be a medical technician. Anastasia, my second, is in school in PK. Volvo and our dear little one, Angela, are still at home. Three girls and one boy. I am Naventacrov, the Woman Who Brings Girls from the Mountains."

Lydia paused again. "It is hard work for me to talk at you in so much English. Many days I don't talk at so much English. In Vyvenka most days we don't ever have visitors like you. I am happy you came. I am happy you bring Chris, your beautiful wife. That is good. I am tired now. It is time to sleep."

Our hosts left and Misha, Chris, and I laid our pads out on the living room floor and nestled into our sleeping bags. As I closed my eyes, thinking through the day's events, I reflected on how well Lydia's story complemented Moolynaut's, forming a more complete, composite whole. But I also knew that the story wasn't finished and that I needed to find a surviving clan of reindeer herders somewhere on that vast, snowy, windswept tundra.

Preparing to Leave

The following morning, Oleg, Sergei, and Simon came by to discuss plans for our expedition to find a tribe of reindeer herders. I spread out my map on the dusty carpet and we all got down on our hands and knees. No one spoke for a long time. Finally, Sergei drew a circle with his finger around a huge section of the interior. "Maybe someplace in here."

Great. The circle was a hundred miles in diameter and crossed innumerable squiggly brown topographic lines that looked benign enough on paper until I mentally converted them into mountain ranges, emptiness, and cold, until I saw blizzards blowing snow across the ridges and through the passes.

Oleg and Sergei knew every undulation of the land within a distance of one tank of gas, round-trip, from home. But beyond that, despite having lived in the village for their entire lives, it was all *terra incognita*. My chart showed a solid red line leading northward from Tillichiki with a legend: "Winter Road." I suggested that we return to Tillichiki and follow the road. Maybe reindeer people were camped along the road so they could transport their meat to the coast and trade for supplies.

Oleg shook his head silently.

Sergei explained, "We never heard of this road. But even if there is a road, it heads north from here. The Holy Stone is west. If we're looking for reindeer, we have to go to the Holy Stone first."

My friends left no space for argument or discussion, and since we were all guessing and I wanted to go to the Holy Stone anyway, I smiled and agreed.

Oleg laid plans: "We will take two snow machines, my Yamaha and Sergei's Buran, and two drums of fuel [110 gallons]. One extra motor for the Buran because it is old. Food for two weeks. If we find reindeer people, fine. If we don't find anyone, we will come back home."

Chris and I explained that we really didn't like riding on snow machines because the noise, the smell, and the lack of activity all detracted from any tactile and personal relationship with the tundra. After much discussion, we all decided that Oleg and Sergei would haul the fuel, food, and camping gear while Misha, Chris, and I would follow on skis.

We went to the store and bought supplies. Oleg and Sergei added salmon caviar and dried fish from their winter caches and then raced off to tune their machines. Misha, Chris, Simon, and I returned to Goshe's kitchen and prepared tea while Lydia went to fetch Moolynaut.

The old grandmother entered, took off her winter coat, sat down, and looked at me with a penetrating gaze, as if seeing me for the first time. I always find her just a little scary when she looks at me like that, but I concentrated on staring straight back into her eyes.

"Are you going with Oleg and Sergei to find reindeer on the tundra?" she asked.

When I nodded, she continued, "That is good." She lifted her hands into the air and looked upward. "Someday the deer will come back to Vyvenka. They will come here after the bad times are over. They will come from the south."

Then she drank her tea in silence. No one else spoke, so I sipped my tea without asking any questions. Moolynaut stood up abruptly, slipped back into her frayed coat, and walked toward the door. With her hand on the knob, she turned. "You will find reindeer people. In the old days we would give fish to the people who live on the tundra, because we have a lot of fish and they have none. They would give us reindeer meat, even though we had a lot of meat ourselves. I told Oleg to take some fish on the sleds to give to the reindeer people. Then maybe you will bring me some meat. I have not eaten reindeer meat for a long time."

She paused. "You will bring me some meat?"

I assured her that if we found the reindeer people, we would return with meat.

Then she chanted a short blessing in Koryak and Lydia escorted her back home.

Simon spoke after the door closed: "Yesterday, you asked the old grandmother about life with the deer?"

"Yes, but she didn't tell me many stories."

"I know; maybe I can help.

"I grew up in Vyvenka but went to the university in PK, became an engineer, and worked in western Russia, among white men, for twenty years. White men talk about their past more than we do. Now I've come back home, to live among my people, but I'm a writer, like you. Our job is to write about things that happen. Good times—bad times. Our job is to write about all times. Times in the past. Please, come to my house for dinner tonight and I will give you a story I wrote about living with the deer."

Simon's Story

THE ALBINO DEER

At dinner, Simon gave me his manuscript, typed on a manual typewriter.

The spring sun tenderly washed the boy's sleepy face as he lay in his reindeer-skin sleeping bag. His breath was deep and rhythmic and his smile greeted the spring morning. Fingers of sunlight reached through the fur tent, starting life again after the long winter hibernation.

His father called: "Wake up, my small one. The bushes are waking just as you are; they are pulled upward toward a star, as their branches float on an ocean of warm spring winds. Among the calm colors of the red spring sunrise, you can hear the plaintive voice of migrating swans. If you listen closely, you can even hear the earth singing as she breaks the bonds of frost and gives birth to the new grasses that will feed our reindeer."

After breakfast, the father and son harnessed the sled deer and set off. The father liked fast, exhilarating driving. Laughing, the boy nestled against his father's wide back. A herd of reindeer grazed in the distance.

In April, the reindeer give birth. Everyone is happy. Even severe silent men begin to sing, and children are too excited to play games with their friends.

The sun shone brightly, but the father knew that a snowstorm was coming. He urgently needed to move the herd close to a hill that would deflect the mighty blast of the northern blizzard.

The boy tugged the father's elbow and said, "Look, there is something white on the tundra. It is not snow, because it is moving. Maybe it is a swan."

The father stopped the team and looked through his binoculars. "It is a newborn albino reindeer."

"May I help the baby deer?" the son implored.

"Let your will be your way."

The boy jumped for joy. The father thought that they should treat the deer as they treated all deer. If he was healthy, he should live. And if he was sickly, he should die. But the father also knew that it was time for the boy to learn to rely on his own decisions, in order to grow into a man.

As they approached the herd, the father talked to the deer in soft clucking sounds. The deer knew the father's voice and were soothed by it.

The son was persistent. "Papa, promise me that we will allow this albino to live to old age. Promise, that we will not make parkas and hats out of his fur in the autumn."

"I promise," the father agreed kindly.

The father's weather prediction was correct. By afternoon, the tundra was buffeted by gale-force wind and a furious snowstorm. The next morning, when the blizzard had subsided, the father decided to check up on the herd.

"Can I come?" fussed the boy.

"Stay home. The weather is unreliable," the father commanded.

The son started to cry. The father could not bear this crying and gave in.

The sled moved slowly through the deep, new snow. The father called to the deer, whistling and clucking softly. A small group of stray deer was on the opposite side of the river. At the sound of the father's voice, they began to cross. The baby albino was with these deer. But the spring ice was weak and under the weight of so many animals the ice fractured. Part of the herd crashed into the frigid current. The adult deer swam strongly to shore, but the current was too strong for the baby albino and he was swept away. The boy cried out and ran to the riverbank.

"Stop!" shouted the father.

The albino reached firm ice, but his legs were already tired from frantic swimming in ice-cold water. The current began to drag him under. Having felt fatal danger, the albino cried plaintively. The boy threw himself down, seized the baby's head, and pulled against the current. He felt himself weakening. Then, with a final burst of energy, he rolled over on his back, pulling the cold soggy deer on top of him.

The new fawn stood and rubbed his warm lips against the boy's cheek. Then he shook his head, ran to his mother, and began nursing voraciously.

"Father, you saw. The albino said good-bye to me," the son cried.

"All can be," replied the father.

The son continued, "Our souls have met, our souls have met!"

April slid into July and nature hurried to finish the next life cycle. Clouds of mosquitoes, no-see-ums and botflies plagued people and deer alike. The people moved their deer to the mountains where they found cool winds and patches of snow.

Autumn brings the colors of a dying nature: Iridescent sunset, pearl dews, yellow grasses, red cranberries, bluish fog obscuring carpets of blueberries. In August the deer grow fat and grow heavy coats. This is the time to prepare winter clothes. It is also the time to dry meat because the sun and the wind are still warm.

Shepherds brought the herd close to camp. Everyone in camp collected to form a living corral. Then the men urged the deer to walk in circles within the corral. They lassoed the deer that they had chosen for killing. For the first time in his life, the albino feared the people. He snuggled closely against his mother. A herder lassoed the albino and dragged him toward the place for slaughter. The boy cried out and the father shouted, "My son saved this deer from the icy river and I promised him that we would not kill it."

So the man removed the lasso and let the deer live.

Five years passed. One cold day in January, a messenger came and told the herders that a large pack of wolves was nearby. The men ran to the herds and set an ambush near a small ravine. At midnight, the boy's father heard the faint breathing of wolves in the cold, still air. He saw a dark head in the moonlight, then five bodies rising onto the ridge. He took steady aim, and fired, but he missed because the distance was too great and the light was too poor. The deer heard the shot, sensed the wolves, and took flight. The wolves attacked, killing three deer in an eyeblink.

The albino raced in an opposite direction from the rest of the herd. A wolf was close behind. The albino clearly heard his pursuer's hot breath. Destruction seemed inevitable. Then the deer turned abruptly and lashed at the wolf with his antlers.

In the nighttime, no one could see the final outcome of the fateful battle. The following morning, the herders counted their losses. Three deer killed, and two missing, including the albino.

The boy sadly remembered his friend and the hours they played together.

Three years passed since the albino disappeared. The shepherds forgot him. Only the boy, now a young man, remembered his white friend. Then, in the autumn, when the deer were in rut, the albino returned.

The reindeer males were fat and strong. They walked through the herd, sizing each other up, pumping their muscles, and smashing their antlers into trees, in preparation for the battles ahead. Then the fighting began. Trumpeting mixed with the dry crash of horns.

The lead deer stood proud on a prominent hill, looking strong and beautiful. He bugled, passed before the herd in a ritual dance, dug his hooves into the ground, and smeared his face in clay.

A youthful challenger charged. The fight lasted one hour, but neither contender conceded. Then, as they sparred vigorously, one of the lead deer's antlers shattered. The conclusion seemed certain, but the old fighter was cunning. He began to depart, feinting defeat, but when the challenger relaxed his guard, the lead deer charged from the side. The young opponent fell, with a broken leg.

All this time, the boy and the albino stood aside. The albino had grown into a robust, forceful adult. The albino stepped forward and challenged the lead deer. The albino made a desperate charge, which the lead deer coolly deflected. But the lead deer was tired and the albino fresh. After a short violent struggle, the lead deer fell. The albino climbed the high hill where the lead deer had stood imperiously.

Then the albino gathered the herd and began to lead them away from the shepherds. One of the older men shouted, "That deer has been wild for too long. It will not obey our commands. It will take the deer away from us to live wild in the tundra. We must shoot it."

In an instant, the boy undressed, swam the icy river, and sprinted to intercept the herd. He ran and ran, desperate to save his friend. The boy saw, as if in a dream, that the albino would listen to him, and only him. Hidden by a hill, he circled in front of the herd. When the boy stepped into the open, he was only a few meters from the albino, with the herd strung out behind. The deer steadfastly looked at the naked boy, as if trying to remember back to his infancy, when this human rescued him from the icy river. Then the deer turned and brought the herd back to the home base.

Journey to the Holy Stone

April 9th dawned clear and windless, with the temperature hovering around zero degrees Fahrenheit. Chris, Misha, and I strolled down the street like celebrities, with our skis over our shoulders, waving to friends who were shouting, "*Shasliva* [good luck]." I looked for Svetia in the crowd but never saw her. Oleg and Sergei rode their snow machines behind us, as if we were in a May Day parade, towing heavy sleds made out of a ragtag synergy of welded steel and lashed birch, canvas, and reindeer skin—all tied together with strips of rawhide, yellow polyethylene, cotton clothesline, and a precious braided climbing rope that I had brought as a gift. Two rusted drums of fuel dominated the load, in both weight and volume. Oleg's faithful dog, Wolfchuck, rode on the back of his Yamaha, surveying the landscape with calm equanimity.

We climbed to the whale's neck and clicked into our skis. Misha was wearing a white military Arctic camouflage suit that made him look like a Russian commando sneaking across the North Pole to attack the soft underbelly of Pennsylvania Avenue. Chris and I were wearing bright yellow and orange ski parkas that made us look like fashion-crazed *piste* bunnies who took a wrong turn on our way to Chamonix. Oleg told us to ski toward Goose Mountain, which he pointed out in the distance, and then the two men fired up their machines and zoomed off to go hunting, leaving a gray-blue cloud of exhaust hanging in the vastness.

When the smoke and silence settled, the cosmos seemed to stop vibrating. I looked across the silent vista of rolling snow-covered hills and ridges, crisscrossed with broad valleys that were sliced by narrow streambeds. A world without motors. Windblown drifts, called *strastugi*, spread out seemingly forever like miniature sand dunes. Bushes grew in sheltered nooks while on the exposed plains tufts of yellow grasses poked tenuously through the snow. Right now, they were anchored in frozen soil, but when the summer sun warmed this land the ground would thaw, the roots would absorb precious moisture, leaves would green, and seeds would form.

I breathed in the frigid air, allowing my body to exorcise warmth, comfort, and security and to adjust to the rigors of travel across the Siberian tundra. Signals raced through nerve endings, expanding and contracting blood vessels and capillaries—adjusting, seeking a new equilibrium. A familiar, joyful, tingling alertness took control.

The mostly treeless landscape before us stretched westward farther than the expanse of the Pacific Ocean and, north to south, roughly the distance between Miami and Washington, D.C. We were looking for a tribe of reindeer herders who were wandering around out there somewhere, and we had absolutely no idea where they might be.

"OK," I assured myself. "One step at a time."

I pointed my skis downhill and accelerated into the fall line. Switches turned inside my brain, replacing worries about the outcome of our expedition with the cathartic cleanliness of motion. Too quickly I reached the bottom of the hill and turned back to watch Chris gracefully carving figure eights through my tracks, as if our paths were forever intertwined, in a carefully choreographed dance, crossing, separating momentarily, but inexorably returning to touch and intermingle again. Misha followed Chris, with his skis wobbling through the morning crust, arms waving to maintain balance, and shoulders hunched forward like a gorilla on a motorcycle, as if he could stay upright if he grasped the air in front of him. We gathered at the bottom, put climbing skins on the bases of our skis, and headed slowly toward Goose Mountain.

A few residual urban images and thoughts squirmed through my brain, but the cranium wasn't strong enough to retain them, and they escaped into that infinite tundra and sky, like air whooshing out of a punctured balloon. The tundra isn't a discrete form, like a calendar-perfect waterfall, a glacier-clad peak, or a rocky crag with a wild goat standing defiantly against scudding clouds. Rather, it is the space between forms. A formlessness so vast that time and distance become distorted. Is that rock fifty yards away and as big as a dog or a mile across the sea of undulating whiteness and as large as a soaring skyscraper? It doesn't matter, because for this instant the most salient feature of the landscape is the frozen crystals of my last breath that expand before me, reflecting sunlight into microscopic dancing rainbows and then dissipating into nothingness, carrying trivial, unneeded, and unwanted worries into the ether, where they will be washed away by the cosmic winds.

We reached Goose Mountain, lying on its chin and surveying our slow march. The temperature rose rapidly as the April sun ascended a cloudless sky.

"Where do we go now?" I asked.

Misha explained that Oleg had directed us to proceed for several hours along an old snow-machine track, cross a stream, and continue over unmarked tundra toward a prominent hill. The hunters in Vyvenka maintained a small shack, called a *serei*, on the flanks of that hill, near a thick patch of elfin cedar, and Oleg assured us that he and Sergei would join us there in the evening.

By early afternoon, the crusty snow softened and pools of water formed around exposed rock. We crossed a small stream, bubbling over crystalline ice that was frozen to the rounded cobbles below.

Misha and I skied side by side in silence for a few moments. Then, not breaking his stride, he commented, "Jon, you saved my life by taking me back to the Wild Nature in our kayaks. Now it is good to be in the Wild Nature again."

I laughed. "Yeah, but I almost killed you a few times on the kayak journey."

"*Da.* This is true. But I was ill in the city making too many papers. You made me alive again. Now I am feeling alive one more time."

In the distance, elfin cedar hugged the flank of a small hill. Small bands of birch trees grew in a protected river bottom.

I asked Misha if this was "the hill" and "the patch of cedar" that Oleg had included in his directions, but he assured me that it was not. Misha spent many years as a field geologist and his understanding of the directions Oleg had given in Russian was much better than mine, so I trusted his navigation.

After climbing a second pass and crossing another broad valley, Chris and I began to tire, so we stopped for a snack and some water. When we started up again, the adductor muscles in my groin began to ache, and I feared another episode of my recurring and debilitating pelvic pain. I thought back to my visit to Dr. Schutte's office and his raised eyebrows when I told him that I was planning to travel across the Siberian tundra, but it was too late to question my resolve, or sanity, and I concentrated on maintaining my pace to keep up with Misha.

By late afternoon my pain intensified, but just as I was about to suggest another rest we found Oleg and Sergei's snow-machine tracks and saw smoke rising out of a small shack, nestled into a stand of low-lying cedar on the flanks of a small hill. The *serei* was small, dark, dirty, dingy, smelly, smeared in animal fat and fish oil. It was furnished with a rickety table, a few benches, and a wall of bunks covered with old, worn, fly-bitten reindeer skins. But it had two critical components: a waterproof roof and a functional wood-burning stove. Luxury is a matter of perspective. The most miserable night of my life occurred when I was caught in a storm in the North Pacific, in an open-cockpit boat no bigger than a Kayak with no shelter or sleeping bag, no place to lie down, and under constant immersion from frigid waves rolling over my head. When one looks outward from that baseline, a tent becomes luxurious and a *serei* is opulent. After the *serei*, you can spend $5 million on a bona fide North American white man's mansion and you won't actually gain that much comfort.

We took off our sweaty parkas while Oleg and Sergei strung wires from their snow-machine battery and hung a 12-volt lightbulb above the table. After dinner, we made tea and sat on the bunks to chat. When we were in town, Oleg was taciturn, but the tundra and the *serei* made him loquacious. Warming his broad, muscular hands around a teacup, he reminded us that we weren't allowed to take photos of the Holy Stone.

"Remember, I told you before about the last person who took a picture of the Holy Stone. He died."

I assured Oleg that I wouldn't take any pictures.

To be certain that I understood the forces of evil that we were dealing with, Oleg told me a story:

"One time I traveled up the Vyvenka River to go ice-fishing and I was camping with several men. Suddenly, in the middle of the night, one man woke up, screaming desperately, 'Pai! Pai!' which means, 'Go away, Devil! Go away, Devil!' The Devil went away and we all fell back asleep, but then suddenly a soft furry animal sat on my chest. I tried to cry, 'Pai! Pai!' but the thing had its hand over my mouth and I couldn't cry out. I couldn't breathe. The thing grew heavier and heavier until it was crushing my chest. I thrashed back and forth until the young man next to me woke up. He shook me vigorously and the thing lost its grip for a second, just long enough for me to yell, 'Pai! Pai!' As soon as I yelled, the furry thing disappeared."

Oleg was silent for a moment and then continued, "I was fine. But the young man who saved me became sullen and sad. He died ten days later."

I asked Oleg if he knew what the furry thing was and he said that he wasn't sure, but he thought that it was sent by a *cherney caldoon*, a black witch. He went on to explain that *cherney caldoons* are people who create evil spells without provocation.

We talked about *cherney caldoons* and their counterparts, *belee caldoons*, white witches or shamans.

I asked, "If *cherney caldoons* are powerful enough to kill, are *belee caldoons* powerful enough to heal?"

"Oh yes!" Oleg assured me. "Moolynaut's grandmother was a powerful *belee caldoon*. Once a man was very sick. He came from far away to be healed. But he was so sick that he died right at her doorstep, before he could enter her *yuranga* and be healed. The old woman immediately grabbed a knife and cut out her own heart and died. Now that she was dead, she traveled quickly to the Other World and found the dead man. She healed him and the two of them left the land of the dead and returned to the land of the living. Then she put her heart back inside herself and sewed up her chest and there was no scar and both of them lived for many years."

I don't know what prompted me to ask the next question. I guess I was thinking about my pelvis, which ached slightly after our long, tiring day. "If

Moolynaut's grandmother could make a dead man come back to life, could Moolynaut heal my pelvis?"

Oleg asked for more information and I told him the story of my avalanche, the surgery, the plate, the recent episodic pain, and the X-ray showing the broken plate.

Oleg listened carefully. I half-expected him to dismiss my request as foolish whimsy, but he took me quite seriously.

"Moolynaut is not as powerful as her grandmother, but she is a powerful *belee caldoon* nevertheless. She has healed many people. But she has never healed anyone with a metal plate. It will be difficult. Our gods here know about many things, but they have no experience working with metal plates. Maybe she can help you, but maybe she can't. She will have to ask Kutcha, the Raven God. Kutcha is the messenger. He will travel to the Other World and ask if you can be healed."

I looked at Misha, and he smiled back, as if all of this were quite normal. I didn't want to voice doubt and I couldn't think of anything to add, so I thanked Oleg, and we all just sat there, lost in our own thoughts. After a few moments, Sergei announced that we had a hard day ahead of us and we should sleep.

I lay back on my bunk, closed my eyes, and felt radiant energy emanating from the thin sheet-metal stove. Oleg and Sergei were quintessential pragmatists, adept at maintaining machinery without spare parts and surviving in this frigid Arctic landscape. Yet ever since Misha and I arrived on the shores of Vyvenka the previous summer, seeking shelter from surf and gale, all our Koryak friends told tales of shamanic power. Of course, spirituality and pragmatism aren't incompatible, but in twenty years of travel across Arctic lands I had never before encountered such guileless belief in magic from the hardened northern people I had camped with.

The next morning Oleg gave us directions again and he and Sergei went fishing. At lunchtime, we met the two men on a windswept pass. After the meal, they drove toward the valley. We carved rounded turns over sun-warmed corn snow and then followed the snow-machine tracks across a featureless plain. An hour later, we reached a rhyolite obelisk, only about twenty feet high and five feet in diameter. Oleg and Sergei were waiting for us: Sergei puffing on his cigarette and Oleg gazing peacefully into space.

The Holy Stone reminded me of an ancient core of a Lilliputian volcano, wrinkled and bent over, like Moolynaut, with age, speckled with a patina of bird droppings and windblown snow. Without the hoopla I might have passed it without a second glance. But for some weird reason, I had come a long way to see this particular rock, reaching from the earth's hot, plastic mantle into Kutcha's infinite tundra sky.

People had left offerings of money, candy, matches, and cigarettes. I pulled a small red glass bead out of my pocket. I had carried this bead with me for many years, and now, when I looked into it for the last time, I saw a distorted fish-eye view of my face, covered in soot-smudged white stubble and peeling frostbite scars, with icicles dangling from my moustache. I slipped the bead into a crack in the rock and asked, in return, for the strength to understand, to make a safe passage, and to bring reindeer meat back to Moolynaut.

I imagined dun-covered skin *yurangas* spread across the plain, reindeer grazing to the horizon, and relatives, friends, lovers, shamans, and enemies beating their drums and dancing before this diminutive, crooked obelisk that was mysteriously so portentous. But today there were only four quiet men, one woman, and two gas-guzzling, oil-belching machines.

The five of us were here because each, in his or her own way, had come to embrace "the Wild Nature" that somehow made us "feel alive." But at the same time, we all lived in square, permanent structures, watched television, and drove cars or snow machines. Chris, Misha, and I had been skiing across the tundra for two days. A minuscule slice of time.

Before we had left Vyvenka, Simon, the mayor, told me that energy flows from the magma-filled bowels of the earth to the Holy Stone. At the same time, people absorb positive energy from the tundra and also feed it to the stone. Thus the stone is a focal point, a storage unit, and a transfer station for good energy. People give energy to the stone, but they also take energy. If I concentrate a little power from the landscape, modulate it through my body, and deliver it to the stone, then a friend, a stranger, or even an enemy can assimilate some of that goodwill, amplified by the receipt of additional energy from the deep earth.

Simon had explained further that to receive energy from the earth, a person must be in tactile contact with it, by walking, skiing, living in a *yuranga*, or herding reindeer. A generation ago, when people moved to towns and started to travel by machine instead of by dog and reindeer sled, some of this primordial bond was severed—so they lost some of their ability to extract energy from the tundra—and the cycle was weakened.

According to Simon, human beings have learned to rely so much on their technological power that they no longer feel the need to seek energy from the earth. As a result, we take from the Holy Stone without counting what we take and without giving back. Without reciprocity, the Holy Stone will eventually lose its power.

I walked over to Chris and put an arm gently around her shoulder. I thought about our rich and varied life together, writing textbooks in our cozy house in the Montana wilderness, skiing in British Columbia, traveling to remote places, supporting each other, laughing, loving. We took off our gloves and each placed our free hand on the Holy Stone, forming a coherent, tactile circle, stone, Chris, Jon, and back to stone. Chris thanked the stone for its energy and for the tundra that spread out before us. I asked it to store a tiny bit of my American, dropout chemist's essence and pass it on to some other traveler, as a bridge across cultures.

The Holy Stone didn't talk back. Or maybe it did.

Lost

We traveled slowly the next day, because Oleg and Sergei were reluctant to venture beyond the boundaries of their known universe. We spent the night in a second *serei*, and after dinner Oleg explained that he had never traveled beyond this place, but friends told him that there was a third *serei* about fifteen miles to the north. He thought that reindeer herders might live in that direction, so he drew a small x on my map: "The *serei* is here." The contour lines in the vicinity were broadly spaced, indicating that we were heading toward a landscape characterized by wide valleys and gently rolling hills. Oleg had placed the x mid-slope on one of the hills. But he had never been to the *serei* before, and the people who gave him verbal directions had no map, compass, sextant, altimeter, or GPS.

In the morning, Sergei clattered and crashed pots as he prepared breakfast. Yesterday's brilliant sunshine was replaced by low clouds, and a frigid wind blew from the north. Oleg and Sergei rode ahead of us and we skied in their tracks. In places, the wind had blown all the snow off the tundra, leaving jumbled bunchgrass and sedge. In other places, the snow was so hard that we could barely discern the fresh snow-machine tracks. We skied up a broad valley until we reached a tributary entering from the north. I veered up the smaller valley and Misha asked, "Where are you going?"

I looked at him quizzically. "Oleg showed on the map that the *serei* was up this valley."

"Yes, but the tracks go that way."

Misha was right; faint tread marks led straight. I felt uncomfortable with the discrepancy between Oleg's x and his snow-machine tracks, but we had to follow the tracks. A few hours later we found Oleg and Sergei waiting for us in a dense patch of elfin cedar. Oleg explained that the *serei* was *bleezkee* (very close), but he wasn't exactly sure where it was. He suggested that we ski over an adjacent ridge, veer left, and look for the building. The hill was too steep for the snow machines, so he and Sergei would drive around the ridge and also locate the *serei*. They'd have a fire and hot tea waiting for us.

I didn't like that plan. In winter, I always carry survival gear in my day pack: emergency food, a shovel to dig a shelter in the snow, a down jacket, and a space blanket. But that morning, Sergei had vehemently insisted that we put all of our extra weight on the snow machines. As a result, I was carrying only cameras, a tiny bag of dried fruit and nuts, a liter of water, and matches. The temperature was around –5° F and the wind was blowing fiercely. Our friends had instructed us to wander over an unnamed ridge, in unfamiliar country, and find a shelter that none of us had ever seen.

I suggested that we stay together, but Oleg and Sergei ignored me. Misha behaved as if Oleg was the expedition leader and we must follow his orders. Chris and I discussed our situation and decided that we should adapt without causing too much of a fuss.

The snow machines raced off and we ascended the ridge. Normally, I embrace isolation, exposure, and emptiness. But standing on that ridge, I was spooked. Below us to the north, we saw nothing but white—no *serei*, no tracks, no snow machines, no Oleg, Sergei, or Wolfchuck. Below us to the south, the sheltered patch of bushes appeared black against the overexposed whiteness of the tundra. White and black—good and bad—*cherney* and *belee caldoons*. I thought about the colors of Halloween: black and orange—night and candlelight. Our line of safety out here was just as stark—a warm night in a cozy *serei* with a full belly or a desperate struggle for survival against the hostility of lethal cold.

Misha suggested that we ski into the valley, angling slightly left as Oleg had instructed. Chris and I agreed. Then I realized that over the past few hours we had turned in a broad half circle. I was sure of it. In the morning the wind had blown against my right cheek, and now it was howling against my left. We had turned 180 degrees. In fact, we were skiing into the tributary valley that we had deliberately passed in the morning.

Oleg had assured us that there was a gully somewhere with a *serei*. But I didn't know if we were in the right valley or the wrong one. And if we were right, should we drop into the river bottom or ski along the contour, as the x on the map implied? If we chose the latter, at what elevation should we contour?

The history of polar exploration contains many accounts of competent explorers who have become disoriented and died of exposure a few miles from shelter. Chris suggested that we climb back up to the ridge and survey the landscape with binoculars. With a growing sense of unease, we followed her suggestion. When we reached the top, the wind had increased to a blizzard and the cold knifed through my light jacket.

I heard a sharp reverberating crack, and the snow undulated subtly underfoot.

Chris turned with a worried look on her face. "Did you hear that?"

It was the earth talking—the permafrost expanding with falling temperature. In most wintry places, soil freezes a few feet deep. For example, in my home in western Montana my water line is buried two feet deep and it has never frozen. In Anchorage, Alaska, water mains are buried ten feet. In contrast, in the Arctic the winter cold is so intense and summer heat so ephemeral that the soil never thaws completely. Over the millennia, the layer of ice and frozen soil has crept downward, reaching its icy finger toward the great mass of hot rock in the earth's upper crust. In some places in Siberia, this zone of permafrost is a third of a mile thick.

I mumbled, "The soil freezes approximately a thousand times deeper in Siberia than it does in Montana." Following that unsettling image, I continued, "Jeez, we're not even carrying warm parkas."

Misha suggested that we return to the patch of bushes where we had last rendezvoused with Oleg and Sergei, but we found no tracks or people. It was 4:00 P.M., afternoon shadows were lengthening, and we had to make a choice. If we turned back now, we could reach last night's *serei* before dark. Then we'd be separated from our friends and we would bivouac without food or sleeping bags, but we would be sheltered from the wind. We had matches, so we could build a fire. We'd be hungry and a little cold, but nothing serious. If we continued to wander aimlessly looking for a tiny dot on the nearly infinite tundra, we might get lucky and find either the *serei* or Oleg and Sergei. But if we failed to find shelter or our friends, we would spend a dangerous night out with no survival gear.

I form critical decisions by weighing probability and consequences. What was the probability that we'd find shelter out here? We sat on our packs in the lee of the bushes, shared a snack, and drank some water. What were the consequences if we didn't find the *serei*?

Chris pressed against me and snuggled her head against my chest. "I think we should turn back," she suggested.

We returned wearily to the *serei*, built a cheery fire, and went to bed without dinner. In the morning, Misha found one blueberry candy in his pack, which we split three ways for breakfast. Then we stoked the fire and went back to sleep to conserve energy. When we woke, I found a few spoonfuls of white flour and a pinch of salt tucked in a corner of the *serei*. We started the fire again and cooked five dime-size pancakes for each of us.

Misha held his stomach and groaned, "Oh! I am so full. I can't eat another drop."

I joked back, "Please. It's Christmas. Have one more piece of cake. I made it myself."

We were at a known location, and since Oleg and Sergei were surely looking for us, our only alternative was to wait. At 2:30 in the afternoon, we heard the sound of a snow machine and Sergei stomped into the building.

He was exhausted and annoyed because he had been looking for us all night, but he was also relieved that we were safe and not frozen stiff out on the tundra. The way he saw it, we were incompetent because we couldn't find the *serei* and we were foolish to return to this shelter when we could have simply waited on the ridge and he would have found us yesterday afternoon. We were the fools. Internally, I felt that the blame, if we wanted to go that route, should be shared. But I kept my mouth shut.

Sergei towed us to the third *serei*, which was less than a mile from where we had turned back. Oh well. I still thought that we had made the right decision, given the information and conditions at the time.

Our first two *sereis* had been hunter's shacks, but this was a real house with an entry area, a large kitchen, and a dormitory room. Smoke rose out of a brick chimney. There was a brush corral for reindeer, a stack of firewood, and an outhouse. A rawhide lasso hung from a nail by the door, and a small doll lay abandoned in the snow. Families had lived here recently, working with their herds. Excitement overcame the embarrassment, annoyance, and discomfort of the past twenty-four hours. We were only ten miles from the outer boundary of Oleg and Sergei's home territory and were already within the migration path of nomadic reindeer people. I stepped out of my skis and walked through the front door into a dark foyer that smelled of freshly tanned hides. A second door led to the kitchen with a warm fire burning in a substantial brick *petchka*.

Oleg was relieved that we were safe and he only expressed mild displeasure about our incompetence. He had a pot of water boiling and suggested that we rest while he cooked dinner. We passed through the kitchen and I lay down on one of eight steel-frame beds, complete with saggy springs and thin threadbare cotton mattresses.

Why had Oleg and Sergei never visited this *serei* before? We had walked here in three days from Vyvenka. A man could drive a snow machine here in half a day. Koryak herders had been living here recently. Weren't Oleg and Sergei curious about their fellow tribespeople? Were communications so poor that they didn't know about relatives living so close by? Or were the herders intentionally staying clear of their town-bound neighbors?

I had so many questions but felt reluctant to ask. Tension still hung in the air, and because I was the de facto captain of the white man's contingent, all the mistakes rested on my shoulder. I felt the need for time and silence to redeem myself.

We ate a large dinner with noodles and moose meat, followed by sugared rice, butter, and apricots. As the evening progressed, I realized that Oleg and Sergei didn't hold a grudge. *"Paiyette."* A mistake had been made and now we were all safe. We were five people and a dog, alone together, looking for reindeer people, and anger isn't a useful survival tool on the tundra. Four days ago, when we had left Vyvenka, we didn't know if there were any reindeer people nearby. Now we at least knew that the herders existed. We just had to find them.

Surrounded by the signs and smells of reindeer herding, Oleg became reflective. Slowly at first, then more passionately as he warmed to his tale, he finally explained why the people of Vyvenka lost their herds:

Before the Bolshevik Revolution, the Vyvenka herders lived the nomadic, subsistence life that Moolynaut, Simon, and Lydia described. The Soviets collectivized and modernized the industry while still maintaining many elements of the old ways. Under the Stalinist brigade system, the herders built a string of houses, like the one we were in now, across the tundra. They herded their reindeer on the same migration path every year and moved from house to house, living in relative comfort during the coldest winter months. Then in the spring and summer they left the houses and continued the migration using their traditional tents and *yurangas*.

While the Koryak managed the herds, Russian merchants arranged shipping and marketing. At predetermined times, the Koryak brought their animals to sheltered bays along the coast, where a refrigerator ship waited. People slaughtered the deer, loaded meat and hides on the ship, and collected their wages. But after perestroika, the Russians left abruptly and the ships didn't show up. The Koryak knew that vendors in PK or Vladivostok would buy their meat, but they had no idea how to raise capital, lease ships, organize markets, obtain permits, and so on.

The herders got discouraged.

Freewheeling Russian bandito merchants offered ridiculously low prices for the meat. If the Koryak refused to sell, the merchants left and the herders received no money at all. If they did sell, the Russians got rich and the herders barely survived. Often "whiskey traders" offered vodka instead of money. Using a timeless form of exploitation, they first traded a few bottles of vodka for one deer. When the herders got drunk, the thieves traded one additional bottle of vodka for many deer.

The herders got more discouraged.

Rogue tax collectors claimed that the Koryak owed taxes, and then collected the imagined debt in meat. When whiskey and lies weren't effective, armed poachers shot deer and hauled the carcasses away in their *visdichots*.

Discouragement led to despair.

Once despair set in, herders drank even more vodka, weren't vigilant in guarding their animals, and suffered huge losses to wolf predation. Oleg explained that Moolynaut's father had poisoned wolves with strychnine that he bought from the Americans. When the strychnine didn't work, he shot them with his Winchester rifles. During the Soviet period, soldiers hunted wolves from helicopters. But after perestroika, the herders couldn't afford poison and the Russian troops no longer allocated expensive helicopter time to aid indigenous herders. When economic hard times deepened, the Koryak couldn't even afford bullets for their rifles. Wolves decimated the herds.

I broke in with a question: "Let's imagine the time when Moolynaut was a little girl, when there were few Russians, few tax collectors, few poachers, and little vodka. The Americans supplied the Koryak with rifles and the herds thrived."

"That's right," Oleg agreed.

"Now let's go back even farther, before the Americans, before Winchester rifles, before strychnine. How did the people control wolf predation during the old times?"

Sergei answered quickly, "Words."

"Words?" I queried.

"Yes. The *belee caldoons* knew chants. They could sing to the wolves. The wolves would listen. They ate some deer, but not too many, and everyone lived together."

We sat quietly for a moment, listening to the crackling of the fire and the howling wind that rattled the windowpanes. Then Oleg spoke thoughtfully: "In the earliest times, wolves were much admired and honored. The she-wolf was always the head of the family. She trained and taught her wolf pups to hunt and the pack lived by her knowledge and cunning. If a human hunter killed a she-wolf, the people gathered to greet the wolf's spirit. The hunter reverently laid a hank of her fur in the fire. If the fur burned quickly, the fire indicated that the hunter honored the wolf. People felt joy. Then the hunter brought the carcass close to the fire, within the circle of the people. He placed dry birch twigs in the wolf's eyes and ears, so she couldn't see how many reindeer lived near the house. The people held a feast and gave the she-wolf the most delicious, fattest piece of meat. In this way, people honored the wolf pack. In turn, wolves honored the people.

"In those times, when our great-grandparents were alive, we had many reindeer. Wolves killed when they were hungry, but when their bellies were full they didn't bother us. People hunted wolves, but people are slow and they had poor weapons, so the wolves usually escaped unharmed. Today there is a war between wolves and people. For a generation, people have shot wolves from snow machines and helicopters and murdered them with poisoned bait. Now the predators kill not only from hunger but also to harm people. And we have no elders who can make peace with the wolves."

Oleg paused for a moment and then continued, "Even with all the troubles, maybe we would still have deer if we could have found some words or songs to keep the vodka away. A long time ago, the Holy Stone had more power than it does today. It gave our *belee caldoons* enough power to keep the wolves away with chants. But there was no vodka in those olden times, so the Holy Stone didn't give us any chants against vodka. Now most of our *belee caldoons* are dead, and the few who are alive, like Moolynaut, are old and they have lost some of their power. All of our young people grew up in Soviet schools and learned from the wooden-headed people, so they, too, have no power. There is no one who can speak to the Holy Stone and learn a chant against vodka. When herders are drunk from too much vodka, then the wolves come and kill the deer. So this is why we have no deer."

I tried to sound hopeful: "But herding people were here, in this house, just a few weeks ago. There are still people on the tundra who herd reindeer."

Oleg looked at me thoughtfully, and then he smiled. "Yes, that is why we are here, on this journey. To find these people. Thank you for buying the gas."

Then, after a moment of silent reflection, he concluded simply, "We have a long day's travel ahead of us and it is time to sleep."

Across the White Desert

I stepped out of the house as the sun was rising, red and flattened, on the eastern horizon. It seemed alternately close enough to touch and then as distant as the farthest galaxy. The wind, blowing wisps of snow across the hardened drifts, had been such a harbinger of danger when we were lost, but now it was another familiar companion, providing a chorus for this strange tribe wandering aimlessly across an adamantine landscape.

Up until now Oleg and Sergei had a plan—to find reindeer people by seeking direction, or approval, from the Holy Stone and then to continue onward toward the most distant *serai* that they knew about. But now there was no plan, only open space and spring snow that crepitated underfoot. To my Ph.D. chemist's mind, this all sounded a bit too crazy, but no one was listening to my ideas and suggestions anyway. That was fine. While none of this made sense to me, I reminded myself that the Koryak people, or their ancestors, had survived in this harsh land for millennia. Now I was learning to discard my Western prejudices and to open myself to a mysterious way of thinking.

After breakfast, Oleg and Sergei siphoned fuel from one of the drums to fill the machines. When they were finished, the drum felt light and sounded hollow. Sergei argued that since Chris, Misha, and I moved slowly on skis and since we were prone to getting lost anyway, we must ride on the snow machines. Oleg honored Chris with her queenly perch behind Wolf-chuck on the Yamaha, while Misha and I made miserable lumpy nests on the sleds by cramming reindeer skins between fuel drums, the metal stove, and Sergei's spare engine.

All day, we wandered northward, swooping in broad arcs. Chris called the landscape the Frozen Ocean because she imagined that our snow machines were like diminutive yachts sailing precariously across the waves. Misha insisted that the landscape was more closely akin to a White Desert, because we had been traveling for five days without seeing any signs of life. I found the paucity of game curious, because I've seen a lot of animals when I've traveled in the Alaskan and Canadian Arctic and there was enough vegetation here in Kamchatka to support a rich and varied fauna.

Oleg and Sergei are indigenous hunters who eat well if they shoot game and eat poorly if they fail. I'm also a hunter, and if there were tracks of reindeer and moose in the snow I would have seen them. Misha has the best distance vision of anyone I have ever traveled with and almost always spots objects long before I do. Chris doesn't talk much when she's traveling; she observes. Wolfchuck has his dog's sense of smell and was trained to alert Oleg to the presence of game. The dog understood that a successful hunt is followed by abundant food for all. I contend that the six of us, with our combined knowledge and senses, weren't missing much. Sure, there were rodents living under the snow and we saw some sign of fox and ermine. Occasionally Wolfchuck leapt off the machine to flush ptarmigan and Sergei pursued, kneeling on the snow machine, with his right hand on the throttle, and firing his shotgun from his left hip, like a cross between Wyatt Earp in Tombstone and Sylvester Stallone on a commando mission. But other than that, we saw few tracks and no large ungulates.

Oleg explained that, three years ago, he shot many geese in April. Last year he killed only a few. "If there were ducks and geese flying around," he concluded, "I would stop right here, lie like a stone in the middle of the valley, and remain motionless all day if need be. Then when a bird flew overhead, I would rise and shoot it. They call me Duck Devil," he bragged proudly. Sergei explained that two years ago he caught eighty fish a day near the second *serei*. Now he was lucky to catch two.

I was curious about these population declines, so when I returned to North America I tried to find a scientific study of wild game populations in the region. The closest source was a report published by the United Nations Development Programme. The scientists wrote: "Specifics of species loss and indicators of degradation of fauna and flora over time are needed to assess the magnitude and direction of change." And: "The understanding of baseline scenarios is problematic." In other words, the biologists don't know what's going on—and that's in the study areas, which are all hundreds of miles south of Vyvenka. When I was in PK, I asked one of the scientists on the project, Vadim, if he could direct me to someone who was monitoring animal populations in northern Kamchatka, near Vyvenka. Vadim told me that it was too expensive to work in the area, so, to his knowledge, there were no studies.

As a result, we're left with a mystery. Vyvenka residents hunt and fish aggressively within a twenty-five-mile radius of Vyvenka, so human excesses could easily decimate faunal populations close to town. But as we traveled beyond the normal hunting range, there were only a few scattered bands of herders, so I couldn't imagine that there was much hunting pressure. My friends all explained that during the Soviet era soldiers shot deer, bear, wolves, and even wildfowl from helicopters, thereby decimating game populations. But that was ten to fifteen years ago, and you would think that populations would have had time to recover.

I can't explain the population balance of the modern ecosystem, but the landscape seemed vast and desolate without the thrill of cresting a hill and watching a herd of wild reindeer, or even a solitary moose, breath freezing in the morning air and hooves pawing in the snow for succulent mosses and sedges. Yet we had been traveling for only five days, my friends were all cheery, and the spring sun had finally begun to slice through the armor of winter, bathing us all in welcomed warmth. We stopped for lunch and Sergei built a fire to brew a pot of tea. I sat apart from the group to absorb the radiant energy in solitude and to write in my journal. With thoughts of the "White Desert" on my mind, I tried to imagine the tundra as it was a generation ago, with thousands of domestic reindeer moving slowly across the landscape. I could understand how, with hard and changing times, the people in Vyvenka would have lost some of their deer, half their deer, or even most of their deer, but I found it hard to fathom how the people lost all of them.

Disappearing markets, bandito capitalism, tax collectors, poachers, vodka, and wolves.

I thought about Oleg's stories recounting how, in recent years, wolves scattered reindeer herds and killed wantonly. If you don't believe that old shamans had spells to communicate with the wild canines, then another explanation might be that in the olden days, before people had poisons, guns, and helicopters, the ecosystem was intact and wolves had a variety of prey to sustain them. After the ecosystem became fragmented and imbalanced, wolves starved. Then, when they encountered a large herd of reindeer, they killed more than they could eat. Thus, according to this reasoning, people a few generations ago didn't protect their herds with chants but with an entire lifestyle based on respect and preservation of the ecosystem.

Homo sapiens have lived in the Arctic for approximately thirty to forty thousand years. During most of this time, our ancestors hunted in this harsh and frozen land using long sticks, with small pieces of bone, stone, or ivory tied to the ends of these sticks. Maybe you don't believe that energy flows from the earth to the Holy Stone and to the people, and that people must also receive energy from the earth and return it to the Holy Stone. But the fact remains that these people, who were anatomically similar to us, survived in a very harsh land with absolutely minimal technology. They lived through ice ages, migrated into unfamiliar lands, and populated the earth. I thought about the day Misha, Chris, and I were lost and I realized that if you gave me a spear and nothing else, I would die rather quickly out here. Even the most cynical Western observer has to appreciate that Stone Age hunters survived through keen observation of their surroundings and intimate connectivity with the landscape and its creatures. And out here, I felt that if people opened their senses wide enough and became sufficiently in tune with their surroundings, I have no trouble believing that they could make tribal pacts with wolves.

Sergei interrupted my reverie by calling me for tea and lunch, and then we continued our procession, following a broad valley simply because it looked like a reasonable pasture for reindeer. Later that afternoon, my legs felt cramped from sitting on the sled and my back ached from the constant jarring, so when our procession stopped for a rest I climbed a low ridge to stretch out my muscles and photograph our procession from above. In the still air, the silence was broken only by my labored breathing and by the crunch of boots on crusty snow. No smells wafted above the snow-covered landscape. All that remained was the now-familiar void of open space. I reached a convenient vantage point and took my video camera out. Soon the purr of one engine and the cough of the other permeated the silence. Then the procession started: machine-sled . . . machine-sled . . . form interrupted by space . . . four tiny dots crawling across Chris's imagined frozen ocean. Even though the machines were traveling at about 15 miles an hour, they seemed still against the vastness, as if there were no past or future, no place where we came from, and no destination that we were headed toward.

I shot a minute of video, walked to the far edge of the ridge, and began to descend, as planned, to intercept the procession. With gravity on my side, walking felt so effortless that I lengthened my strides, and then, thinking about the ease and fluidity of skiing, I broke into an easy lope. Suddenly one boot punched through the crust and I stumbled. I had too much momentum to catch my balance, so I let myself launch into a somersault, landing on my shoulder. I stood, brushed myself off, and waved to indicate that everything was fine; I had just taken a little fall on snow.

Everything wasn't fine. My pelvis had jarred loose. Dr. Schutte had warned me, "Don't run," but for an instant I forgot those bad times and had felt the irresistible pull of gravity. I regained my feet and returned to the snow machines, forcing myself not to limp. No one—not even Chris—saw the pain inside me.

We camped that night and on the morning of the sixth day we climbed a hill and surveyed the empty landscape. Oleg thought that reindeer might be camped in a broad plain where forage was abundant, whereas Sergei assumed that they would seek shelter in a protected valley. We had left Vyvenka with two machines and 110 gallons of gas, and we were all aware that when we burned the last precious drops the pistons would rotate to a cold, silent halt.

We set out again, following Oleg's hunch, traveling efficiently on wind-hardened snow. But whenever we crossed a ravine or streambed or descended the lee side of a hill, the machines bogged down in sugary snow. To add to our troubles, Sergei's machine suffered a mechanical malfunction several times every hour. When a machine broke or got stuck, no one spoke, cursed, accused, or complained. If it sank into soft snow, we shoveled and pushed; if the guide rollers on Sergei's track slipped off their moorings, we flipped his heavy machine on its side and jammed the worn parts back into some semblance of position. When Sergei's engine overheated, we packed snow on the carburetor and waited. I was amazed at how many times you can cajole a dying machine back into temporary operation without installing any new parts.

Now I understood, again, why Oleg and Sergei didn't stray far from home. Snow machines are potentially faster and easier than human- or animal-powered travel. But when you're running on ten-year-old spark plugs and thirty-year-old guide rollers, when your machine is so worn-out that you feel compelled to carry an extra engine, when three-quarters of your load is fuel, and when no locals have enough money for gas anyway, then snow machines are a royal pain in the ass, not a quick, efficient way of traveling. Factoring in all the machine problems, we averaged a little over 3 miles per hour, about the same as skiing speed. I was reminded that in the Stone Age people mushed their dog teams or reindeer sleds for hundreds of miles to gather at the Holy Stone for the spring festival. Today, with the eclectic mixture of poverty and twenty-first-century technology, people rarely stray more than twenty-five miles from home.

That afternoon, one of the fuel drums developed a leak and spilled gas onto our tent and sleeping bags. "*Paiyette*. No big deal. That's life." The drum was almost empty anyway, so we siphoned most of the remaining gas into the machines and drained what was left into the good drum. Then Oleg pushed the old, worn-out, rusted drum on its side and kicked it. It rolled down a slight hill and the wind carried it across the snowy tundra. As the drum bounced and cavorted like a playful calf, disappearing within a miasmic cloud of windblown snow, I imagined that I was witnessing the end of the Fossil Fuel Age and the beginning of a scary or titillating uncertainty.

We had burned half of our gas. I reasoned that we would have to turn back because we would need the remaining half for the journey home. But Oleg explained that he and Sergei had used a lot of gas looking for us on the night we were lost and that, furthermore, we were traveling outward on a circuitous route. Oleg estimated that we could burn the gas that was now in the machines, plus one additional tankful in each, before we needed to retreat. That wasn't much. I steeled myself for the probability that we would return to Vyvenka without finding the reindeer people or bringing meat back to Moolynaut.

On the evening of the seventh day, we drove to the top of a hill and were surprised to see several rickety, ancient abandoned drill rigs rising, rusted and weather-beaten, against the horizon. It looked as if some Martian tricksters had sped back through time in their flying saucers, stolen a little worn-out machinery from the nineteenth century, and deposited it on the tundra.

I recalled that the world's second-largest platinum mine is located near Korpf/Tillichiki. Misha explained that we were traveling through a mineral-rich zone of metamorphic rock and he suspected that exploration geologists were drilling cores to find gold and silver.

Meanwhile, the sky was darkening, the wind was building, and dense, menacing lenticular clouds indicated that a blizzard was approaching. The tent was soaked with gasoline from the leaky drum, but when you're traveling with decrepit machinery you, too, eventually smell like a machine. We pitched and secured the bulky cotton tent, set up the small sheet-metal wood-burning stove that would keep us warm, and gathered firewood. Then we built ourselves a windbreak of snow, brush, boards, and ragged pieces of tar paper that we unceremoniously pilfered from the rig. After working for an hour, I stood up to stretch my back and try to interpret the now-constant pain I felt in my pelvis.

What was going on in there? What was broken, torn, ripped, displaced, or rubbing? I couldn't tell, but I felt vulnerable out here on the tundra, so far from medical attention.

I tried to act as if it were no big deal: *"Paiyette."* That didn't work. No, despite my resolve to be stoic, the pain persisted doggedly, centered in the fulcrum of my balance, of my lifestyle.

Shaking the worry aside, I watched the three broad-shouldered men and one tough, diminutive woman, with fur-lined hoods and tanned, wind-scoured faces, coated with rime and frost. We had come together from afar and soon we would return to our disparate lives. But for now, we were building a windbreak against the blizzard, dedicated to a common goal and overcoming obstacles as they arose. I bent my back to the task in front of us.

Blizzard

Since the last *serei*, we had been camping in Oleg's canvas wall tent. If we all lay down on our backs, touching shoulders, there was room to sleep four people, but there were five of us. Oleg slept against one wall of the tent; Sergei slipped into the sleeping bag with Oleg; Misha anchored himself in the middle and Chris next to him. And me? I cuddled up next to Chris, separated by many layers of fabric and down, with my sleeping bag half poking out the side of the tent flap, exposed to the elements. When I awoke the next morning, the outside edge of my bag was warmly insulated beneath a foot of soft, dry snow.

Spindrift had also invaded the interior of the tent, so my friends, still tightly wrapped in their cocoonlike sleeping bags, were dusted with snow, looking like tundra hills stretching toward the horizon. But unlike the tundra, the tent reeked of spilled gas, unwashed bodies, moldy canvas, wood smoke, and poorly tanned reindeer hides. I rolled over carefully so I wouldn't disturb anyone, and felt a sharp pain radiate from my pelvis, ripple across my groin, and lodge in the top of my femur. I breathed deeply, again trying to figure out what was hurt, how serious the injury was, and how I could compensate. Somewhere in my subconscious, I realized that the feeling had been my bedfellow all night, steady, lingering, insistent, intensely worrisome, without actually becoming debilitating.

I closed my eyes, lay still, and tried not to call myself a stupid fucking idiot.

We slept late, started a fire in the stove, ate a leisurely breakfast, and hung our damp bags over the stove to dry. Then we dressed and ventured into the storm to gather more firewood. The first blast of snow-laden air took my breath away, but once I adjusted I realized that the temperature was only about zero Fahrenheit. Tendrils of blowing snow swirled along the ground and wrapped around our feet, like so many octopi on the seafloor. The morning fire had been cozy, but I enjoyed the internal warmth generated as we sawed firewood and shoveled snow. I moved about gingerly, looking to see if anyone noticed that I was walking awkwardly, trying to locate a center of balance that put the least pressure on my injury. But the pelvis is the fulcrum and you cannot stand without it. Loosened cables on the drill rig snapped in the wind, pulleys creaked, and an errant bull wheel rotated slowly, making the rig seem like civilization's ghost clanking its chains.

We completed our chores and retreated inside. The tent was cramped and I had a hard time finding a comfortable position because my pelvis and adjacent adductor muscles ached. Intermittent sunlight was scattered by clouds, reflected by blowing snow, and refracted through the cotton tent, casting a subdued orange glow, like candlelight.

I wrote in my journal while Chris read a damp, crumpled copy of *The New Yorker*. Oleg seemed content to gaze into nothingness, but Sergei needed an outlet for his boundless and restless energy. He fidgeted, drank several cups of tea, stoked the fire, and then asked to see the *Americanski* magazine. Chris interrupted her reading and handed it to him.

Sergei reached into his duffel to find a scratched, dusty, bent pair of reading glasses and then studied each page carefully. He scrutinized the leather interior of a Lexus with the wry commentary: "*Americanski* Buran (American snow machine)." The next page featured an image of a lascivious model in a scant, body-hugging dress, looking orgasmic because she had just purchased a new cell phone. Sergei commented, "She must be cold, dressed like that." We all laughed because she did look silly, clothed only in that flimsy dress and wrapped inside a few pages of *The New Yorker* to keep her warm. I wanted to take pity on her and give her a beaded dog-skin hat, ragged Soviet army fatigues soaked in snow-machine oil, sealskin pants, and some real shoes, for Godsake, because every time she went out to pee those dumb high heels would surely punch through the weak crust.

Sergei turned to the back page, which was a full-color advertisement showing a man in tidy L.L.Bean clothing, walking across a snowy field, headed toward misty, snow-flocked spruce. A black Labrador retriever followed two paces behind the man. The copy read: "American Partnership—American Century."

Sergei was puzzled. "What is this about?"

Chris looked at me.

I smiled. "This photograph says that if you work with this company, you will become very rich. And if you become very rich in America, then you can go for a walk in the snow with your dog."

There was stunned silence; then everyone burst into rollicking laughter. When he calmed down enough to speak, Sergei exclaimed, "My friends the *Americanskis*! Oh, you *Americanskis*! What a strange people! We will never understand you."

When the mirth subsided, we sat quietly, enjoying the peacefulness of a stormy day, listening to the wind and the flapping canvas. Snow eddied around the lee side of the tent, drifted through the buttoned doorway, and hissed as it melted against the red-hot stove. Misha picked up the thread of the conversation: "We laugh, but in this life we all live in towns and cities, and sometimes it is hard to know how much to work and how many things to buy. We all work to buy many things, but maybe we work too much, because we don't need most of the things we buy. You don't need money to walk into the Wild Nature and watch the snow fall."

Oleg added, "Yes, Misha, you are right. Most people want money. I, too, want money. But there are many people in Vyvenka who don't like to work and are troubled by money. Maybe these people are the happy ones. It is hard to know.

"A poor man wakes up in the morning and thinks, 'I am hungry. There is no food in the house.' So he walks out on the ice and goes fishing for *korishka*. [*Korishka* is a small fish, six inches long, which Misha calls cucumber fish.] Maybe he is lucky that day and catches a whole sack of *korishka*. He can't eat them all, so he takes the extra fish to the store and sells them. Now he has a big problem. He has money. 'What do I do with all this money?' he asks."

Oleg held his head in his hands as if he had a huge emotional weight and a throbbing headache. For theatrical impact, he repeated the imagined dilemma.

"'What do I do with all this money?'"

Then Oleg smiled and held one finger in the air to indicate a eureka moment. "'Aha! I will buy some vodka.'"

Oleg giggled uncharacteristically. "So this man spends all his money, drinks all his vodka, and passes out. When he wakes up, he has no money and no vodka. But now life is simple again. He has no worries and knows exactly what to do. He is hungry, so he goes fishing for *korishka*."

We all laughed and then we quietly contemplated the disparate stories and images from two ends of the economic spectrum, on two neighboring continents so far away from each other.

Oleg took the magazine from Sergei's hand and thumbed through it slowly, glimpsing a culture that was so incomprehensible. It was a stormy day, we had nothing else to do, so we all waited patiently. Then Oleg unfastened one of the buttons on the tent door and stared out into the storm. Snow eddied and collected on his broad, passive face. "I told you this before. If the mafia bandits in PK would steal only three-quarters of our fish, all the fishermen in Vyvenka would be rich, like you *Americanskis*. But they steal ninety-five percent, so life is hard.

"And we've lost our reindeer, as well. We spoke about this yesterday. Before perestroika, before that bandit Gorbachev gave our country to the *Americanski* bandits, we had ten thousand reindeer in Vyvenka. Ten thousand, do you understand?"

He waited for Misha to translate and for me to nod.

"Now we have none. Zero. None."

Oleg composed himself, smiled, and said softly, "*Paiyette*."

The conversation, which had started so jovially, had turned somber, and we all retreated into our own private worlds and thoughts.

Reindeer People

The storm broke during the night, and the following morning Oleg skipped breakfast and roared out on his machine, traveling fast, without passengers or a sled. He returned a half an hour later with exciting news: He'd seen houses in a nearby valley, with smoke curling out of one of the buildings.

We wolfed down our breakfast and hurriedly packed our gear, as if we feared that the houses would disappear if we were a half an hour late. As we reached the bluff above the river, a rainbow formed through a mist of frozen fog. It wasn't a summer rainbow, arcing bright and unfettered across a warm, blue sky, but a winter rainbow, held low to the ground by the cold and pointing—like everything else around here—toward the distant horizon. The colors were muted and subdued, but they were the first natural reds and yellows we had seen in this stark landscape of white on white and they greeted us like summer flowers. I had never seen a winter rainbow before, but Sergei smiled and announced, "A winter rainbow is a sign of good luck. We will find reindeer people today."

Beyond the rainbow, a cluster of houses lay half-buried in drifting snow. We skidded the machines down the steep bank and followed fresh snow-machine tracks upriver, past skeleton houses adorned with loose tar paper and torn roofing that flapped against fractured rafters. The smell of wood smoke emanated from a small enclave of intact buildings. As we approached, the sun burned through the fog, revealing hillsides scarred with crude roads and deep trenches cut by heavy machinery during mineral exploration.

Two men stepped out of a building, blinking into the morning light. Constantine was well over two hundred pounds, effusive and talkative, dressed for the below-zero temperature in a thin plaid shirt, cotton sweatpants, and slippers. His sidekick, Nikolai, looked like he had just walked out of a gulag— silent, tall, bearded, and emaciated, with sunken cheeks and a glazed, hunted look. Constantine and Nikolai had worked for the exploration geologists and then remained after the geologists left, choosing isolation and nature-clad poverty over the banal slum-infested poverty of urban life. Constantine shook my hand with bone-crushing enthusiasm. Nikolai extended a withered, destroyed stump, probably blown up, crushed, or smashed in a mining accident. Even though he hadn't seen another soul for God knows how long, he didn't say a word.

After an American company had found commercial quantities of gold here, the Koryak leaders told them that they could truck the entire mountain to the coast and carry it away on their ships if they wanted, but they couldn't build a cyanide leach facility to concentrate the ore on the tundra. So the company never opened a mine. They hired Nikolai as a caretaker to protect the dilapidated ruins of the exploration camp from nonexistent intruders. Constantine was a freelance poacher, trapping the few remaining fox, wolverine, and ermine that lived along the valley bottom.

Constantine invited us into the shack and served tea and homemade bread. When we returned outside, the sun was hot. I felt that the blizzard had been the last blast of winter and now spring was finally asserting itself. Small rivulets of water dripped off the roofs with a cheery, tinkling melody. When we asked about reindeer people, Constantine pointed across the plain: "Go west, until you reach a thick line of bushes. Turn south, cross three frozen creeks, then turn back west toward the mountains. You'll find reindeer and a small tribe of herders."

An hour later we crested a small rise and Sergei whistled softly: "*Eileen* [reindeer]." I hopped off the sled, painfully stood with my cramped and injured pelvis, and trained my binoculars in the direction that Sergei indicated. In the distance, reindeer were grazing peacefully on the tundra, with their intricate branched antlers silhouetted against distant, snowy hills. Near the herd, four men were standing close to a fire. One of the men was looking at us through his binoculars. I felt like waving a cheery hello, but it seemed silly. Chris walked over and stood beside me, so I handed her the binoculars and leaned slightly to press against her, and she gently pressed back. It was a simple, wordless moment of intimacy, a celebration of our success, muted but more memorable and poignant than a hand-slapping hullabaloo. We had been traveling across the tundra for nine days, which is a lot or a little, depending on your perspective, and despite the improbability of it all, we had found reindeer people in this vast and empty landscape.

We crossed a creek bottom, got stuck in the soft snow for half an hour, and then regained solid crust on the open tundra. Oleg tied Wolfchuck to the sled so he couldn't jump off and chase the deer. Then we proceeded very slowly. The deer looked up and started to bolt but didn't run far. We stopped. The deer calmed down. We continued cautiously. The young men were waiting. Three were dressed in Soviet army fatigues, and one wore an incongruous red and blue nylon ski suit. One of the men had blond hair and blue eyes, indicating Russian ancestors, but the others had the almond eyes, high cheekbones, and dark coloration of the Koryak.

We stopped and faced the men with an awkward silence. After coming all this way, we had nothing to say. The herders, too, were silent. Beyond their faces, I watched a deer paw through the snow to find hidden morsels of grass and moss. Finally, Oleg introduced us briefly. The men nodded and didn't say much. Then they conferred among themselves.

The oldest spoke: "We don't have visitors very often."

The man in the red and blue suit interrupted: "We've had visitors once in my life. They were Japanese and they came in a helicopter. They asked us a lot of questions and then they flew away after an hour or two."

The first man continued, "The deer are starting to give birth. There were two new babies this morning. Now the herd is very nervous because wolves often attack during the birthing. You are strangers. The deer don't know you and you don't know how to talk to them. You must return to the base and speak to Nikolai, the brigadier. Alexander will show you the way."

The man in the ski suit introduced himself as Alexander and then sat on Oleg's sled and pointed southward. Oleg and Sergei started their machines and we eased slowly away from the herd, toward the base. After crossing two creeks, getting stuck once, fiddling with the guide rollers once, and taking one cigarette break, we traveled five miles to a small encampment of tar-paper shacks snuggled into drifting snow. At the sound of the engines, a tall, lean, handsome man in his mid-fifties stepped outside to greet us. Oleg explained our mission and the two men talked. Misha didn't translate, and from what little I understood, Oleg was recounting our passage and the reasons for our visit. I wasn't sure exactly what Oleg said, but I was glad he was doing the talking, because if someone asked me, I couldn't readily explain why we had journeyed so far to come here.

A year ago Moolynaut had looked me in the eye and said, "Please come back. It will be good for you." So Chris and I had traveled from Montana to New York, Moscow, PK, Korpf/Tillichiki, and Vyvena. Momentum, love of travel, and curiosity had carried us onward to find these reindeer people, but now that we were here, I felt like a nosy intruder rather than a sacred pilgrim.

The stranger had a triangular face, with high cheekbones narrowing to a pointed chin, highlighted by a wispy moustache that drooped toward an even wispier goatee. But the most prominent feature was his smile, which seemed ever present, subtle, genuine, and benevolent.

He addressed me directly in Russian, his hand extended: "Hello, my name is Nikolai. Please to meet you."

I shook his hand and introduced myself. Then he greeted Chris with a grandfatherly smile and said, "You have traveled from far away. You must be hungry. Please, come inside."

A battered cassette deck, connected to an old car battery, played scratchy music, a hot fire burned in a rusted sheet-metal stove, and furs hung everywhere, exuding a soft, now-familiar, animal muskiness. The ceiling was so low that I stooped defensively, even though I had an inch of clearance if I stood straight. My eyes, accustomed to the bright tundra, slowly adjusted to the cavelike room, illuminated by scattered sunlight filtering through small, dusty windows. Two men introduced themselves while two women remained silently in the shadows near the stove. Nikolai offered the least rickety stools to Chris, Misha, and me. Oleg and Sergei shared a bench that threatened to collapse at any moment.

There were twelve people in camp: Nikolai and his wife, Nadia, six men in their twenties and thirties, two young women, and two toddlers, age five and three. Eight hundred deer were grazing on the tundra.

The young women moved silently and shyly to serve heaping bowls of warm, rich reindeer meat and rice. When we finished our soup, they brought diced fried liver ladled over buckwheat, a huge pile of greasy bannock (fry bread), and dark, sugary tea.

Nikolai never asked why Chris and I had traveled three-quarters of the way around the world to arrive at this isolated outpost. The length and ardor of our journey, the salutary space of the tundra, and the immediacy of spring blizzards had exorcised reasons and motivations. Now we were in a warm house, eating wholesome food, embraced by the kindness of strangers. I was happy to relax, liberated from the jarring snow machines, the only epicenters of noise and air pollution for hundreds of miles in any direction.

Nikolai explained that their brigade migrated along on a cigar-shaped route that they repeated every year. During Soviet times, when money and materials were plentiful, they built a string of houses to make their winter encampments more comfortable. The current camp was the most elaborate, with five structures: the commons where we were now, a small private cabin for Nikolai and his wife, a *banyo* (Russian sauna), a toolshed, and a small tipi-shaped structure for preparing meat and hides. The brigade settled here every year for the birthing. In early May, when the calves were strong, they left the base and headed toward the Sea of Okhotsk, where ocean breezes protected people and deer from the intense hordes of mosquitoes that plagued the inland tundra. During the summer, they supplemented their diets with salmon and seal meat. The brigade lived in tents during the warm months, returning to the most northerly of their houses in late October.

The brigade also maintained apartments in Manily, a small city on the Sea of Okhotsk. The older children stayed in town for schooling and some of the mothers remained with them, with the women rotating in shifts between town and the tundra camps.

Nikolai explained that before perestroika the brigade owned two thousand deer, which was the carrying capacity of their pasture. During the mayhem following the demise of the Soviet infrastructure they lost more than half their herd, and now they had only eight hundred.

Nikolai seemed upset over the loss until I complimented him by commenting that the brigades near Vyvenka had lost all their deer: "You must be a strong leader to have held the brigade together and preserved your tradition."

I had paid the right compliment and Nikolai nodded slowly, his face filled with pride. Then he grew somber and reflective. "Yes, it was hard times. For several years we hid on the tundra, far from poachers, tax collectors, and other bandits. And far from vodka. But we lost a lot of deer anyway. With our herd so small, we stopped selling meat. Now conditions are improving. We will build the herd back up to two thousand. Then we can sell deer again."

I looked around the room. Even though the scene was desperately poor by North American standards, our hosts had served store-bought rice, buckwheat, tea, sugar, and bannock. Nikolai had a fairly new snow machine parked out front. Thus the clan operated on a small but viable cash economy. If the brigade didn't sell deer, how did they obtain money?

Nikolai explained that they lived communally and everyone contributed what they had. Some people worked part-time in Manily. He and his wife received government pensions. And the rich operating platinum mine offered meager compensation for permission to mine 80 million dollars' worth of ore from Koryak lands every year.

After our meal, we went back outside. Nikolai and the younger men examined our loads: the dented fuel drum, rusted stove, and greasy spare engine.

Nikolai asked to try my skis. I sat in the snow and exchanged my ski boots for his mukluks. Both sets of footwear represented a pinnacle of technology in their own land and for their own purpose. Mine were molded out of high-tech plastic, with forward-lean adjusters and side-to-side cant levelers. Nikolai's mukluks had soles of hardened, waterproof sealskin, fur side in, to make warm, comfortable foot beds. The lower part of the boot, which was in constant contact with snow, was also made of sealskin, but with the fur out, to shed water. The tops were reindeer skin, also fur side out, sewn artfully into a patchwork of white and brown. Nikolai's wife had packed dry moss inside the boots for additional warmth. The boots were light, comfortable, and warm. More than that, they were made of a carefully selected combination of naturally available materials, blended with elaborate, loving, time-consuming artwork. But most important, they represented a tactile, integral part of the marriage contact: I provide you with meat; you hand-stitch my boots and make them comfortable and beautiful.

Nikolai skied away, feet far apart, arms forward, in an awkward crouch. Undaunted at his instability, he shushed down a small hill, crossed his tips, and crashed headfirst in the snow.

Stone Age Hunters in the Arctic

About 2 million years ago, small bands of hominids marched out of their tropical homeland in Africa. Although some settled in the Middle East, a few restless adventurers moved past the warm paradise of the Mediterranean, crossed the fertile Asian steppe, and eventually headed north.

In the 1980s, Russian archaeologist Yuri Mochanov investigated a Stone Age campsite on the Lena River in northeastern Siberia just south of the Arctic Circle.[1] Even during the warmest interglacial period, this site, called Diring, was a harsh place, with hot summers and bitterly cold winters. Yet hominids set up home here and raised their families, a quarter of a million years ago. In that distant and shadowed past, these earliest Siberians were probably *Homo erectus.*

The Diring residents didn't have sophisticated tools or language. We assume that they communicated to some extent and we know that they knapped stone tools, but their technology and culture were quite simple compared with Stone Age people who came later, such as the Cro-Magnon, for example, who painted breathtaking art on cave walls in Europe. Yet their survival assures us that something about their technology and culture must have been more advanced than what immediately meets the eye. One investigator commented that the Diring settlements in the Arctic "imply a range of behaviors and adaptations that we have never given *Homo erectus* credit for, from making mitts and boots, to controlling fire and having winter survival strategies."[2]

The Diring people weren't alone. Two hominid settlements in northeast China have been dated to 260,000 years ago. Skulls show anatomical traits intermediate between *Homo erectus* and *Homo sapiens.*[3] Much later, *Homo sapiens* settled just south of the Arctic Circle in western Siberia by 40,000 years ago[4] and north of the Arctic Circle by 27,000 years ago.[5] These people left no written record, only a few skeletal remains, some stone and bone tools, and charred detritus from long-extinguished campfires. One window into their behavior, however, is to analyze the process of gathering food.

Igor Krupnik, a Russian anthropologist who works at the Smithsonian Institution, estimates that in the Arctic, where there are limited plant resources, coupled with high caloric requirements due to the cold, each person needs to eat 18.5 reindeer a year to survive.[6] That means that a hunter with a family of five must kill 92.5 deer every year, or a little less than two a week. Our ancestors settled in the Arctic before the invention of the bow and arrow and hunted with pointed rocks, bone, or ivory lashed to the ends of long sticks.

Occasionally, when conditions are perfect, I try to see how close I can creep to a deer or elk. Three times in my life, I've managed to sneak within spear range, almost close enough to touch. Three times in forty years. Yet if I were a Stone Age hunter, I would have to get that close twice a week, summer and winter, every week of my life—or die.

So how did Stone Age people survive?

In some locations, whole tribes of Paleolithic hunters worked together to stampede large prey, such as mammoths, over cliffs. We can guess that these people scavenged as well as hunted. Fine. I'm sure that Stone Age hunters had a whole host of tricks up their reindeer fur sleeves. For example, Stephen P. Krasheninnikov, one of the earliest Russian explorers in Kamchatka, reports joining a small group of Stone Age Koryak as they located a grizzly bear den, in early spring, when the bear was still hibernating.[7] One brave young man stripped off all his fur clothes, so he wouldn't smell like a reindeer. Naked, he crawled into the den, dragging a rawhide rope. When he reached the bear, he carefully tied one end of the rope around its massive paw—without waking the brute. Then he crawled around the bear and on a prearranged signal he pushed on its rump while his partners pulled on the rope. When they had cajoled and coerced the bear into the open, the men pounced on it with spears.

Fine. These stories only increase my sense of wonder.

Several modern Koryak had told me that their immediate ancestors "sang" or "talked" with wolves to arrange a mutually acceptable survival pact for both species. Lydia had told me that Moolynaut "conjured" up the storm that brought Misha and me to Vyvenka the previous year. You can take these words literally or metaphorically, as you please. But as I aimlessly wandered around the oceans and tundra of northeast Siberia, I came to believe, beyond a shadow of doubt, that our Stone Age forebears possessed not only incredible strength but also a consciousness and a communication with nature that I could only vaguely comprehend. I'm sure that I could never completely understand this consciousness, but I could come closer, as I spent more time here.

For me, there's another mystery, which goes beyond the question "How did people survive in the Arctic?" That is: "Why did they go up there in the first place?" Planet Earth was not densely populated when *Homo erectus* or later *Homo sapiens* moved into Siberia. The lush beaches of India and Southeast Asia weren't all that crowded. So why would ancestors move into the Siberian Arctic? Were they following a pragmatic agenda? Perhaps they were chased out of their homeland by famine or warfare or lured to the cold because there were fewer parasites and disease organisms. Or was it something else? Curiosity? Love of adventure? Were they following some religious or shamanistic vision quest? We'll never know, and any attempt to forge an answer would involve anthropologically irresponsible speculation, so I demur. But the simple act of musing about the question was enriching my journey and my life.

Despite incredible survival skills, Stone Age life in the Arctic was desperately hard. Our earliest accurate birth- and death rates were collected in the 1800s. From this data, we know that all across the circumpolar north populations suffered frequent catastrophes. For example, in Siberia birthrates were high and relatively constant, but death rates were also high, spiking with sporadic warfare, famine, and epidemics. In bad years, death rates exceed births and populations declined. Among the Nenets people, each woman gave birth to a mean of eight to nine children, but only two to three survived to become adults. Each newborn infant had only a 6 to 10 percent chance of surviving to the ripe old age of sixty-five.[8]

About twelve thousand years ago, cultures in several tropical and temperate regions developed agriculture and built cities. Gradually, civilization spread its fingers. In 892 C.E. a Norwegian chieftain named Ottar sent a letter to King Alfred of Norway, telling the king that he owned six hundred domestic reindeer. This is the earliest evidence that at least one tribe of Arctic people had made a shift from hunting to pastoralism. The idea and technology spread rapidly across Eurasia, and over the following centuries inland Arctic people across eleven time zones prospered along with their ever-increasing herds. (Stone Age Arctic people in North America remained hunters and never developed reindeer herding.)

The Koryak were decimated by war and disease during the Russian conquest. Then they readjusted and prospered under czarist rule. Lydia's grandfather, I remembered, owned twelve thousand reindeer. Hard times returned under the Soviets, followed by perestroika.

Now we were hanging out with Nikolai, leader of one of the few reindeer-herding groups in northeast Siberia to have survived all the oscillations and ravages of millennia. After his crash on skis, I helped Nikolai to his feet. Undaunted and determined, he climbed back up the hill, skied down, and crashed again. Then he smiled, released the bindings, and invited us in for tea.

Nikolai

The next morning, Nikolai decided that he'd better make radio contact with an official in Manily and tell him that two *Americanskis* were visiting— just so he didn't get into trouble. The entire tribe gathered as one of the young men sat on a bench and rotated a squeaky hand-cranked generator to activate a crepitating box filled with World War II–era vacuum tubes. Nikolai shouted into the transmitter, a garbled voice replied, and Nikolai explained our presence. I listened apprehensively, because you never know how an encounter with bureaucrats will play out in modern Russia. Luckily, the official laconically asked a few questions and apparently decided that he would have less work to do if he wrote our names in a big book—and then ignored us. The young man stopped cranking, the noise subsided, and the isolation of our tundra camp once again replaced that distant world of law and permissions. With that business out of the way, Nikolai explained that he would harness four sled deer to two sleds so Misha, Chris, and I could travel back north and visit the herd. Oleg and Sergei elected to rest at the base camp.

Sled deer live close to camp and are fed richer food than the animals in the herd. They are also considerably tamer than herd deer because they work with people. The deer are harnessed side by side, two deer to a sled. When a sled deer is young, the herders cut the left antlers off half the animals and the right antlers off the other half. Then the animals are harnessed so their antler-less sides are adjacent and they don't spear each other. The deer wear a halter fitted with small brass pegs that press against the animal's temples. When the driver pulls a rein, the peg presses against that side of the deer's head and the deer turns in the opposite direction. Each driver also carries a birch whip, tipped with a prod of fossillized mammoth ivory.

Nikolai's wife, Nadia, insisted that Chris dress in something warmer than white man's clothes. She slipped a beautiful reindeer-skin *kuchlanka* (overcoat) over Chris's head, but before I could admire the artistic patch-work of white and brown fur, Nadia added a blue canvas *kamlecha* (wind-breaker). Later, Chris told me that this was the warmest clothing she has ever worn. Nikolai made beds of reindeer skins on the birch sleds, which were lashed together with rawhide.

After we made ourselves comfortable, Nikolai strapped a rifle across his shoulder and we took off, with Misha and Chris on one sled and Nikolai and me on the other. I watched Misha, who was a successful, suit-wearing, cell-phone-carrying, computer-savvy businessman, serenely content bouncing along and gently poking a deer in the butt with a Pleistocene chunk of mammoth tusk tied on the end of a long stick. His joy made me think of the *New Yorker* ad that we had laughed at a few days before. If you are successful, save your money, and become rich, then you can go for a walk on a snowy afternoon with your dog.

Years ago, when I lived in the Alaskan bush, I learned that sled dogs love to pull and howl in delight when you harness them for a journey. Running is their joy, recreation, avocation, and reason to be, and when I've driven a sled behind an enthusiastic team I felt like a forest gnome riding on the back of a lead wolf as it chases a stag through the snow. Deer, however, are sullen and reluctant. It's obvious that they have no interest in pulling and that they would much rather hang out, nibble on moss, and chew their cud. We chugged along at 4 miles an hour, marginally faster than cross-country skiing and about half the speed of a dog team. But deer are the draft animals of choice on the tundra because they eat vegetation, which is usually available. If you don't care how fast you are going and when you'll "get there," wherever "there" is, then reindeer are the most efficient and cost-effective mode of transportation in this land.

We drove for half an hour, stopped in a sheltered thicket, and Nikolai lit a cigarette while the deer rested. He started talking in mid-story, as if he had been telling the narrative to himself and suddenly turned up the volume in the middle.

". . . So, one of our sons is a welder in PK and our daughter works in the doctors' laboratory in Vladivostok."

"They are far away," I commented.

He nodded and waved his hand to indicate that the story was finished. If I wanted more, I could fill in the details with my imagination, while he returned to the immediacy of tundra survival.

"It's a beautiful but dangerous time. The deer are calving and the wolves are hungry after a long winter. If the wolves attack and frighten the deer, mothers will run away from their babies and the stampeding herd will trample the helpless and bewildered calves. After a week or two, the calves will be strong enough to run, but right now is a dangerous time."

Nikolai waved his mammoth ivory, the deer resumed their laconic pace, and we all plodded northward. After another half an hour, we crested a small rise and saw the herd, grazing peacefully on the tundra. Nikolai tied the four sled deer to a bush and gave us instructions; "You wait here while I go forward and reassure the herd. When I hold up my hand, you can come, but slowly, and no talking or sudden motions, please."

Nikolai walked toward his beloved animals, clucking softly, until he was in the midst of the herd. The deer looked up from their grazing and then continued to feed. After about five minutes, Nikolai signaled us to join him and we moved carefully until we were surrounded by the sight, sound, and smell of deer. Then we sat. Deer pawed through the snow and ate. Two bulls sparred briefly over a choice patch of moss. The tundra was complete and alive.

Nikolai tapped me on the shoulder, with a broad smile on his face, as he pointed toward a cow about thirty yards away. Her head was lowered toward a small dark spot on the snow. A newborn calf rose from a steamy pile of afterbirth and, only minutes old, it took its first steps on wobbly legs. It lurched forward, fell on its face, and lay in the snow while its mother licked it dry. Somehow that few moments of rest miraculously gave the calf enough strength, coordination, and confidence to stand again, shake, and survey its world—deer, snow, distant hills, silence, and blue sky. Then it resolutely took a few steps to its mother, found a teat, and drank its first mouthful of warm, rich milk.

We watched for a half an hour until Nikolai motioned for us to move on. Two men had been guarding the herd all night. Now, in the warmth of the noonday spring sun, as drops of meltwater collected on the stalks of willows and grasses that poked through the snow, they were lounging by a fire and drinking tea while reclining against an overturned sled that acted as a windbreak. Although they looked casual and relaxed, their rifles were handy and every few minutes one of the men scanned the horizon with binoculars. Nikolai added snow to the kettle, put a few sticks on the fire, and motioned for us to sit. While the water was heating, he explained that the guards were on watch for twenty-four hours and then were replaced with a new shift from the base camp.

I asked, "Do the guards remain on duty all night, even during a winter blizzard?"

"Especially at night during a winter blizzard."

Nikolai explained that guards never used tents, even in the most inclement weather, because even a thin wall of nylon or reindeer skin closed out the environment and isolated them from the herd. A guard in a tent wouldn't be alert enough to detect lurking wolves. One of the men remarked that night watch was pleasant in the springtime, when the night was short and the cold less intense. But winter was harsh, with sixteen hours of blackness, temperatures plummeting to fifty below, and frequent blizzards.

Nikolai continued, mirroring the conversation we had had with Oleg a few days earlier, "After perestroika, many guards in other brigades drank too much vodka and passed out during night watch. Then wolves ate the deer. We have kept our herds because we work hard and have avoided vodka. Someone is always on guard, night and day, every day of the year."

The water came to a boil and Nikolai fished four battered tin cups, sugar, and tea out of his pouch. With my fingers around the cup to absorb the warmth, Chris resting gently against my shoulder, and the deer grazing peacefully all around us, I tried to imagine what it would be like to bivouac in this tundra void every other day throughout all four seasons, in the company of reindeer and wolves, plagued by blizzards in winter and marauding mosquitoes in summer.

During my tenure as an adventurer, I've bivouacked on numerous occasions, sometimes intentionally and often out of unplanned necessity. A bivouac is a bittersweet experience. Tied to a narrow ledge on a rock wall or cramped into the damp cockpit of a kayak in a stormy sea, you're cold, wet, scared, and most likely hungry and thirsty. But at the same time, you're in the most intimate contact imaginable with the natural world. To say that the land or seascape is beautiful may be true, but beauty is almost beside the point. It's not so much what you see but what you feel. Stripped clean of all the distractions—and comforts—of your normal urban existence, you are left with a sense that you are vulnerable yet powerful, insignificant but connected to all the wonder around you. And through all this, you are left with a cathartic clarity and intensity of perception.

Now, sitting by this fire, I tried to imagine how my personality, and even my senses, would be different if bivouacs on the sea, the mountains, or the tundra were a near-daily occurrence—if my entire life were framed by a herd of deer, the lurking of wolves, and our mutual sharing of the tundra void. In his story about the albino deer, Simon told us that in the darkness of midnight the boy's father could hear the sound of wolves breathing amidst thousands of deer, all at a distance too far for an accurate rifle shot. In a parallel observation, Wade Davis describes how Amazonian hunters can not only smell animal urine at forty paces, but they can also tell you what species it belongs to. Living in houses and cities, I have forfeited that ability.

In *The Alphabet Versus the Goddess*, Dr. Leonard Shlain, a surgeon at California-Pacific Medical Center, argues that people are affected by how they communicate with the world as well as by the content of the information they exchange.[1] Specifically, a person who receives information directly from nature has a different perceptual gestalt than a person who receives similar information primarily from books and computer screens. This conclusion is obvious enough and I think that everyone will agree that reading a great lyrical passage about a storm is fundamentally different from standing on a ridgetop as a frigid wind blows snow across the cornices.

But Shlain takes his argument one step further. According to modern neurological research, the left side of the brain controls the human propensity to process abstract symbolic concepts. Science, mathematics, logic, and philosophy are left-brain activities. Reading and writing are also left-brain activities because they replace concepts, emotions, and pictures with symbols. The squiggly blobs of ink on the paper that spell the word "dog" don't smell, look, or feel like a four-legged furry animal that wags its tail, but our left brain makes the connection between the letters and the animal that licks—or bites—our hand. In addition, the left brain controls past and future as related to our sense of linear personal history. Awareness of this history has benefits, of course, but it also carries the propensity to concentrate and organize all the hassles and stress that make up our personal baggage and project them into future anxiety.

In contrast, Shlain writes that the right side of our brain processes *"non-verbal clues, concrete gestalts, music, art, inflection, spontaneity, simultaneity, aesthetics, emotion, and gesticulation."*[2] (The italics are his.) Clearly, a Koryak reindeer herder relies heavily on right-brain intuition. In icy winter darkness, the herder might never see a wolf, but he must sense danger. What does it mean to sense danger? Perhaps it's something simple, such as observing the nervous motions of beloved deer. Or it might be an acute sense of smell or hearing, as a blind person compensates for loss of sight. However, some people would argue that the herders protect their deer with an indefinable sixth sense—or a shamanic song that secures a nonaggression pact with the wolves. Whatever your beliefs, during the night a rifle is useless, so the herder must communicate assurance and tranquility to the deer, so they won't stampede, and at the same time he must somehow divert the wolf attack.

The identification and avoidance of a wolf attack is a Present activity. With a wolf lurking on a nearby ridge and windblown snow reducing visibility to near zero, you must be totally alert—in a wholistic right-brain manner—to every sensation that fills the present moment. When I contemplate these modern Koryak herders, I hold the same respect, admiration, and wonder that I feel about Stone Age Arctic hunters. Personally, I don't want to trade my current opulence for the short, hard life of a tundra herder—with poor food and nonexistent medical attention—but I believe that I have a lot to learn from these people.

I grew up in rural Connecticut, on the shores of a lake, surrounded by a New England forest that extended as far as a six-year-old's legs and imagination could fathom. In my earliest memories, Donny Cohen, Spiker Feen, and I splashed endlessly in the lake and built forts in the woods to protect rescued damsels from tireless demons. I started first grade in a musty wood-frame schoolhouse, but in the middle of that formative year the school board condemned our building and built a new brick and concrete block structure, cheerily named Park Avenue School. On moving day, we all lined up, shortest to tallest, boarded the yellow school bus, lined up again, and marched toward the building, without talking or fidgeting. When I crossed the portal, I stared down a long parallel hallway built of symmetrical, monotonous rows of block, punctuated by steel doors that opened into identical classrooms. Suddenly terrified, I stepped out of line, sat on the tile floor, and burst into tears.

I could never have formulated the angst in words I use now, but I must have intuitively recognized that at that moment I was being wrested from the right-brain world of my childhood—and my hominid ancestors. If I followed the path that my society was outlining for me, those halcyon days in the forest would be forever reserved for weekends and summer vacation—if I were lucky. The rest of time I would sit at a desk, mind my manners, learn to add columns of numbers and do long division, and memorize fifty state capitals—all so I could perform efficiently in a left-brain society where I would operate computers and fill out tax forms.

Most of my friends recall a similar, seminal moment of dread and angst as they first comprehended that they must adapt to the precision of modern society. One close friend, Nina, talks about the day when she escaped from kindergarten and walked home, stopping to play, alone, in the mud beside an irrigation ditch.

Lydia's life began when she fell out of the womb into her mother's deerskin boot. As an infant and young girl, Lydia lived on the tundra with the deer. But when she was six the Soviets tore her away from her mother and her tribe, eradicated her name, imprisoned her in a dormitory, and taught her rules and lessons from a distant land she had never seen and couldn't comprehend.

Jill Bolte Taylor was a neuroanatomist who performed cutting-edge research at the Harvard Department of Psychiatry. On the morning of December 10, 1996, a blood vessel exploded on the left side of her brain, impairing the function of that hemisphere and vaulting her instantaneously and unknowlingly into right-brain perception.

She writes:

It was beautiful there. Imagine what it would be like to be totally disconnected from the brain chatter that connects you to the external world. So here I am in this space and any stress related to my job was gone. And I felt lighter in my body. And imagine all of the relationships in the external world and the many stressors related to any of those; they were gone, too. I felt a sense of peacefulness. Imagine what it would feel like to lose 37 years of emotional baggage!

*I believe that the more time we spend choosing to run the deep
inner peace circuitry of our right hemispheres, the more peace we will
project into the world and the more peaceful our planet will be.*[3]

In my adult life, I've oscillated between vastly disparate worlds—as a
Ph.D. research chemist and a science writer on one hand and an adventurer on the other. As I grew older, when reason might have dictated that
I seek comfort and security the call to adventure became increasingly poignant. Many people think that outdoor adventure is mainly a confronta-
tion with danger and adrenaline-laced fear. Those elements exist, of
course, but for most of us expeditions provide an arena where we are forced
to use our right brain to intuit complex situations in mysterious landscapes,
much as the herders learn to avert a nighttime wolf attack. Thus expeditions summon a joyful reliance on deeply buried senses, where failure is not
an option.

In mid-afternoon, two men arrived from the base to relieve last night's
guards. For about an hour, the old watch and the new worked together to
move the herd a few hundred yards closer to the base camp. Nikolai explained
that they moved the herd a little distance south every day to bring the deer to
fresh pasture. The herd would arrive at base camp in a few weeks and then
continue their untiring, ceaseless, incremental migration. When the deer
were five miles south of the base, far enough that it was no longer convenient
to commute to the herd, the entire brigade would pack up their tents, leave
the permanent structures, and migrate with the animals for the duration of
the summer.

We watched the deer for several more hours and then plodded back to
the main camp and settled into the warm house, with its dark, soot-coated
walls. Sergei asked me what I thought of the herding life. I told him that I
saw the beauty but also the hardship. Sergei nodded and smiled, apparently
happy that I understood. He explained that he'd been a herder for seventeen years in a Soviet brigade. I thought it was strange that he had never told
me before, but Sergei usually talked about the moment, not past histories or
future plans. Now that he had revealed this memory, he explained that he

preferred the seasonal intensity, excitement, and richer rewards of commercial fishing. Sergei then reflected that the language of coastal Koryak has a melodious singsong cadence, reflecting the innate happiness engendered by the abundant salmon runs that make life relatively easy—despite the modern ravages of the mafia bandits who steal most of the money. In contrast, the herders' language is abrupt, cropped, and full of consonants, brought on by their beautiful but brutal and never-ending struggle for survival.

Fractured Ice

After five days with the herders, Oleg and Sergei had a bad case of homesickness. We asked Nikolai if we could buy some deer meat, but on the one hand, he wouldn't sell any until his herd increased to the post-perestroika complement of two thousand. On the other hand, he didn't want us to return home empty-handed, either. We gave him fifty pounds of rice, along with some dried fish, butter, and cooking oil. Nikolai reciprocated with the front shoulder of a reindeer for the people of Vyvenka and skin shoes and gloves for Chris. That evening, the women prepared a festival dinner with stacks of fried bread, a huge kettle of boiled moose meat, plates of dried salmon and salted wild onion, dishes of cloud- and blueberries, and cup after endless cup of dark black tea with copious amounts of sugar.

The next morning, we woke early, ate breakfast, and prepared to travel. My pelvis felt stronger now, after several days of relative rest. The subzero morning cold tickled the hairs inside my nostrils while a red-orange-purple sun rose across the bleak snowy plain, so prominent that it almost seemed to pulsate as it climbed into the sky. Everyone in the camp gathered to see us off. Nikolai urged Chris, Misha, and me to return when we had more time. If we sent a message ahead through the brigade members in Manily, he would prepare special reindeer teams for us and we could travel as far as we wanted.

We said good-bye and Sergei pulled the starter cord. The noise and smoke made me think of the long journey home, from this reindeer camp on the tundra, through Moscow and the huge, bustling immigration facility at JFK Airport in New York, to mine and Chris's small brown house in the Montana forest. I turned and waved as we sped away until the fur-clad figures grew smaller and darker against the receding background. The sun ascended with a promise of warmth and we stopped to stretch our legs and free Wolfchuck from his tether. Huge feathered ice crystals had formed on exposed bushes during the cold, clear night. As the bushes undulated gently in the morning breeze, the sun refracted through the ice to project sparkles that danced across the snow.

We plotted a direct course through the mountains toward Vyvenka. Moving steadily, in good weather, with no detours, we covered as much distance in one morning as we had covered in several days on the outbound journey. After crossing a mountain pass, we descended into a warmer, more maritime climate. It was the 20th of April. Snow and ice were melting and water was flowing in the creeks, while behind us reindeer were giving birth and somewhere, Sergei assured us, bears were rousing from their long hibernation.

In the early afternoon, Sergei maneuvered his snow machine down a steep bank onto a frozen creek. But when he gunned the engine to climb the opposite bank, his track spun on the ice, causing the bulky machine to drift sideways and jam tightly against a rock. I slid down the bank to help muscle it onto firmer footing.

As I lifted the back end of the heavy snow machine, I heard an ominous crack as the ice fractured. Before I had time to react, I dropped a few inches into ankle-deep water and landed on one leg. I had only fallen a few inches and a normal body would have absorbed the impact, but something tweaked inside my patched, bolted-together, reinjured, and temporarily healed pelvis. I fell to my knees, writhing in pain.

I half-rolled and half-crawled onto the bank and lay there, cradled by snow. Snow that brought so much joy to my life, snow that I lived with nearly every month of the year, snow that had avalanched and crippled me. When I tried to stand, my legs barely supported me, but I managed to hobble to the sled and sit down.

Chris sat beside me and asked if she could help.

"No, thank you. There's nothing to do. I think I'll be OK."

Oleg asked if I would be strong enough to travel.

I smiled and nodded, adding that I was riding on the sled and as long as I didn't have to ski I'd manage. Anyway, I had no other choice.

I rearranged the reindeer-skin padding and made myself as comfortable as possible on the birch sled while Sergei and Oleg transferred gas from the drums to the machines. Then Sergei walked over, kindly placed a hand on my shoulder, and assured me that Moolynaut would heal me as soon as we returned to Vyvenka.

I looked at him quizzically, but he returned my stare with a guileless smile. I remembered the conversation we had during the first night in the *serei*, when Oleg explained that Moolynaut would travel to the Other World and ask Kutcha, the Raven God, to heal me. At the time, I didn't believe this promise, and I still didn't, but I had nothing to gain by expressing doubt. In any case, I'd weathered these episodic pains before and they usually healed in a day or two, so I was concerned and upset but not terribly worried.

With a cigarette dangling from his mouth and a friendly backward glance, Sergei stood on the running board and pulled the starter cord. The engine sparked to life one more time and our tiny procession resumed its lonely journey across the trackless wilderness. We stopped at 5:00 to make camp, but then Oleg and Sergei decided that we should proceed to the third *serei*. I had stored the coordinates in my GPS and checked the distance.

"It will take us six hours to get there," I protested. "It will be dark."

"Not if we drive fast," Sergei assured me, with a wry grin.

Oleg and Sergei had the homebound blues and they wouldn't be dissuaded. We drove at breakneck speed but also got the machines stuck several times and had a few mechanical breakdowns, finally reaching the *serei* well after dark. Everyone was exhausted, so we shared stale bread and dry cheese for dinner and dropped into sleep.

In the middle of the night, I heard the firebox door banging and the clanking of pots. "What the hell is going on?" I wondered. By 6:00 A.M. the house was so hot that I unzipped my sleeping bag to cool off. As soon as I stirred, Sergei shoved a bowl of food in my face with the command: "It's time to go! Wake up! Eat!"

There was no reason for the rush, but Misha was cheerfully bustling about and it wouldn't do any good if I acted rebellious or irritated. When I stood, my pelvis felt much better than it had the previous evening and I walked into the kitchen with only a slight limp. I felt relieved that the pain had subsided but disturbed that my body was so fragile. Someday, if I continued my adventurous lifestyle, this episodic, recurrent fragility might land me in big trouble.

We loaded the sleds, drove to the second *serei*, and stopped for a few hours to fish. Sergei caught a grayling and a pike, then spit on the snow and announced that the fishing was horrible and that we may as well head home.

Before dark, we drove up the familiar street and stopped in front of the now-familiar duplex that housed Goshe, Oleg, and Lydia. Lydia had been worried and was overjoyed to see us. During a happy homecoming dinner, Oleg told the story of my injury and rapid healing.

Lydia nodded and laughed good-naturedly. "Maybe it's the mice."

"The what?"

"The mice. They are the animals that make foolishness on people."

"Oh, like the coyote, the trickster, of the American Indians?"

"I don't know about this coyote person, but I think that maybe the mice are making foolishness on you, just like they make foolishness on Kutcha the Raven God.

"Once, a long time ago, when the world was new, Kutcha was walking on the beach with his wife, Miti. They saw a dead seal lying on the beach and Kutcha said, 'Oh, let us take this dead seal home and we will have meat for our dinner.'

"A little mouse stood up on its back legs and shouted, 'Squeak,

squeak! I am sorry, Mr. Kutcha, but we found the seal first. It is our meat. You cannot take it home.'

"Kutcha ignored the mouse and took the meat home and he and Miti ate a big dinner and fell asleep. When they awoke in the morning, the rest of the seal was gone because the mice had snuck in during the night and stolen the meat.

"Kutcha was very angry and left home singing, 'I will kill all the mice and take my meat back. La-di-da. I will kill all the mice and take my meat back.'

"The baby mice were very afraid: 'Squeak, squeak. Oh! He will kill us.'

"But a wise old mouse met Kutcha at the door and greeted him, 'Oh, Mr. Kutcha, it is so good to see you. Please come in; we have prepared a feast for you.'

"Kutcha smelled the cooked meat and forgot that he had come to kill the mice. Instead he sat down and ate a big bowl of seal-meat soup. While he was eating, the mice tied the seal's stomach to his bum.

"When he returned home, Miti said, 'Oh, Kutcha, what happened? You stink.' And then she saw the seal stomach tied to her husbands' bum and she laughed and laughed.

"Now Kutcha was really angry and left home again, singing, 'I will kill all the mice and take my meat back. La-di-da. I will kill all the mice.'

"The wise old mouse greeted Kutcha at the door again, "Oh, Mr. Kutcha, it is so good to see you. Please come in; we have prepared a feast for you.'

"Kutcha came in and the mouse fed him a huge plate of boiled seal ribs, which was Kutcha's favorite dish. Kutcha ate until he was so full that he lay down and fell asleep. While he was sleeping, the clever old mouse smeared red berries on Kutcha's lips and black ash on his eyes, so he looked like a beautiful woman. On his way home Kutcha looked into a river, and when he saw his reflection he thought

*that a beautiful woman was beckoning him from beneath the water.
He jumped in and chased the woman but never found her. He looked
for this woman for the rest of his life, but he never found her."*

Lydia finished her story and smiled.

"That was a good story, Lydia, but I don't understand. Are you telling me
that I am like Kutcha and the mice are playing a foolishness on my pelvis?"

Lydia smiled mysteriously. "It is all the time difficult to know about that
things."

Kutcha, the Raven God

Lydia arrived early the next morning with fresh bread, tea, and the announce-
ment: "Our grandmother will visit to us that morning. Do not remove far
from this place. She will come to this place to fix your ill."

Lydia had set a plan in motion and the situation was out of my control.
On the one hand, I'm receptive to faith and prayer and believe that many
diseases can be healed with medicines found in native plants, but there's a
limit and I didn't believe that anyone could weld metal with words or change
scar tissue to cartilage with chants. On the other hand, Moolynaut wasn't
going to hurt me and it would be rude to refuse her offer. Besides, I was
curious—and maybe even something more than that.

Sergei stopped by to ask if Moolynaut had agreed to see me. Apparently
she's selective about the cases she accepts, and Sergei was pleased that I had
passed the admissions test. Chris, Misha, and I waited, drinking tea and
listening to the clank of machinery as men dragged nets out of storage in
preparation for the upcoming fishing season. Soon Lydia and Moolynaut
walked in. We told Moolynaut about our journey, explained that we had
brought her some meat, and talked in detail about our visit with Nikolai and
the herders. She responded by hoarsely whispering, "Ahh! Ahh!" at critical
junctions in the story.

Then she asked about my injury.

I related how the avalanche had ripped my pelvis apart and that surgeons had bolted me back together with a titanium plate, but the healing had been incomplete, leaving me with episodic pain. An X-ray showed that the metal plate had broken. Now the accident on the tundra had tweaked my pelvis again.

During my narrative, she stared at me intently, barely acknowledging Misha, who was interpreting. I felt a little timid to stare back but more frightened to break the contact, so I held her gaze.

When I had finished, she motioned me into Goshe's bedroom. Lydia followed, and as she was about to close the door I turned back to catch Chris's worried glance, remembering our eye contact as the nurses wheeled me into the operating room for the surgery. I smiled to reassure her and Chris smiled back.

Lydia closed the door and I took my bearings in the Spartan room with its threadbare rug, narrow, saggy bed, and old footlocker that stored all Goshe's clothes. Moolynaut said something in Koryak to Lydia, who translated.

"Our grandmother says that she will travel to the Other World. There are five levels in the Other World. Two *belee* (white or good) above us, then our world in the middle, and two *cherney* (black or evil) levels under us. Moolynaut has not enough strong to go to the *belee* world on the top of all the mountain. But she will talk to Kutcha, the Raven God. Kutcha can fly to the place where the Old Woman lives. This woman has great power. She will walk to the top of the mountain and talk to the Old Woman Who Lives on the Top of the Highest Mountain. Maybe that woman there will fix your ill. Maybe she does not do this. We do not know. But you must believe. If you do not believe, bad things will happen. Kutcha will be angry. It will be bad for Moolynaut. It will be bad for you."

Before I had time to digest all of this information and the dangerous threat behind it, Moolynaut told me to strip naked, stand on one foot, hold my right hand behind my back and my left arm pointed straight in front of me.

I had entered this room with a mild sense of journalistic curiosity, an attitude, at least in part, of "wow, this will be cool to write about someday." But Moolynaut was intently serious.

I'll never know exactly why she asked me to strip naked, but I suspect that she wanted me to enter the Other World devoid of pretense, just as I had entered this world. I took a deep breath and removed my shirt and socks. As I was about to unbuckle my belt, I felt oddly embarrassed and vulnerable. In front of whom? Moolynaut? Kutcha?

I thought, "I'm a chemist from suburban Connecticut. I went to high school with George W. Bush. So it all has come to this; I am about to pull my pants down in front of two women I barely know, so I can stand in front of them on one leg while one of the women summons help from the spirit world."

I composed myself. I needed to be in the present. Doubt and cynicism morphed into an acute mixed sensation of exhilaration and trepidation, as if I were about to launch my kayak through dangerous surf.

I slipped my pants off, tossed them on the bed, and lifted one foot gingerly, wondering if my injured pelvis would support my weight. Then I focused on my center of gravity, feeling foolish looking in the required yogic pose.

Moolynaut approached until she was a few inches away. She was bent over and wrinkled, wearing layers of worn canvas clothes, colored ribbons, and a jaunty kerchief with gold thread woven among red roses. I concentrated on maintaining my balance. Moolynaut—small, wrinkled, and old— was staring at me.

Moolynaut had asked me to believe, warned me of dire consequences— for both of us—if I didn't. Then she had removed my armor, stripped me naked, leaving no hiding places. Now she was staring straight at me, probing into my soul.

I panicked. In truth, I didn't believe that thought waves, Kutcha, or Kutcha's buddies could perform orthopedic surgery. Yet I would break the spell if I said flatly, "No, I don't believe." But, I felt certain that Moolynaut would detect a bold-faced lie. I couldn't think. I had to concentrate on not falling over. But I had to think. What did I believe in? I believed that Moolynaut and all my Koryak friends lived a simple and honorable life. I had come here to learn and understand, not to judge and criticize. I felt deeply honored that everyone was making such a big fuss over me.

I had to rely on my blink instinct, so I started talking without initially knowing where my thoughts and words were taking me.

I spoke to Lydia but held Moolynaut's stare: "Tell our grandmother that I come from a different place. Far away. My mother never taught me to believe in Kutcha. I have never learned about the Old Woman Who Lives on the Top of the Highest Mountain. My mother never taught me to understand your ways. I do not know about these things. But I will try to believe. I will try with all my heart."

Lydia translated and Moolynaut nodded wordlessly. Then she pulled a small piece of rabbit fur out of her pocket and cupped it in her hands. Lydia draped my Polartec jacket over the old woman's head. Moolynaut stared into the rabbit fur and chanted in the ancient tongue. Soon she closed her eyes and rocked back and forth, slowly and rhythmically, still chanting. Her palms opened and the rabbit fur drifted to the floor.

I balanced over my one grounded leg and imagined myself as a tower, an *axis mundi* rising toward the Old Woman's mountain. My leg began to tire. Moolynaut was hunched over, chanting, and oblivious to everything in this temporal universe. My quadriceps muscle trembled and I focused all my attention on balance and strength. My extended arm wavered, but I forced it to remain rigid.

I was reaching for something. A spot of light perhaps? The blue sky that peered at me from so far away, yet so close, when I was catapulting in the maw of that avalanche. I was too puny to touch that sky, but maybe if I waited for that eddy to lift me . . .

I lost track of time. I was no longer a cripple. I was a maypole, a Torah, a minaret, a Christmas tree—erect, proud, and straight. I could stand here forever, if need be, balancing on a thin branch that wavered in the breeze, my outstretched arm wingtip to wingtip with Kutcha, the Black Raven, reaching toward the Other World.

Even though time was lost, it still passed by anyway.

Moolynaut stopped chanting, looked up, and smiled. Lydia told me that I could stand on both legs now. That confused me for a second, because my conscious mind had shut off altogether and I had somehow forgotten that I was balancing on one foot. I lowered the raised leg and shifted my weight until I was solidly and firmly connected to this earth.

Lydia explained that Moolynaut went to the Other World and met Kutcha. Kutcha relayed our request to the first Old Woman. This Old Woman said that she would take my request to the Old Woman Who Lives on the Top of the Highest Mountain. The Old Woman who spoke to Kutcha said that she would like to help me, but it would be difficult because of the metal plate. She had no prior experience healing injuries partially and improperly patched together with metal plates. She would see what she could do. Come back tomorrow.

Moolynaut held the rabbit fur against my scar, which runs across the top of my pubic hairs. Then she rubbed me with a piece of seal fat. Her touch felt soft, almost erotic for an old woman. She chanted again in the old tongue. Then she bent down until her face was close to my penis. I felt arousal, embarrassed, wondering what would happen next. Moolynaut chanted a brief phrase in the old tongue and spit on my pubic hair. Then she stepped back, spit on the rabbit fur, and told me to keep the fur in my pocket, forever. Finally, she struck a match and stepped close to me again. Our faces were about a foot apart and I looked through the tiny flame into her wrinkles—wrinkles that held the secrets of a century, the secrets of reindeer, dogsleds, wolves, salmon, winter, revolution, death, famine, upheaval, hardship, springtime, family, and tribe. Moolynaut slowly gathered her lips into a small circle, as if she were about to kiss me. With a gentle puff she blew out the match, and the smoke danced between us. She wrapped the blackened match in a piece of paper and told me to burn it in my *petchka* when I returned to Montana. And one final admonition—I was not to make fire during the entire healing process, which might take two or three days.

I dressed and reentered the kitchen. Chris and Misha were drinking tea, chatting. Chris raised her eyebrows. I smiled and held my palms up, to indicate "I'll tell you about it later." Moolynaut left the house without say-ing good-bye or looking back. Life suddenly returned to normal, as if there had been no séance and no naked journey with Kutcha. Lydia asked if Chris and I would talk to the schoolchildren about our lives in Montana. I was confused, still half in a trance, reluctant to fully reenter this world. But, as travelers, we can contribute by carrying the news and teaching the children.

We walked down the street toward the school. I put my hand in my pocket to make sure the rabbit fur was still there protecting and healing me. Just a few days ago I had been crawling in the snow, unable to stand. Now I was walking, surprisingly pain free. But my pelvic pain had been episodic for a year. One day last winter I had to crawl around the apartment to go to the bathroom—and two days later I was skiing aggressively. The orthopedic surgeons in America were confused. I was confused. No matter, on the way to school I felt a boyish bounce in my gait that I hadn't felt in years.

Chris and I spoke to the school assembly and passed around photos of our home, the Montana mountains, and the animals that live in our forest. The children asked thoughtful questions about our lifestyles, our reasons for traveling, and the habits of various animals. They gave us hand-sewn potholders and we reciprocated with postcards of elk, bear, mountain lion, and bighorn sheep. After class, we joined the children for recess. Like chil-dren in all northern latitudes, they had packed snow to make a jump on the hillside above town. We watched the older, more athletic boys slide down on pieces of plastic, launch, and somersault through the air.

Suddenly I wanted to fly through the air—like the boys, like Kutcha. I wanted to be a boy again, at recess, to sneak down to the pond behind my school, catch a frog, and run around the playground chasing Molly Sue Fript. I wanted to fly back through time, remove the avalanche from my his-tory, and be healed, completely and forever. I danced lightly on my feet, pain free.

"Hey, Chris, let's get our skis and play with the kids."

We raced back to Goshe's, returned, and both executed a feeble spread-eagle off the jump. Chris and I were never good at aerials.

Three boys were infected with our energy and charged home, returning quickly with crude ski-bobs that looked like tricycles with short steel skis instead of wheels. They challenged us to a race and we all climbed back up the hill. They were giggling, plotting, and strutting in front of the girls. I intuitively understood that this was a no-holds-barred, full-contact, Roller Derby type ski race, for big stakes.

Chris shook her head and tapped me on the elbow. "Jon, I don't think this is a good idea. I'm not going to race and I don't think you should, either. Whatever happened in that room with Moolynaut, your pelvis is still half held together with scar tissue and a broken plate. Someone's going to get hurt, and most likely it will be you."

I shook my head. Pain is such a strange bedfellow. When it's present, it overruns the castle and dominates all conscious thought. But let it slip off into the night and—poof—only vague memories remain. Right now I felt fine. More than fine. I had stood on one leg, reaching for the magic light that shone from the Other World. I had perched wingtip to wingtip with Kutcha, and we were buddies now. And anyway, I'm too much of a stick-throwing, spear-wielding male to back down from a few skinny-necked, punk-nosed preteenagers on inferior equipment.

One of the girls counted, "*Adeen, dva, tree,*" and the boys pushed off. I intentionally held back for half a second, accelerated from behind, and clipped the front-steering ski of the closest competitor, watching with satisfaction as he cartwheeled over the handlebars. The racer on my right veered toward me with a banshee yell, but I dodged and he oversteered his machine and wiped out. There was just one more left. We were going pretty fast now, headed straight for an alder thicket, but I saw a sinuously open line, so I slalomed directly into the bushes. The poor kid just didn't have the technology to make tight turns. He hit a branch and self-destructed amid a horrible racket of snapping wood. I reached the bottom, held my ski poles in the air, and all the girls cheered.

The vanquished slid down, bedraggled and snow covered—but with mischievous grins. They plotted briefly among themselves—and challenged me to a rematch. Just as recess was starting to be fun, a stern teacher in a gray overcoat appeared, clapped her hands, and called the children back to the classroom.

Chris sidled up to me and put her arm gently around my waist. "Jon, that was stupid."

I grinned. "Stupid is a value judgment. I'm better. And by the way, who won?"

Mukhomor

With recess over, Chris and I returned to Goshe's. Moolynaut was sitting at the table with a small bundle that was wrapped in an old magazine, tied with red string. She greeted us, opened the bundle, and spread out a pile of shriveled dried mushrooms. I immediately recognized the faded red tops and white specks of hallucinogenic *Amanita muscaria.*

These mushrooms, commonly called fly agaric, or soma, have been used for millennia across the circumpolar north and as far south as India and Greece. Viking warriors ate *Amanita* before battle to attain a berserker state of fearlessness and strength. According to one Web site, "There is significant circumstantial evidence that the Santa Claus myth originated somehow with *Amanita muscaria.* Think about this now . . . red clothes with white trim just like the cap of the mushroom . . . reindeer flying all around . . . a whole lot of 'ho ho ho-ing' . . . "[1]

Remember. Jesus was born in Bethlehem, but the Christmas image of flying reindeer arose from the Far North, not the Middle East.

Moolynaut announced, "We will eat these mushrooms together." She smiled a broad, warm smile revealing a few teeth and abundant empty space. I was relieved that the intense stare was gone.

Lydia asked, "Do you know about these?"

"Yes. We call them *Amanita.*"

"We call them *mukhomor.* Have you to eat *mukhomor* before?"

"Nyet."

Moolynaut reverently divided the mushrooms into five portions, for Misha, Chris, Lydia, herself, and me. Each portion contained an equal share of tops and stems.

Moolynaut explained, "If you eat only the tops, you will feel that you lose your legs. If you eat only the stems, you will feel that you lose your head."

She laughed a deep-throated belly laugh until her whole body jiggled with mirth. Then we made piercing eye contact and I assured her, "I don't want to lose my head—or my legs." And we laughed again.

Moolynaut instructed us to dice our portions into small pieces, but I didn't cut mine properly, so she took over, staring at the plate with great concentration. We each threw one piece over our left shoulder with our right hand and one piece over our right shoulder with our left hand.

Moolynaut explained, "This is for Kutcha. He likes the *mukhomor*, too, and it is better if he eats the *mukhomor* with us."

We all agreed heartily.

I grasped a few small chunks of diced mushroom between my thumb and forefinger and lifted them toward my mouth. As an adventurer and a journalist, who came to age during the sixties, I felt a little mushroom high would be a fun escapade on a spring morning out here in this precarious village nestled between the tundra and the sea. But no, I had a queasy feeling as if I were removing my clothes again.

Where were these people taking me? Was I getting in over my head?

The mushrooms tasted smooth and earthy, without any bitter alkaloid overtone. We ate boiled potatoes, drank tea, and finished our portions of *mukhomor*.

We talked about our journey and about Nikolai's clan. After about an hour, the drug began to take effect. I stared at the white tablecloth, decorated with prints of generic purple, red, and orange flowers. In a hallucinogenic vision, the flowers shimmered in the fading afternoon light and rearranged into bushes, windy camps, *strastugi*, snow machines, skis, and reindeer sleds.

Moolynaut appeared to sit far away, on the other side of the table, on the other side of the tundra, on the other side of time, and she looked so small out there, barely above the distant horizon. The tundra between us was cold and windswept yet familiar and friendly, cradling and cathartic. Then she levitated, hovering above the table, the tundra, as if she were soaring on errant winds, with Kutcha.

She began to talk.

"Long ago, when I was a little girl, big trouble came to our land. Russians had been in our land for many years. Even my great-grandparents knew Russians. But usually, these Russians didn't cause too much trouble. Sometimes they brought us good things like knives, traps, and cooking pots, and sometimes they came to collect taxes. But usually they weren't too much trouble.

"Then something important happened in that big village they call Moscow, involving one man called the Czar and another named Lenin. People were killing one another, but I was a little girl then and I couldn't understand why. Some people were Red and others were White, but when I asked my mother if they were wearing colored masks my mother told me that this was no business for a ten-year-old girl.

"One day, we heard that the Yankee traders were coming with their big ship. The Yankees had come every year since I was a little girl. They always brought flour, sugar, and tea. The flour was white and clean, the sugar came in small cubes all stuck together, and the tea wasn't bitter like Russian tea. Sometimes they brought metal things, too. My father had a knife that he bought from the Americans. It was always sharp, better than the Russian knives. Sometimes the Americans brought horses. White horses. My father was a rich man and he wouldn't buy brown horses. He had five hundred white horses. He bought these from the Americans. In exchange for all these things, we gave the Americans reindeer meat and hides, dried fish, fox skins, and walrus tusks. The Americans always asked for more walrus tusks.

"Usually, the whole tribe came down to the shore to see the Amer-

icans and watch the trading. The Americans always gave candy to the children and colored beads to the women. But on this day, my father said that the women and children must stay home. I told my mother that I was walking onto the tundra to pick cranberries, but when I was out of sight from our yuranga I took the old path to the ocean and climbed a hill above the beach. Something bad was happening. My parents were very worried and I wanted to see what would happen when the Americans came.

"That was a long time ago, but even today, when I am an old woman, I remember that my heart raced when I first saw the tips of the masts rising above the hilltop. Then, after a pause, I climbed the last few feet and peered down at the iron ship moored in the middle of the bay, with steam billowing from its smokestack. I remember the deep-throated rumble. Metal clashed against metal. It was a motorized schooner with both engine and sail."

Moolynaut stopped her narrative and looked at me. I could feel the *Amanita* and sensed that she was slipping away, but the narrative continued.

"So much metal," she marveled. "My mother treasured her one cooking pot, but these people had a whole ship made of metal.

"The men gathered on the beach with two hundred reindeer, while the rest of the herd grazed on the tundra, behind a hill. I knew these deer; I could identify individuals by their gaits and faces and often remembered stories about mother and calf or bull and cow. In this, I was no different from any of the other children. I was a Koryak, a reindeer herder."

Moolynaut proudly straightened in her chair.

"A large iron arm swung across ship's deck, stopped, and lifted a rowboat on a rope. Men climbed into the boat; the arm swung around, and lowered the boat into the water. The boat and the men looked so

small; maybe they weren't real. But I knew they were. The men hefted long oars and rowed toward shore. It would take several minutes for the boat to reach the beach, but time was abundant on the tundra, and I was accustomed to waiting.

"When the boat arrived, my father stepped forward and shook hands with the headman from the boats. After they talked, my father turned and shouted a command. The herders whistled, ran, and waved their long rawhide lassoes until the deer pressed together into a tight group that looked like a single animal. But I knew it was many deer because antlers waved in the breeze like trees with broad branches. We don't have many trees here because our land is tundra, but I know what a forest looks like because I see the antlers.

"Soon the tight circle of deer thinned into a line, like a lake flowing into a river, and one of the cows started leading the herd back toward the tundra. Men shouted and diverted the herd to move in a circle. I felt my body tingling inside because the circle walk was always a prelude to action. When deer become nervous, they run. If they have no direction, they scatter. But if they are already walking in a circle, then they run in a circle. In a land with no fences or corrals, we force the animals to run in a circle before we select some to slaughter.

"I wanted to run down the hill and throw small clods of moss at the herd to be sure that none of them escape, but today, for the first time in my life, the men had not asked the children to help.

"The Americans watched the herd for several minutes and the headman talked with my father again. Then the strangers lifted several wooden boxes out of the boat, set the boxes on the beach, and pried open the lids. My father reached down, grasped a shiny new rifle, and cradled it gingerly. My uncle walked down the beach, set three sticks upright in the sand, and stepped aside. Three shots rang out and three sticks fell over. My father nodded.

"The men lassoed several deer and tied their hooves together. Then the Americans grabbed the animals and unceremoniously threw them into the boats. I started to cry. My people frequently sold hides and meat, but they never sold live deer to anyone. *My father once told me that he would never sell live deer to the Americans because these men weren't loving enough and they didn't know how to care for deer.*

"*One young bull shook its head free, struggled to its knees, and looked up at the hilltop where I was hiding. That was my deer; I had tamed it, fed it succulent mosses, and even brought it pieces of salty dried fish as a delicacy. My mother taught me special chants and spells to protect this deer from marauding wolves—and the wolves listened.*"

Moolynaut fell silent and then chanted briefly in the old tongue. A few tears rolled down her cheeks. "*But my spells had no strength against all these things that were happening to us.*"

Moolynaut wiped the tears away with a corner of her shirt. When she began talking again, her voice sounded as if it were coming from someplace far away.

"*The rifles were Winchesters. Winchesters are very good rifles. Have you ever heard of Winchester rifles?*"

I nodded and she continued, repeating an aphorism she had told me at our first meeting:

"*And my father bought many cartridges that day. You know, rifles are no good without the cartridges.*

"*We kept some of the rifles and buried some in the ground. Bad times were coming, and during bad times you need to have good rifles. You rub the working parts with seal fat and wrap everything in sealskin and hide the rifles in the ground where they sleep like bears. And when the hard times come, at least you have the rifles. Then you can live.*"

Moolynaut paused again, longer this time.

"Maybe I knew—on that day—that our lives were about to change. I don't know. I remember what I saw, but I don't remember what I thought or didn't think. It was a long time ago. I was a little girl."

Moolynaut finished the story quietly:

"But I do remember that I wanted to cut my deer free and lead it into the autumn tundra. I saw myself, alone, with the young bull, huddled behind an outcrop of rock as the first snows swept across the land. I would lead the bull to rich pasture and it would protect me. We would grow old and strong together. But this was just a dream. I was a little girl and my father was on the beach, counting rifles."

Moolynaut appeared to settle slowly back into her chair. Even though Chris, Lydia, and Misha were close by, they all seemed small and far away. I wanted to reach out and touch Chris, just to be sure she was still there, but I wasn't sure that I should. Before I could decide what to do, I realized that Moolynaut was talking to me, directly, in Russian.

"How old are you?"

"*Pyet-decyet pyet* [fifty-five]," I answered.

Moolynaut laughed a rollicking full-body laugh as if I had just told the best joke of the century.

"And you are still traveling across the tundra." She laughed again, rocking gently from side to side as if she were dancing. "And you paddle your kayak across the ocean. What is your secret to youth and long life?"

I laughed uncontrollably, as if some great tension had been released. Tears filled my eyes and I let the cathartic laugh run its natural course, cleanse my insides, and exorcise worries, problems, and the niggling affairs of life. I had come three-quarters of the way around the world to seek wisdom from this century-old shaman. The *mukhomor* was racing through my brain and *she* was asking *me* the secret of long life. When I calmed down sufficiently, I managed to exhale a single word in Russian:

"*Leesja* [skiing]."

Moolynaut nodded serenely as if she understood completely, but Lydia looked at me, expecting a more complete explanation.

I spoke in English now, allowing Misha to translate: "Skiing keeps my body strong, my mind alert, and my heart full of passion. Skiing keeps me young."

Talking didn't seem to be on the agenda anymore. Lydia stepped out and returned with a *boubin*, a ritual ring drum. Moolynaut took the *boubin*, beat a soft melody, and sang in simple, monosyllabic tones:

"Ya, yaaah, ah ya, ya, ya."

As the melody reverberated, I thought with wonder about my healing, shamanism, and my friends in the room. Then the music and the *mukhomor* pushed aside the protective folds of reason, transporting me to the rain forest with a band of primates prancing in the moonlight and thumping on logs.

"Ya, yaaah, ah ya, ya, ya."

Now I was flying alongside Kutcha, headed to the Other World. We passed over endless expanses of ocean. Ocean that had given me strength and had nearly killed me. Ocean that I had traversed in real time, on the real planet.

Moolynaut started dancing, athletically for a ninety-six-year-old woman. In the dim room, I drifted into a trancelike state, without words, wavering on the edges of unknowable mysteries.

For the next several hours we passed the drum around, speaking through ancient rhythms and wordless chants.

In the middle of the night, when the drug euphoria was beginning to wane, Chris, Misha, Lydia, and I walked Moolynaut home. Then I wandered off by myself, listening to the creaking of my boots on cold, frozen snow. After some time, I saw Chris's form in the night shadows. She was walking along the beach, moving with her characteristic athletic grace. I intercepted her path and met her just above the surf line. A few clouds scudded across the sky. The glistening surf reflected starlight and a sliver of moon, but I couldn't see the horizon where black sea met the night sky. I drifted into a hallucinogenic dreamworld where Chris was both by my side and, simultaneously, in other places at other times. We were lying in bed together, cuddling with easy familiarity before getting up and facing the day. We were standing on a snowy ridge, grinning with frost-encrusted smiles. We were cooking dinner, with the smell of baking bread emanating from a wood-fired stove. Then the dreamworld slipped away, I put my arm around her shoulder, and we walked back to Goshe's together, still without talking.

Man with the Fast Shoes Mountain

I slept soundly until gray dawn penetrated the dusty windows. Before I had fully opened my eyes and gotten out of my sleeping bag, Lydia opened the door and came inside, wrapped in a blast of frigid arctic air. She told us to get up quickly because Moolynaut was coming for a second séance. Then, with a sense of impending urgency, Lydia disappeared back into the cold and I sat up, feeling simultaneously disoriented and energized. After I dressed and splashed cold water on my face, Moolynaut shuffled in, smiling and leaning on her cane. I smiled back, remembering her as she appeared to me yesterday afternoon, hovering above the worn tablecloth that had become a vast and inscrutable tundra plain.

Without any discussion or preamble, Moolynaut led me back into Goshe's room, where I once again undressed, stood on one leg, and held my right hand behind my back and my left hand straight in front of me. The focus and balance came easily this time, as if it were quite natural that I should be perched on a tree limb, wing to wing with Kutcha. We were buddies now—we had eaten *mukhomor* together—and I felt his warm intimacy. I was rooted to the floor with my one leg, but my outstretched arm reached across the tundra—that white living emptiness that I was crossing but could never cross, laced with cold yet as soft and warm as a newborn calf rising from its steamy afterbirth. Moolynaut pulled a blanket over her head and began chanting in the old tongue, trembling slightly as she transported herself quietly into the Other World. The three of us, Moolynaut, Kutcha, and I, were a team, journeying together into the unknowable.

After some indeterminate amount of time, Moolynaut stopped chanting and when I put my raised leg on the ground I was instantly transformed back into a skinny, white-haired old man, naked and foolish looking in Goshe's haunted bedroom.

Moolynaut talked to Lydia in Russian and Lydia explained that Kutcha had discussed my case with the Old Woman and other acquaintances in the Other World and they agreed to try to heal me. Moolynaut rubbed seal fat on my scar. When she bent down to spit on me, as before, I felt as if I were the recipient of a gentle caress from an old lover. Then she stepped back and told me to return again for one more séance the next day.

I put my clothes back on and we all returned to the kitchen for breakfast, which consisted of tea, bread, butter, and salmon caviar. After the meal, Oleg suggested that Sergei, Chris, Misha, and I travel upriver to a hunting cabin. Chris, Misha, and I had ridden on the bouncy, jarring sled for too many miles, so this time we elected to be towed behind the snow machines, like water skiers on snow. After traveling across the smooth river ice for half an hour, the men stopped to cool their engines and smoke a cigarette. I was still energized from the mushrooms and the two séances and didn't feel like standing around in the cold, so I took off alone, skate-skiing upriver across the hard, crusty spring snow. Working my skis easily, I took great relaxed, rhythmic strides, pushing off my edges and my poles, gaining momentum and glide, and feeling my muscles warm with the welcome exertion and the rising sun.

Engine noise broke the morning silence, and when the machines caught up to me I bent down, grabbed the towrope, and continued upriver without stopping. When we reached the hunting cabin, Chris pulled me aside.

"Jon. Back there on the ice . . . You were skating!"

"Yeah. I didn't feel like standing around in the cold. Was there a problem with that?"

"No problem. But Jon! Don't you realize what happened? When we first met, you loved to skate-ski. But you stopped after the avalanche because your pelvis hurt too much. Jon! Don't you remember? You haven't skated since your avalanche!"

I looked into Chris's familiar face, wrinkled by decades of exposure to sun and wind, staring back at me, lovingly and earnestly. At first I didn't understand what she was saying, but she was so excited that I forced myself to comprehend.

To skate, you push first with one leg and then with the other. The sweeping side-to-side motion is hard on the pelvis and the connecting adductor muscles. I hadn't skated much since the accident—even on my best, pain-free days. Back home in the Rocky Mountains, when we were returning from a mountain ski tour Chris and our friends would often skate the last mile of flat road. I would try to keep the pace, but the pain would eventually dominate and then I'd trudge along, frustrated and grumpy that I was a slow, crippled gimp.

But today I had skated, and when the snow machine came by I picked up the towrope and glided off. Incredibly, I had forgotten avalanche, pain, and healing and had skated for the pure joy of the motion—body connected to skis, skis plying edges onto hard, crunchy spring snow.

Chris and I stared at each other.

Of course it was impossible that some old lady had healed me by rubbing rabbit fur and seal fat across my scar, by spitting on my pubic hairs, and by chanting ancient prayers to Kutcha the Raven God. Even before my encounter with Moolynaut, I had experienced good days and bad. This was a good day and I was operating on a little residual energy from the *mukhomor*. There's nothing like a pain-free day and a mellow mushroom trip to put a person in a good mood.

No, this was different. I was no longer an injured person having a good day. I was better. I had stood on the branch with Kutcha and beaten the drum with Moolynaut. I had raced those boys on their ski-bobs and won. And now I could skate again. My mind went blank, able to feel joy but unable or unwilling to analyze what had happened.

Soon Misha and Sergei joined us. Sergei pointed to a small mountain rising incongruously out of the flat tundra a few miles away, and Misha translated.

"They call this 'Man with the Fast Shoes Mountain.'"

"Yes, Lydia spoke about this place. Wasn't Moolynaut born near here?"

Sergei nodded, obviously happy that I remembered.

"But Sergei," I asked, "how did the mountain get that name?"

"A long time ago, a Koryak man invented a new kind of snowshoes, made of long, narrow pieces of birch. This man could slide downhill on these snowshoes. We called him Bistro Torbaza, *Fast Shoes."*

"You mean he invented skis?" I interjected.

Sergei smiled. "This man spent all winter climbing mountains and sliding back down. He had *bistro torbaza.*"

"I think I understand this man."

Chris tapped me lightly on the elbow, with an impish grin on her face. "Let's ski it, Jon."

Sergei objected. "It's steep, rocky, and dangerous. It will take you all day to reach the summit and you'll have to walk back down in the dark. Remember, you two get lost easily."

I looked at the mountain. It wasn't big, steep, or dangerous. For the entire trip, Oleg had been the captain of the expedition and Chris and I had been aliens, geeks, tourists. Yes, we had gotten lost. Yes, I had slipped in the icy stream and writhed around in the snow muttering, "Oh fuck!" and other unpleasant epithets. Yes, we acted like uncomprehending morons half the time, because without Misha we couldn't understand what people were saying. But now I could forget all that because a snow-covered mountain beckoned. For me, skiing is more than a sport; it is a release from temporal worries and an affirmation of self. Yesterday's race with the schoolchildren was just the preamble. Now I needed to climb a real mountain, turn my skis into the fall line, and let gravity lure me into its own secret chamber in the Other World.

I looked back at Sergei. "No, my friend, we're not going to get lost and we're not walking back down anything. We're going to climb that mountain and ski down."

Sergei grinned, nodded, revved up his machine, and towed us across the tundra toward Man with the Fast Shoes Mountain. When the slope became too steep for his machine, he turned off the motor and told us he would wait, all night, if we didn't return on time. Chris and I affixed climbing skins to our skis as we had so many thousands of times in the past and gained the summit easily in an hour and a half. We cuddled together silently in a wind-sheltered nook formed by sun-warmed rocks and shared a few dried cucumber fish, looking across the tundra where, unseen over the horizon, Nikolai and his brave band were diligently guarding their deer from human and animal predators. Then we slid along the skyline over windblown snow until we came to a broad west-facing couloir.

Chris and I stood side by side. Skiing was the anchor and epicenter of our marriage. We skied on our first date. We skied on our wedding day. And on our honeymoon. After we had settled into our new life in the home we purchased together, we spent the winter carving turns on a gentle slope in the Bitterroot mountains near our Montana home. One day, Chris casually remarked, "I hope being married to you doesn't mean we will only ski these meadows and glades for the rest of our lives." She had said it without anger or rancor, without discernable challenge. But with worry. I kissed her gently and promised that we would ski the great ranges of the world together. So we carried our passion to the Alps, Central Asia, Bolivia, British Columbia. And we always knew that whenever we faced seemingly insurmountable relationship problems, we could put on our skis, walk across a frosty ridge, breathe cold air, and let mountains work their cathartic magic. Now we were together and in love, on top of a mountain, with skis on our feet and a snowy mountain beneath us.

Chris looked at me, "How's your pelvis, Jon?"

"You want to know the truth?"

"Yes."

"Well, maybe I've gone off the deep end. Call me crackpot. But I feel absolutely, completely, one hundred percent wonderful. Pain free."

"Well then. This is your special moment. You ski first."

Man with the Fast Shoes Mountain was the highest peak in the immediate vicinity and it had been blasted by Arctic blizzards that had swirled the snow off the flanks, leaving sharp rocks exposed. Some of this transported snow had collected in a broad couloir that now stretched below me. The wind drifts formed their own fluid topography, curvaceous and soft when compared to the harsh edges of the exposed dirt and rock on either side. But the snow was hard and my ski edges barely gripped the icy surface.

I dropped off the ridge and accelerated with skis flat, pointing straight downhill, until I was going too fast to function through analytical, left-brain channels. Since there wasn't enough time to think about how to ski, I just sent one final conscious signal down to my body: "OK, let's get this operation under control." Then my body took control and my knees rolled into the first turn, driving sharp steel edges into a parabolic arc on icy snow. Muscles pressed comfortably against ski boots as familiar impulses raced through well-oiled synapses.

I hope that everybody has some activity that gives their body so much joy that it can tell the mind to shut up. And then the mind finds itself on vacation, without the perceived need to output a lot of silly chatter. And lo and behold, when the output spigot is turned off, uncensored input flows in—sky, wind, compression of the muscles, the raw joy of motion.

After the first few turns, the couloir curved into the sun and the snow became warm and soft, swishing gently beneath me. I let the skis run freely between widely spaced turns.

I was dancing, flying; I was whole. Then, for just a moment, a familiar but horrible memory surfaced out of the past, arriving as a complete instantaneous image. I was lying on the snow at the bottom of that avalanche gully, unable to stand. Chris and my friend Mitch were racing up toward me. I looked across at a ridge that dominated the skyline, tracing ski lines through tree glades and rock outcrops. In my memory, the ridge became fuzzy as I began to lose consciousness. A voice deep inside me cried out that this was not the time to lose control. I shouted down to Chris and Mitch, "Hurry, I need your help!" They arrived breathlessly: "What can we do?" I answered, "Hold me. Give me energy and love." Chris gently lifted my upper body and lay beneath me, to raise me off the cold snow, while Mitch blanketed me from above, to keep me warm. I concentrated all my energy on that fuzzy ridge. Gradually, the outline drifted into focus. When I could discern a sharp skyline, offset by snow-covered trees, when I could trace the ski lines again, I whispered softly to Mitch, Chris, and the mountains around me, "OK, my friends. I'm hurt, but I'll be back. Wait for me. I'll be back."

And now I was back, carving turns through soft corn snow on a couloir in northeast Siberia, letting my muscles do the thinking, centered over a pain-free pelvis. Finally, through a mysterious and circuitous route, I had fully honored my hopeful, irrational promise.

I reached the bottom and stopped in front of Sergei who was waving excitedly, yelling, "Kielbasa—Montana," the two most wonderful words in our mutual lexicon. Kielbasa, sausage, the richest, most fat-filled food, and Montana, the best place, our wonderful and mysterious home in America. "Kielbasa—Montana!" I yelled back.

We looked up and Chris had started her descent, shoulders pointing steadily downhill, body angulated, knees and skis flowing gracefully and seamlessly from one turn to the other. Sergei pointed to Chris and ran his hand through the air in a wavy motion to imitate her tight, controlled turns, and then he pointed to me and drew longer arcs to indicate my faster ski line. Then, with a broad grin, he repeated, "Kielbasa—Montana."

After Chris reached the snow machine, Sergei towed us back to the cabin. Oleg and Misha were waiting, smiling. Oleg announced, "Oh, we watched through binoculars. It was very dangerous. We were frightened for you."

"No, it wasn't dangerous. We ski slopes like that all the time."

But Sergei disagreed and excitedly held up his hand to indicate that we had just plummeted down a sixty-degree precipice.

I didn't care. I had skied Man with the Fast Shoes Mountain with my sweetie. Without pain.

We returned to the *serei*, had tea, and motored back to town. The following day was our last in Vyvenka. Moolynaut came by for another healing session. For a third time, I undressed and stood on one foot, with one arm folded and the other stretched toward the dreamworld. This time I was ski-ing down the mountain, wind in my face, edges biting into soft snow—healed, better, pain free. Kutcha was flying with me, wings outstretched, gliding a few feet off the slope, dipping one wing and then the other, as if he, too, were carving turns. Then Kutcha swooped away to tell Moolynaut that the folks in the Other World thought I was an OK guy and so they had fixed me up, broken metal plate and all. I asked Moolynaut to thank Kutcha for me and she complied. It was a done deal.

I dressed, trying not to think analytically about the healing process, and walked into the kitchen, on my own two legs—pain free.

After Moolynaut left, we went to the store to buy her a gift. The Vyvenka grocery store is a dark, dusty, hollow-sounding room with three shelves be-hind a single low counter. A few people lurked in the shadows like gnomes who guarded the bridge in some distant fairy tale. We ordered fifty pounds of rice, ten pounds of sugar, and five bottles of precious fruit juice. The clerk shook her head. "You bought fifty pounds of rice two weeks ago. What are you doing with all that food? You think you're in the big city? We don't have enough food in this store to sell it to you, just because you have a lot of money."

A voice rose out of the shadows: "They're giving food to the people. They gave rice to our cousins, the herders, who live on the tundra. They're giving this food to Moolynaut, so she will have more to eat than cucumber fish. Sell them the food."

The clerk apologized and placed our order on the counter. Then she tallied up the sum with her abacus and we paid the bill.

We brought Moolynaut the food along with needles, thread, postcards, light gloves, woolen mittens, and warm socks. She nodded appreciatively.

Lydia held a potluck feast that night, and after dinner Chris inflated two balloons, which we batted around without any structured game or apparent rules. People were delighted and Moolynaut joined in enthusiastically, always passing the balloon to the children, who shrieked in excitement.

Before I went to bed, I wrote in my journal: "A lot of happiness was generated with simple friendship, a little food, and two colorful balloons."

In the morning we walked to Moolynaut's house to say good-bye, but a neighbor told us that she had gone fishing. We loaded the snow machines for the journey to the airport and then drove upriver.

Moolynaut was sitting on a stool beside her dog team, peering through a hole in the ice, with her fishing line rolled up on a stick, jigging for cucumber fish. The temperature was just below freezing and she was dressed in a full-length cotton windbreaker without her reindeer-skin *kuchlanka*. She was wearing rubber boots with reindeer-fur liners and the light green gloves we had given her.

We exchanged pleasantries. During all the time I had known her, Moolynaut had never directly passed down words of wisdom, mystic mantras, or lofty advice from her century-long view of life.

When I thanked her for healing me, she smiled and nodded. When I said good-bye, she replied, "Come again. It will be good if you do."

Then a fish nibbled on her hook. She ignored me, her body tensed, one finger played the line to feel its vibrations, and she waited while her unseen prey feathered its fins—indecision swirling in its tiny fish brain. The fish bit; she snapped the line taught and wheeled in a four-inch-long, three-ounce cucumber fish. She held it against the ice with one foot, smacked it on the head with the back of her long knife, and took the fish off the hook, smiling broadly.

Maybe Kutcha had sent the fish to create a final image and to pass on words of wisdom that Moolynaut would never verbalize. "If I live to be one hundred: I hope to be strong enough to hitch up my dog team and drive across a frozen river on a spring day with a damp, foggy sea breeze and light wind drifting snow across the ice. I hope to be lucky enough to catch a few cucumber fish for dinner. I hope to be wealthy enough to be surrounded by friends, children, adopted children, grandchildren, and great-grandchildren. I hope to be respected enough so that some rich foreigner travels from far away to give me a new pair of warm gloves. And I hope to be content with these simple pleasures."

Part 3

Return to Thank Moolynaut

The doctor cures the sick by
the laying on of hands, and prayers
and incantations, and heavenly songs.

—Sarah Winnemucca, Paiute

The Funny Thing

The funny thing is that I was healed. Better. Fixed up. Pain free. As my orthopedic surgeon, Dr. Schutte, would say, "returned to full athletic performance." Between the healing, in the spring of 2001, and now, when I am
sitting at my computer on a damp December day in 2008, I look back on
seven arduous expeditions: I kayaked a technically difficult white-water river
in the Himalayas, sea-kayaked through shifting pack ice in the Canadian
Arctic, and then kayaked, twice, in the open water of the South Pacific,
skied steep glaciers in the Bolivian Andes, made a long ski traverse in Siberia, and mountain-biked across the Altai Mountains in Kazakhstan and
China. In addition to these expeditions, I've skied aggressively for seven
seasons in British Columbia and Alaska, did a little rock climbing, some
recreational mountain biking, and white-water kayaking.

During all this time, I've had no pain in my pelvis except for the mi-
nor aches and muscle pulls that are normally associated with my age and
lifestyle. Every time I ski and feel my body flowing in sync with complex
and undulating terrain—sharp snow crystals blowing in my face—I thank
Moolynaut, or Kutcha, or luck, or somebody, or something for my joy. But it's
not just about skiing. Sometimes when I walk down the aisle in the grocery

store, trying to decide if I want broccoli or cauliflower for dinner, I suddenly feel my old energy flowing through my epicenter, my pelvis, in uninterrupted spirals. Then I realize, as if I hadn't verbalized it before, "It doesn't hurt to walk. I'm whole."

Back in the Montana Forest

After leaving Vyvenka, Chris and I returned to our home in the Montana forest. The mountain snowpack was melting and the creeks were nearly flooding. We slept with the bedroom window open so we could enjoy the cool night air, smell the forest coming alive, and listen to the water crashing over rocks as it rushed toward the more populated valley below.

On a typical morning, after breakfast I would grab my reading glasses and head out the door for my commute to work. Frequently Chris handed me an imaginary set of car keys, kissed me gently on the cheek, and warned, with mock seriousness, "Now, drive carefully, dear. Don't get sucked into road rage." Then I walked down the hill, listening to the birds, 150 feet to my rough-hewn office building, started a fire, and turned on my computer. Chris worked in her office upstairs to help me with research and secretarial tasks. At the same time, she wrote her own magazine articles and she planted a spring garden. At noon we ate lunch together, at 2:00 we walked the mile round-trip to the mailbox, and then after answering the daily mail and e-mail we hiked, rode our bikes, or kayaked the West Fork of the Bitterroot River, a peaceful stretch of nonthreatening white water. One or both of us went to town once a week for groceries and errands, but in the interim we often saw no other people for days at a time. Chris was such a calm and innately content person that she created an emotionally stable platform that was big enough for both of us to stand on. This was our time-out from the world, where we could enjoy our intense closeness and feed our creativity.

I thought about my healing every day: as I walked to the office or split firewood, when I closed my eyes to sleep, or when I opened them in the morning, cuddling gently against Chris's warm body as the rising sun cast the first shadows over the mountains.

I told Moolynaut that I would try to believe, yet surrounded by the trappings and beliefs of Western culture I no longer stood wingtip to wingtip with Kutcha, and I found it hard to ignore a lifetime of scientific logic. I'm a Ph.D. chemist, after all. In his book *Returning to Earth*, Jim Harrison succinctly summed up the bias behind my feelings: "I had always stuck to the idea offered by my ninth grade science teacher that all genuine phenomena must have a natural or scientific explanation."[1]

Of course, I had read about shamanic healings and mysterious powers of holy men and women, but I had never paid much attention or given those accounts much credence. Now I had experienced my own healing. It didn't make sense. How could I write textbook explanations of the Second Law of Thermodynamics and then run around believing that some wizened shaman and her sidekick, Kutcha, had patched up an obviously scrambled array of bone, cartilage, scar tissue, and metal?

So, I was torn between two worlds, magic and logic. Which would I choose?

One day, as we were hiking along a familiar game trail, marveling at the abundant bear grass, with its elegant stalks and conical caps of succulent white flowers, Chris suggested that I get a new X-ray of my pelvis. We already knew that my titanium plate was broken, the screws were loose, and something inside me had cracked, just a teensy-weensy little bit. But that was before the injury on the tundra followed by Moolynaut's séance. Would a new X-ray be different from the one taken before I left for Siberia? That's what a scientist does, after all: observe the system before and after the perturbation and collect as much information as possible before he or she comes to a conclusion.

I knew that eventually someone was going to suggest that I seek the opinion of a Western doctor. I stopped and faced Chris, feeling naked, balanced on one leg, arguing against my entire culture, against everything I had ever learned or believed in.

"Nope. I'm not going to get an X-ray. I promised Moolynaut that I would try to believe—with all my heart."

Chris shook her head incredulously. "What? You're a scientist. Let's collect the data."

"Sorry, I'm not going to risk getting Kutcha all pissed off."

"Holy cow, Jon! You do believe!"

"Well, I'm better. It doesn't hurt. Why fix it if it ain't broken?"

She looked at me as if I were a stranger. In her face I saw my lover on the pillow and also the skier, eyebrows frosted on a windblown ridge.

I softened my voice. "Sorry, Chris, I mean it sounds crazy. I know that, but I'm not going to get that X-ray. I stood naked in front of Moolynaut and told her, 'I will try to believe.'"

We turned and walked along in silence, and I recalled that day, decades ago, when my professor walked into my office in the chemistry building, as I was typing my thesis, and asked me why I hadn't scheduled any job interviews for continuation of my career after graduation.

Although I hadn't used those words directly, essentially I said, "Nope. I'm not going to schedule any interviews. I promised my dog that I would smell the earth instead."

And in that moment of refusal and affirmation, when I abandoned rationality because rationality wasn't the issue anymore, I changed my life and set a course that eventually led me to stand in front of Moolynaut.

As a scientist, my job was to dissect mysteries, poke and probe them, blast them apart with electrons, smash them into detectors, crunch them through computers, mentally reassemble the pieces, and then—the Holy Grail of Western logic—eviscerate them into Hypothesis, Theory, and Law. Mystery with a sword in its belly. QED.

But now I was faced with an alternate paradigm. As Ken Kesey famously said, "If you seek the mystery instead of the answer, you will always be seeking." I wondered how many times in my life I had teetered on the brink of a magical moment but had never even known it was nearby because I was too closed minded, unobservant, or busy worrying about responsibility, reason, or security to be aware. Now I was walking on a pain-free pelvis, and what was wrong with replacing "QED" with "Hallelujah"?

But, it wasn't that easy, either. The western, left-brain side of me wasn't going to give up and allow some old woman to instantaneously change the worldview that I had inherited from my ancestors and my culture. On the one hand, I refused to get the X-ray. On the other hand, despite my refusal, part of me needed the explanation that the X-ray might provide. So I sought something I would never find, even as I simultaneously repudiated the search.

Before I left for Siberia, neither Dr. Clark nor Dr. Schutte could explain why I was experiencing episodic, intense pain. Clearly, the plate was broken, but there are no nerve endings in a titanium plate. Despite the mostly healed hairline fracture through bony scar tissue, my pelvis remained properly aligned.

I never went back to see Dr. Schutte, but Ron Clark is a friend and I spoke to him about the healing several times. Finally he summed up his best professional diagnosis:

"Something mysterious caused the pain. Then something mysterious ended the pain."

Could it be that the original pain was imagined, psychosomatic? It's easy to label people with chronic pain as neurotic. But pain is real; pain is elusive; pain often defies scientific explanations. In her book *Pain: The Fifth Vital Sign*, Marni Jackson explains that there is a direct relationship between physical trauma and immediate, acute pain. You drop a rock on your toe, and your toe hurts. Drop a bigger rock, and your toe hurts even more. But long-term, chronic pain, the kind I was experiencing, is infinitely more complicated. Frequently doctors observe no quantifiable relationship between physical parameters, such as an X-ray, MRI, or CAT scan, and the level of chronic pain.[2]

Pain is a sneaky little devil. The brain can register pain when there is no detectable trauma, or alternately it can act as if everything were hunky-dory when actual trauma exists. People who have had limbs amputated frequently feel chronic pain in appendages that no longer exist. Thus if you amputate an arm, the part of the brain responsible for communication with that arm refuses to admit that the arm no longer exists. Instead those brain neurons are eager not to lose their job, so they sound the alarm that the arm is hurting.

So, maybe Moolynaut had healed me or maybe I wasn't really hurt in the first place. Or maybe some mysterious communication had transpired and I had instantaneously willed myself to be whole again.

Scientists explore these and closely related questions when they test the efficacy of new drugs or therapies. Typically, they select a number of people with a given ailment and divide the subjects randomly into two subgroups. They treat one group with the real drug and the second with a pill that contains inactive ingredients called a placebo. The people who take the placebo think that they are being treated when in fact they are not. In one summary of many studies, 32 percent of patients were healed or partially healed by a placebo.[3] These experiments imply that just as a child stops crying when you soothingly place a Winnie the Pooh bandage on a cut, nearly one-third of adults suddenly get better when you tell them that they should be getting better.

It's possible that my body was physically healed when I was in North America, long before I met Moolynaut, but some part of my brain was confused by all that hardware and scar tissue. As a result, my brain *had the opinion* that I was still injured and should experience pain—and presto, I had to stay home from skiing. Personally, I have a hard time believing that my original pain was imagined, or psychosomatic, and that I crawled around the apartment the previous winter because some pesky thought process was getting in the way of a good time and that the problem was solved when an old lady made a big fuss over me and spit on my pubic hairs. But who's in charge here anyway: Moolynaut, Kutcha, me, or my brain?

I have a close friend and ski partner, Andy Zimet, who is a physician. Andy reminded me that the pain was episodic and that I wasn't hurting when I went to see Moolynaut. A few days before we returned to Vyvenka, I slipped on a rock, fell in the creek, and reinjured my pelvis. The pain disappeared on its own volition the next day and I was pain free when I walked into the first séance. Andy hypothesized that possibly, the previous winter, the broken plate may have twisted just a tiny bit, but enough to rub against bone or soft tissue and cause significant pain. The last violent fall may have moved the broken plate, perhaps ever so slightly. This movement caused immediate pain but readjusted the plate so now it was doing no good but no harm, either, and the pain dissipated. Thus my "healing" with Moolynaut and Kutcha coincidentally occurred a few days after I was healed through a sequence of unusual but physically explainable events.

One afternoon, six months after visiting Moolynaut, I sat down with a piece of scrap paper to scribble a short summary of what happened to me, followed by the possible explanations:

First I wrote: "I was healed. As Misha would say, 'This is really.'"

Followed by: "Some people will believe that Moolynaut and Kutcha performed magical outside intervention. Alternatively, pain specialists might propose that the magic came from within, as my mind and body exorcised the real or imagined pain. As a third possibility, a statistician might argue that this was a rare and fortuitous coincidence."

Then I doodled for a while, drawing stick figures of skiers joyfully descending impossibly steep mountains. Finally I wrote: "I can't distinguish among the three possibilities. Maybe I shouldn't bother to ask the question, because even if I could magically deduce the answer, it wouldn't change anything. Moolynaut spit on my pubic hair and I'm better. No discussion needed."

After a few more doodles, I realized that there was one more issue that I had to address. When I was standing there on one leg in Goshe's bedroom, with Moolynaut chanting in the old tongue, when I was reaching for that spot of light, maybe my outstretched arm spanned across the years I spent as a Ph.D. research chemist, toward something I can't define or put to words. For a brief moment, I believed.

Believed in what?

Shamanism is an ancient practice. In all aboriginal cultures, on all continents, from steamy rain forests to frozen tundra, for as long back in time as anthropologists can deduce human behavior from the fossil record, we have evidence that shamans were an integral part of human culture. And now I had become part of that ancient and venerable tradition.

Hounded by curiosity, I read about Neolithic rituals and animistic religions, searching for clues to understand the complex sequence of events that had suddenly become my reality. But the claims, counterclaims, beliefs, and denials were so contradictory and confusing that I learned nothing. Next, I peeled off another layer and wandered into the Paleolithic until finally I continued my thought-journey to the origins of our ancestry, even before *Homo sapiens* evolved.

I learned that about 1.6 million years ago early hominids began making the first symmetric stone tool, a hand ax, manufactured by knapping a blade onto the edges of an oval-shaped stone. Then, incredibly, for a million and a half years, stone tool technology hardly advanced at all. But, during this time, brain size steadily increased. In human evolution, sophisticated tools came much later than something else—something that was more important from an evolutionary standpoint.

When I was in grade school, I learned that the secret to hominid success was our utilitarian hand, with a flexible wrist and a thumb lying opposite our four digits. Mrs. Shepherd, with her purple hair, purple dresses, and stumpy legs, taught us that Stone Age *Homo* were using their marvelous hands to build and use tools and weapons. True enough. More recently some researchers have postulated that we also used our hands to develop the art of throwing projectiles. But all these mechanical explanations can only be part of the story. Mrs. Shepherd dutifully taught us long division and emphasized the folly of looking out the window to watch the autumn leaves, but somehow she neglected to teach us that our ancestors were playing music and holding paintbrushes in their marvelously dexterous hands. I tried to peer past Mrs. Shepherd's bias that evolutionary progress was based on pragmatism alone: tools, weapons, defense, and offense. What was going on in our newly conscious brains as we were climbing down out of the trees and becoming human? Long before our ancestors developed a sophisticated tool kit, they were using their cognitive powers to develop social relationships, bury their dead, collect and store symbolic rocks and seashells, and later adorning these objects with red ochre dye.

So, which was more important: magic or logic? We're missing the point even by asking the question. There is so much we don't know. How do we know if our ancestors were loving or combative, cooperative or competitive? When did language develop? Did parents play hopscotch with their children? And, more directly germane to the mystery that plagued me: Why did people revere, respect, or even fear their shamans? When did shamans begin to heal the sick?

No one can answer any of these questions, but through Moolynaut's love and the glowing embers of Nikolai's campfires I had been privileged to catch a tiny glimpse of the power in the old ways. The Koryak people built no stone fortresses; they never sent armies on wars of global conquest or launched rocket ships to the moon. Distorted by our Western bias toward the word "accomplishment," we overlook and forget.

I didn't need to explain my healing. Moolynaut never asked me to explain. She had asked me only to believe, to open my consciousness to a part of myself that had been there for 2 million years but had been ignored lately, stored in some great dusty leather trunk in my brain's attic, along with a few worn stone hand axes and a sealskin pouch of red ochre dye.

Chris and I had a marvelous ritual of sitting on the couch and touching gently, but not erotically, while discussing any issues that concerned either of us. It was inevitable then that one day we sat down, each leaning apart but intertwining our legs, and Chris asked, "So what exactly do you believe in? Do you believe that Moolynaut healed you? Do you believe in Kutcha?"

We sat in silence for a long time. Finally, I told Chris that I would never understand what had happened inside my bones, nerve endings, ligaments, and patches of scar tissue. All that was irrelevant.

A person is changed every time he or she experiences intense emotional or physical stimuli. Fall in love, go hungry on a windy mountaintop, dance all night and you wake up the next morning slightly different than you were before. I had changed and I felt lighter in my body. Suddenly I was terrified that the latent scientist inside me would build some newfangled catapult that would destroy this wonderful cathedral inside my brain, capture the séance with Moolynaut, try it for heresy, and burn it at the stake.

Magic or logic? Which would I choose?

I will never totally toss logic out the door with a swift kick in the butt. But something special happened that day in Vyvenka, revealing a mysterious connection between my brain, my body, nature, and the spirit world, a relationship that had been there all along but hadn't been there, because it didn't exist until I believed in it.

I'll never know if I believe in magic or not, because I can't define the word in any meaningful sense. Thus I don't have an answer because I've lost track of the question. But I'm certain that if I believe that the world is wondrous, fascinating, and mysterious, then I will be curious, aware, and attentive to everything around me, eager not to miss out on that next special moment. And for me, that's as good a start as anything else I can think of.

I stood up, walked across the room, picked up my dog-eared copy of Joseph Campbell's *The Hero with a Thousand Faces*, turned to the bookmark in chapter 2, and confirmed that repudiation was not an option. Campbell wrote: "[If the hero refuses the call] his flowering world becomes a wasteland of dry stones and his life feels meaningless—even though, like King Minos, he may through titanic effort succeed in building an empire of renown. Whatever house he builds, it will be a house of death: a labyrinth of cyclopean walls to hide from his Minotaur. All he can do now is create new problems for himself and await the gradual approach of his disintegration."[4]

Talk about hellfire and damnation. I was fifty-six years old. I had been injured. Healed. I had believed. I had scrutinized my belief with scientific logic, but nothing made sense. Well, not nothing. If I listened to Joseph Campbell, Moolynaut, Kutcha, and myself, then I had no choice.

Perhaps my lifetime relationship with the mountains, deserts, and oceans of this world had already been changing me for a long time. On my first visit, Moolynaut had asked me to return. Now I could come out of the closet and explore the depth and breadth of her mysterious wisdom.

I decided to return to Vyvenka a third time, ostensibly to thank Moolynaut for healing me but really because I needed to continue a journey that I had started long ago and occasionally neglected.

A Bar Mitzvah and a Boubin

Unfortunately, my finances suffered several disastrous setbacks. My text-book editor died and my words, ideas, copyrights, and career collapsed into a legal morass. At the same time, I couldn't sell any of my adventure/travel manuscripts. The stock market crashed and our savings dissipated daily. I applied for a job as a substitute teacher in physics and chemistry at Darby High School but was rejected because I didn't have any education courses on my résumé. Despite my resolution to return to Vyvenka and thank Moolynaut, I couldn't afford the airplane ticket.

In August 2002, I got an e-mail from my brother, Dan, who lives and works in Tokyo. His son, Benjamin, was having a bar mitzvah in October. Dan knew that Chris and I were broke, so he generously offered to buy our tickets. The timing was perfect and Dan's gift was generous and fortuitous. I decided to fly across the Pacific a few weeks early, detour north to Kamchatka, visit Moolynaut, and then return to join Chris and the family.

My travel arrangements required that I fly to Tokyo, spend the night with Dan, take the bullet train to the west side of Honshu Island, and then board a second flight across the Sea of Japan to Vladivostok. After crossing the Pacific and struggling through a groggy, jet-lagged half-sleep in Dan's apartment, I took a cab to the train station, arriving on the platform at 9:14. At 9:23 a column of women in hospital green uniforms, with pink trim, marched down the platform with military precision, proudly holding brooms and dustpans as if they were parade swords. When the column reached the first white line painted on the concrete, three women stopped abruptly while the others marched to the next white line, where three others fell out of formation. The process continued until the parade-perfect janitors were spaced evenly along the platform, all standing stiffly at attention.

At 9:26 the train arrived and eased to a halt so that the doors opened exactly at the white lines. Commuters filed out and the tidy green women bowed politely to each exiting passenger. Then the women trotted in, double time, and quickly swept out the train. They exited at 9:31 and the outbound passengers, myself included, filed in. The train started up at 9:33:59, one second ahead of schedule.

At noon I opened the lunch I had bought at the Tokyo train station. It was hygienically wrapped in a Styrofoam dish, with a sprig of green plastic parsley to highlight a small serving of rice, one green bean, one Lilliputian carrot, one piece, each, of several vegetables I didn't recognize, and several small potions of fish, some of which were familiar and others that weren't.

This precise, immaculately clean world ended abruptly when my next flight touched down at the Vladivostok airport. We taxied past decrepit gray concrete hangers, with skeletal wood-domed roofs that appeared reluctant to withstand the snowfall of yet another Siberian winter. The plane's reflection was cast in sunset colors by the few remaining windows that had withstood the ravages of time, vandalism, and neglect. In the terminal, rifle-toting soldiers herded the passengers through unlit hallways and our footsteps echoed on the worn, grooved wooden floors. At the immigrations desk, a trim, fit-looking young woman with the uniform of the elite Pogranichniki (the Russian border guards) asked me in English why I was traveling to Russia.

I told her that I was a tourist.

She shook her head and tapped her finger on the counter.

"You are lying."

We stared at each other silently.

She spoke and despite the harshness of the situation I reveled at the back-of-the-throat enunciation and familiar cadence of her Russian accent.

"I see tourists every day. Look at those people over there." She pointed aggressively at a middle-aged camera-toting Japanese couple in clean, neatly pressed casual clothes. "Those people are tourists." She waited a moment for emphasis. "I look at your clothes, but more important, I look into your eyes. You are not a tourist. You are lying."

From long experience with police and border guards throughout the world, I've learned that it is better to act a little stupid by saying nothing than to say something careless. I remained silent.

The Pogranichniki woman went on the offensive, raising her voice. "And don't tell me you're a businessman, either. Look at those men." She pointed to a row of Japanese businessmen lined up in a queue, all dressed in identical gray suits with identical black briefcases, like a row of mirror images of one another, smiling patiently. "If you tell me you're a businessman, you're in big trouble, because then I'll know that you're really lying." She slammed a closed fist on the counter with an assertive bang. "Don't lie to me."

I tried to think of a simple statement that would withstand scrutiny, not a complex, contorted story that would lead into an abyss.

"I'm going to Petropavlovsk to visit some friends."

She smiled. "Thank you. Now I believe that you are telling the truth."

Then she tapped the counter again. "But what kind of men are these friends? Why are they so important that you fly so far to visit them?"

I decided not to tell her that I was going to thank Moolynaut, who had healed my pelvis by having me stand naked on one foot, with my right arm behind my back and my left arm stretched out before me, reaching into the Other World. I smiled and said nothing.

She grabbed my passport, pushed her chair back with a screech of metal on wood, and disappeared behind a worn, drab unmarked door. A new agent appeared and quickly processed the Japanese tourists and businessmen until I was standing alone.

Did her computer tell her that in 1999 Franz and I left our guide behind and sailed through the Kuril Islands without proper permissions until the Pogranichniki relented and finally let us pass, dubbing us the "Two-Man American Suicide Expedition"? Do they have a record that in 2000 Misha and I paddled around the bureaucrats in Anadyr in the dead of night because we didn't have permission to visit the area? Did she know that our case ended up in a general's office and the general let us continue because he respected our expedition?

A bent, shuffling janitor turned most of the lights off, because obviously there was no need to consume all that electricity just for me, and I waited in the semidarkness. Almost an hour later, the woman returned. She silently handed me my stamped passport and smiled warmly as if to say, "Yes, I know about you now. You're a wanderer. You and probably your friends are all minor-league gangsters. But aren't we all minor-league gangsters, out here on the frontier, each in our own way and our own style? Welcome to Russia."

The next morning I continued northward on another flight and met Misha in PK. Then, a few days later, on October 14th, we flew to the even more decrepit outpost airport at Korpf/Tillichiki. It was late in the season and too stormy for Oleg to risk an ocean passage and pick us up by speedboat, but there was no snow, so he couldn't travel by snow machine. As a result, we had to walk from the airport to Vyvenka.

Before we left Korpf, Misha wanted to visit a geologist friend who worked at the platinum mine. The mine is located on the tundra north of town and the office is a few blocks from the airport. The geologist received us warmly in a comfortable, brightly lit room lined with photos of modern heavy equipment working a huge placer deposit, the second-largest platinum mine in the world. Once the geologist learned that I was a journalist, he earnestly described all the environmental protection measures used to ensure that the mine didn't pollute the rich Koryak salmon-spawning grounds. I smiled and secretly resolved to take some water samples back to a lab in the United States.

After tea and a snack, the geologist explained that the winter road to Vyvenka followed shortcuts across numerous lagoons, lakes, bogs, and rivers and wasn't navigable until freeze-up. He recommended that we walk along the beach, and then he assigned a driver to take us as far south as possible. The driver explained that we were leaving too late to reach Vyvenka that evening, but that he would call a friend who was the caretaker of a small coal mine along our route. His friend, Alexei, would feed us and put us up for the night. We climbed into a huge six-wheel-drive diesel military truck, roared to the end of the road on the south edge of town, and then churned over wet sand along the beach. Finally the driver shut off the engine when we reached a river that was too deep for the machine to ford.

My pack was loaded high, like Santa Claus's pouch, with presents: warm clothes, fishing gear, rope, tools, tea, kielbasa, a box of Pampers for Lydia's granddaughter, and a cup for Gosha because he had gotten drunk and broken all the cups in his house. It was 5:30 in the afternoon, the beach was bathed in sunset colors, and a southwest wind was roiling Govena Bay into whitecaps. Misha and I stripped naked to the waist, forded the frigid stream, then dressed and, finally out of the clutches of civilization, started walking down the beach. We immediately fell into easy conversation, reminiscing fondly about our sea kayak expedition along this coast two years ago. After leaving Vyvenka, we had paddled directly across the bay and camped on a sandbar that now shimmered in the distant twilight. Govena Point rose in rocky elegance to the southeast, where steep waves and a dangerous current shear had guarded our passage and forced us to spend a nervous night on a tiny beach in the middle of a grizzly bear trail.

Misha and I walked along the soft sand as sunset gradually lost its colors and night descended. In our normal lives, I often missed the transition into night because I retreated to the warm, electric glow of our homes. However, if I can ignore the growing apprehension of darkness, the change of light is one of the most glorious times of day. Colors and shadows soften into a peaceful background that embraces but doesn't demand attention, allowing thoughts to internalize—or fly outward. It's a time to reflect on the day and think about the adventures ahead. As my eyes adjust, I see more and more with less and less, until finally the retina surrenders and pleads for the harsh glow of a headlamp.

It was totally dark by the time we left the beach and turned inland toward the coal mine, following muddy tire tracks covered with a thin film of ice. A disheveled man standing beneath the feeble glow of a security light directed us to an apartment where Alexei was expecting us. The flat was in an advanced state of disrepair, even by Russian frontier standards, with peeling paint, patched wallpaper, rickety handmade furniture, and coal dust everywhere. But Alexei fed us a rich, welcome fatty stew and a crisp garden salad picked fresh from his greenhouse.

Alexei explained that the mine had recently shut down for the winter, but he remained as caretaker and security guard. He complained that it would be hard to obtain food this winter because the bulldozer had broken down and he couldn't drive to town.

I asked him why he didn't travel by snow machine rather than try to plow a road with a heavy diesel-belching bulldozer.

He seemed irritated at my comment and explained that he hadn't been paid in eleven months and he didn't have any machine—light or heavy— that worked. However you analyzed the problem, it was hard to get to town and buy food—and once he got to the grocery store, he didn't have any money anyway.

I let the matter drop.

The Soviet Union has collapsed, but the beast continued to poison even after it had expired. We were sitting on top of a valuable coal deposit and there was no money to maintain machinery, buy food, pay employees, or paint an apartment. Fifteen miles to the south, the electricity in Vyvenka was sporadic because there wasn't enough diesel fuel to run the generator and the central heating plant had shut down years ago for lack of coal, engineers, spare parts, and resolve.

The next morning, Misha and I hiked along the beach, passing cliffs of sedimentary rock interbedded with coal seams. After a few hours, we reached a tiny harbor with an abandoned fishing camp nestled behind a huge boulder. There were a few house foundations and a rusted steam winch used long ago to haul boats out of the water during storms. Vertical cliffs blocked further passage along the shore, so we followed a faint trail leading up a narrow gully to the tundra plateau. We picked our way along a maze of game trails and narrow footpaths that meandered past low bushes, grasses, and sedges, yellow from autumn frost. Numerous arctic hares scurried for cover at our approach. The sky darkened in the southwest and rain clouds appeared on the horizon. The storm approached slowly, driven by small puffs of wind that presaged a low-pressure system spiraling toward us. If we had been at sea, we would have looked for shelter, but the earth is solid and forgiving and today the storm posed no danger. Two and a half years earlier, Moolynaut had conjured up a storm to bring us to Vyvenka. Now, perhaps, she was talking to us again, urging us to hurry toward the warmth, comfort, and friendship of town.

Light rain fell. Our track led us down a slight incline into a small basin where the bushes were sheltered from the wind and grew to shoulder height. Suddenly Misha lurched forward and fell heavily to the ground, shaking moisture from the leaves and branches. One leg was twisted behind him at an odd angle. I raced up and discovered that his foot was caught in a wire snare. He was confused but not hurt, and I couldn't help laughing.

"Misha, if you were a lynx, I'd have to skin you now."

Misha was half-amused at the joke while simultaneously embarrassed that he had been caught unaware. I released his foot from the wire, thankful that it wasn't a spring-loaded leg trap, reset the snare, and covered it lightly with leaves, so it would remain invisible to the next creature that wandered along this trail.

We stopped for a rest and a snack. We were nearing Vyvenka, within the realm of hunters who were trapping the lynx that preyed on hares. Shortly past noon, we dropped off the plateau to the north shore of the Vyvenka River. As planned, Oleg was waiting us with his speedboat, to ferry us across the river to town.

He greeted us warmly.

"*Oostal* [tired]?" he asked me.

"*Da, conyeshna, chut, chut* [yes, of course, a little]."

I asked about everyone's health and Oleg answered that all was well. Their daughter, Anastasia, had returned, pregnant and without a husband, from PK. She was now living at home and he and Lydia were overjoyed to have a new baby in the now-crowded house.

I asked how the fishing had been that summer—and Oleg's face darkened. He explained that there had been a lot of fish this year, but local fishermen had been denied permission to set their nets.

"What?" I asked incredulously.

A small company had built a fish-processing facility with the notion that Vyvenka locals could add value to their catch by freezing and canning the fish locally. In an effort to establish rapport with the community, the owners of the company shipped basic commodities north and sold the food at reduced prices to their employees and to the fishermen. They donated money to the schools and helped rebuild the library. Unfortunately, the larger urban-based fishing conglomerates, who were accustomed to controlling the salmon run, were annoyed. To punish this upstart company with benevolent ideas, they convinced the government to shut down fishing entirely for the year, in the hope that they would force the mavericks into bankruptcy. While the capitalists battled in the offices and banks of PK, local Vyvenka fishermen were denied the right to fish in their aboriginal river. Instantly their annual incomes plummeted to zero.

"Then how do you live?" I asked. "What do you eat?"

"*Paiyette*. In Russia there is always a way," Oleg replied. "Lydia makes a little money as a schoolteacher. We have potatoes from the garden, cucumbers from the greenhouse, and berries from the tundra. We shoot hares on land, hunt seals in the sea, and catch fish from the river. Next year we will have money so we can buy things. Now we live with the things we already have. Throughout all history there have been good times and bad. *Paiyette*. It's important to stay happy, even during the bad times."

We crossed the river and walked down the now-familiar street to Oleg and Lydia's house. People were demolishing an abandoned Soviet apartment complex. With its outside walls removed and innards exposed, the building looked like a huge, rotten dead beast. The demolition seemed to be one final attempt to exorcise the vestiges of the defunct, hated Soviet regime, and in the exorcism we were exposed, one more time, to its raw ugliness.

Lydia was waiting for us at her doorway. She plucked some thread from our garments, welcomed us inside, and then burned the threads with her incantation of cleansing. She was happy and beaming, with no outward indication that her husband's income had dropped to zero during the past year, dragging them into extreme poverty until the Earth completed another revolution around the Sun, the salmon followed primordial urges to swim upriver again, and the Russian bureaucrats reissued fishing permits.

During tea, I explained that my pelvis was completely healed and I wanted to thank Moolynaut for making me whole again.

Lydia replied, "Yes, this is good." Then she smiled broadly and said, "Moolynaut has made a gift at you."

"That's wonderful. I'm so excited. What is it?"

Lydia disappeared into the back room and returned with a round hand drum. It was about two and one-half feet in diameter, framed with bent birch, and covered with reindeer hide. Crossed strings provided a handle and a light metal chain was attached above the handle to jingle, like the cymbals on a tambourine. The striker was the fur-covered foreleg of a dog.

Lydia handed it to me. "This is a *boubin*. This *boubin* has a woman's voice, which is good, because you are a man and you need women in your life. You must play it so it knows you. When it is your friend, it becomes your *boubin*. Maybe it will become your lover." And Lydia held her hand to her mouth and giggled.

I held the drum and struck it tentatively.

Lydia grabbed the instrument and commanded, "No, like this!" She shook the *boubin* and struck an ancient rhythm. Then she danced around the room with a high-stepping gait, chanting in the old tongue, with her eyes closed.

I tried to emulate—and everyone laughed.

Lydia explained, "Every person may make a drum. But only special persons do make *boubins*. Moolynaut knows this ways. Everything must have happening in a special time with a special song. Moolynaut begins to have making your *boubin* in the spring, because at these time she knows you are coming to our homes. After all the snow runs away, Moolynaut prepares the wood from trees that are just saying hello to the sun after their long winter sleep. The reindeer skin is have to be made from a special deer that is killed in a special way. It came from somewhere north of Korpf. I do not tell you exactly all about these things. Each thing on the *boubin* comes from a special place at a special time. If all is done the right way, it is a *boubin*. If even one thing is done in not the right way, it is only a drum."

"I understand. So now the *boubin* has magic?" I asked.

"Yes. This is correct. But it can have *belee* (white) magic or *cherny* (dark) magic. It is now your *boubin*. You must teach it *belee* voices."

I felt a little overwhelmed at the responsibility, and at the same time the request was stretching my sense of credulity. How could I teach magic to a drum if I didn't believe that drums had consciousness? I could rationalize the whole request as an allegory, just as my high school religion teacher had dissected, analyzed, and explained all the miracles in the Bible in a form palatable to a bunch of smart-aleck eighteen-year-olds. But neither blind literal acceptance nor allegorical rationalization resonated with me. I was among friends, in a foreign culture. Everyone around me was animated, happy, loving, and giving. Cynicism and dissection seemed out of place. I reminded myself, instead, to remain mindful, curious, and observant.

I beat the *boubin*, cooed softly to it as if I were talking to a newborn baby, and tried to communicate happy thoughts.

Perhaps the *boubin* whispered something in my ear, or more likely, the recent conversation finally settled into my brain and triggered a delayed comprehension. "Wait a minute! Lydia! Did you say that Moolynaut started making the drum in the spring, just after the snow had gone away?"

"Yes, do you not remember? Before one minute ago I spoke at you about this things."

"And did Moolynaut know, from the beginning, that the *boubin* was for me?"

"Oh yes." Lydia smiled. "That is the only way to make a *boubin*. When you are making a *boubin*, you must think about the person who will take this *boubin* home. You must know that this person will bring *belee* magic to the *boubin*. So the *boubin* can make *belee* magic for the people. Otherwise bad things will happen."

Lydia stopped and reflected on this, then shook her head gravely. "Very bad things."

I took a deep breath. "In the spring, I didn't have enough money to buy a plane ticket. I didn't know that I was coming to Vyvenka until my brother invited us to the bar mitzvah in August."

Lydia looked at me as if she didn't understand my puzzlement.

"Don't you understand?" I asked. "How did Moolynaut know I was coming before I knew I was coming?"

Lydia smiled and her broad, rosy cheeks framed her small, round mouth. "Ah, yes. This is no difficultness. Many times Moolynaut knows these things before other people know."

I beat the drum softly, trying to collect my thoughts.

Then I realized that Moolynaut, the main character in this drama, wasn't here.

"Where is Moolynaut?" I asked. "May I speak with her to thank her for this *belee boubin?*"

Lydia answered, "You came here to thank Moolynaut for fixing your inside. But Moolynaut did not fix you. Moolynaut is only the talker."

"You mean 'messenger,'" I interrupted. "Moolynaut is the messenger."

"Yes. Moolynaut is the messenger. She talked to Kutcha the Raven God. Now you must thank Kutcha, hisself. But Kutcha does not live in this world. You and Misha must walk at our great-grandmother to the Other World. When you come at the Other World, you can thank Kutcha. Tomorrow it is time for you to talk at Kutcha in the Other World."

I beat the *boubin* slowly, feeling afraid. Back home, in the safety and familiarity of my own culture, I had speculated about the development, function, and power of the hominid brain. But I was about to pass beyond speculation. Tomorrow, I would ask my big brain to take me to a place we had never been before.

Journey to the Other World

That evening, after everyone else retired, Misha and I laid our pads on Goshe's faded, musty Brezhnev-era rug, spread out our sleeping bags, and crammed jackets into stuff sacks to make pillows. We turned off the lights, but before we dozed off I asked Misha what Lydia meant when she said that it was time for us to talk with Kutcha in the Other World. Misha responded that he thought we would eat the *mukhomor* again with Moolynaut.

In the silence and darkness he continued, "Many Koryak people travel to the Other World with the *mukhomor*. You and I, we are Europeans. Maybe we can walk on this road. Maybe we do not. We will know tomorrow."

I remember thinking, "What next?" I had left my home in America, passed through the ultra-clean railroad station in Tokyo, and now was back in Goshe's apartment in Vyvenka. I didn't believe that Moolynaut could lead me to talk to Kutcha, but then I hadn't believed that Moolynaut could heal my pelvis.

The next morning, we hung around, cutting firewood, drinking tea, and chatting. After a light, early lunch, Moolynaut walked through the door, moving with an off-balance gait, clutching her side, obviously in pain.

I greeted her and asked what was wrong.

She coughed softly and held up her hand to indicate that she would speak in a moment. I rushed to bring her a stool and she lowered herself slowly, again clutching her side, inhaling in short, rapid breaths.

After she composed herself, Moolynaut explained that two weeks ago she was feeding her dog team. One of the dogs lunged for the food and knocked her down. She fell against the side of a bucket and broke some ribs. They were healing but remained painful.

I remembered saying good-bye to Moolynaut the previous year. She was ice-fishing and her dogs were sleeping peacefully in harness. I had once owned a team in Alaska and I frequently wrestled dogs to break up a fight, to pull them away from food, or to control the excitement as I led individuals to harness. Clearly, Moolynaut didn't have the strength, athletic speed, and agility to control a pack of raucous dogs, so she must have managed her team mainly through willpower and the force of her crackling, raspy, but assured voice. Yet an accident had happened.

Then I thought, "If Moolynaut is a great healer, why doesn't she chant herself into a trance, visit Kutcha in the Other World, and mend her own broken ribs?"

Clearly, shamans don't have that power. Despite the séances and *muk-homor*, people in Vyvenka become sick and injured. Many die young. Alcoholism and suicide are endemic. Looking back in time, I thought of how even the most powerful shamans couldn't repel the Cossack invaders who conquered the land in the eighteenth century, nor could the shamans cure the infectious diseases that killed 60 to 65 percent of the Koryak at first contact. During Soviet times, diabolic KGB agents pushed shamans out of heli-copters, exhorting them to fly if they possessed so much magic. Now the Russians control the Koryak land and fish and Moolynaut's chants had no effect on the corrupt bureaucrats. So where does her power begin and end? Why was I chosen? Why was my pelvis now pain free?

I broke my reverie to realize that I had forgotten my manners. I raced back to the living room, retrieved my *boubin*, and returned to the kitchen, beating a quiet rhythm and singing a thank-you song. Misha translated, but Moolynaut barely acknowledged my antics and my gratitude. With great concentration, she reached into her shawl and retrieved a cloth bag full of dried *mukhomor*. She spread the fungi on Goshe's table, with its plastic flower prints, shuffled through her collection, and picked an especially large mushroom. For the first time, she smiled.

Moolynaut took a deep painful breath, looked toward the ceiling, and rocked back and forth, with the same motion she had used during our heal-ing trance. After a few moments of reflection, she told me that one day in early summer, as she was walking on the tundra, she heard a voice. She looked around, but no one was in sight, and the voice was unfamiliar. Then she realized that the voice was emanating from the ground, so she looked at her feet and saw this *mukhomor* calling her name. The *mukhomor* explained that it had a special message for Jon Turk and asked Moolynaut to pick it and dry it for me.

She held the mushroom up between us.

I set the *boubin* down and took the mushroom from Moolynaut's wrinkled but steady fingers.

When Moolynaut had dried the mushroom in the hot summer sun, the brilliant red cap had paled to a dull, reddish tan. At the same time, the white dots darkened until they almost blended with the background. But when I looked at the fungus face-to-face, the camouflaged white dots seemed to rise out of hiding to stare back at me, like so many eyeballs. For some weird rea-son, I wasn't particularly surprised that this *mukhomor* knew my name and intuited that I was coming to Vyvenka before I knew about the bar mitzvah and my brother's offer of a free plane ticket. I no longer thought that it might be strange that this mushroom had engaged Moolynaut in a conversation.

Chris, Misha, and I had eaten *mukhomor* before, but clearly that first experience was a casual introduction to the drug. Now, as I gazed at this ticket to the Other World, I was apprehensive but too curious to retreat.

We repeated the ritual of carefully separating the stem from the cap, dicing both, throwing a portion over each shoulder for Kutcha, and then eating the top and the stem in equal proportions, so we wouldn't lose our legs or our head. This time Moolynaut didn't eat the *mukhomor*, because her ribs hurt too much to embark on a long and potentially arduous journey.

This *mukhomor* was much bigger than the one I had eaten the year before and Moolynaut was staring at me intently. Misha sat by my side, cutting and eating his portion, which was smaller than mine. Sergei walked in, eyes glazed over, already journeying to the Other World. Lydia ate a small *mukhomor*. Children wandered in and out. We chatted for a while, but I have no memory of what we talked about.

Moolynaut silently gathered her things and walked out the door, leaving me without my teacher, as if I were naked, standing on one leg, needing to focus on my center of gravity to stand erect, connected to the earth.

I began to feel light-headed. As an anchor to reality, I looked at my watch; it was 1:00 in the afternoon.

Oddly and annoyingly, someone turned on the television. Five iridescent green cartoon animals spiraled in a whirl, reaching out of the screen, exhorting me to buy Kit Kat chocolate. Then an exquisitely clean woman in an exquisitely clean room assured me that my life would be better if I bought Tide detergent. I looked around the room that I was in and at my rough-clad friends and wasn't convinced that cleanliness was my salvation; it certainly wouldn't facilitate my passage to Old Woman Who Lives on the Top of the Highest Mountain.

On the television, a warship was leaving port and several beautiful women with big breasts and tight clothes lined the dock, waving good-bye to their men. One woman threw a bundle into the outstretched arms of a sailor. He opened the package and removed a pair of pink, lace-fringed panties. He waved the panties victoriously as his comrades watched in envy. Then a second woman, even more beautiful than the first, threw a gift to her sailor boyfriend. Socks. All the sailors laughed at the unfortunate goon who had received a pair of socks from his sassy maiden. As the woman turned and walked away, the camera zoomed in on her butt, wrapped tightly in black pants. Then the butt expanded until it filled the entire screen—two cheeks with a line down the middle, wiggling because somewhere beyond the screen a torso and legs were walking. A logo flashed across the wiggling ass and a deep, resonant voice spoke from the television.

I couldn't understand the Russian, but as the *mukhomor* began affecting my brain I imagined that the asshole was talking to me, in a man's voice, enticing me to buy something from Moscow, Paris, or Madison Avenue.

Maybe they were selling magic pants that enabled people to talk through their assholes.

I started giggling. My friends looked at me, but I couldn't explain.

Now great balls of flame exploded on the television and limp, lifeless bodies flew through the air. This was too much.

I tapped Misha on the shoulder, "I'm going outside for a walk."

As I was putting on my parka, Lydia shook her head. "No, this is not good," she exhorted. "Maybe the Woman Who Lives under the Ocean will sing at you. She has a very beautiful voice, like a soft, warm cloud. Maybe you will follow the voice into the sea because you think it is a warm, dry world with many beautiful women. But the water is cold and you will die." Lydia's unique impish smile radiated out of her broad face, full of love and concern.

"I will be fine," I answered.

"No. Maybe the *mukhomor* will talk at you and you will not know what is sea and what is land. Then you will follow the beautiful voice. You are a man and men like to sleep with beautiful women. The Woman Who Lives under the Ocean is very beautiful. This is not good. I will send Angela with you. She will pull you back from the sea when the Woman begins to cry out to you."

Angela is Lydia and Oleg's youngest daughter. She was eight years old at the time, and although always shy around me, she was alert and observant. I had brought her numerous small presents and she always watched me, curious and uncertain. Lydia dressed Angela in warm clothes.

It was a gray October afternoon in the Siberian subarctic. Angela was dressed in a red woolen coat, with wool mittens, a dog-fur cap, and yellow rubber boots. We walked outside and headed toward the beach. I didn't hear a siren's song, but I did pause to watch the waves and reflect—again— on our kayak journey across this ocean and on the storm that had brought Misha and me to this strange and beautiful village. Angela grasped my pants with her tiny hands. I looked down and she was tugging at me, with a grim, determined look, her heels dug into the sand, braced to hold me back, should I decide to bolt for the Woman Who Lives under the Ocean. I smiled, but Angela was too scared and awestruck with her responsibility to smile back. I held back a laugh, afraid that if I relapsed into a convulsion of mirth, rolling in the sand like a madman, poor Angela would be over-whelmed.

We had no true language between us, just a few words of pidgin and the commonality of our humanity. Silently I turned inland, and together we climbed up the back of the sleeping whale that looked like a hill rising above the town. A cold wind blew gently from the north and I turned to face it, welcoming the onset of another winter. Winter is my favorite time of year, when fluffy snow blankets the land and Chris and I ski graceful curving lines in the silent mountains.

A tiny hand pulled almost imperceptibly at my pant leg again and my diminutive but diligent guardian pointed toward the ground. I dropped down to my knees. Angela knelt next to me, picked a tiny tundra cranberry, smaller than a pea, and offered it. I smiled and carefully squeezed the precious berry between my teeth. It had freeze-dried in the autumn cold, but beneath the hardened skin there was a burst of summer sweetness. I smiled and Angela smiled back, with childish delight at a simple pleasure.

I remembered a time, decades ago; I was crawling through the high grass in an abandoned field on our small farm in Maine with two of my children, Nathan and Noey, picking wild strawberries that lay hidden close to the earth. As the three of us wandered on our hands and knees, we gradually packed subtle paths through the yellowing hay, and every once in a while, at a junction in these roads, I encountered a tiny face, smeared with red, intent on this quest to pluck juicy taste explosions from the soil. Returning to the present, I looked into Angela's joyful smile and laughed back, simultaneously regretting the passage of years that had turned my children into adults and rejoicing in the long, alluring path that had made my life rich and had brought me to this tiny village at the end of the earth.

Twilight overtook the day and the *mukhomor* began to dance more strongly in my brain. I stood and felt dizzy, started to walk, but lost focus—sat down. White space washed through my brain and then, in my imagination, the *boubin* was beating and someone was chanting. It was the sirens. Tricky witches. They weren't calling from the real ocean; they were calling from an imaginary ocean, singing inside me.

I sat there, listening.

Faithful Angela tugged at my elbow.

She spoke in Russian, earnestly, and I recognized the words: "Night and cold. Very cold."

She was standing and I was sitting, so her face was level with mine. Her mouth was taut with concern, rosy with frost, and smoothly beautiful with youth.

I nodded and replied in Russian, "Yes, we go to the house."

I stood with great resolve and took Angela's tiny fragile hand in mine. With great determination, she led me down the hill, across the main street of Vyvenka with its frozen mud holes, and toward the house. When I entered the room, the television was off and Misha was sitting, alone, on the dusty green couch, staring vacantly into space, obviously somewhere else. Angela disappeared.

I slumped down into Goshe's musty green easy chair and looked at my watch—5:00 P.M. Then I lost touch with the Real World. I dream-walked into a mazelike cavern with dark, smooth, menacing, nondescript walls. There were many turns and side tunnels, but at each junction I walked toward a small white dot of light that shimmered in the distance. It seemed as if the light should grow larger as I approached, but it remained constant. I began to run toward the light.

Yes, run. I had a mission. In my mind, I knew that I must thank the Black Raven for reconnecting my body with my spirit.

Then I stopped short. What would happen after I reached the Other World? Did I have the power to find my way back? Winter was almost upon us; my pelvis was healed; I wanted to go skiing with my friends.

Like all dreams, especially those that are induced by a magic mushroom, words and logic broke their bonds. I thought, "Maybe I could just step into the Other World for a second. I'll stand in the doorway, hold on tightly to the doorjamb, and peek inside long enough to thank Kutcha. He healed my pelvis and I owe him a thank-you. Then I'll turn around quickly, race back home, and go skiing."

I began holding conversations with myself. "What would happen if the Other World sucked me in like a giant vacuum and I couldn't escape?"

"Moolynaut travels to the Other World and returns with apparent ease."

"But I'm not Moolynaut."

"Where is Moolynaut?" I asked myself. "Why did she leave me? Isn't she supposed to be my guide?

"I need a teacher and a guide. I need someone to introduce me to Kutcha and then to guide me out of the Other World once I cross the threshold."

But I was alone. I was suddenly terrified that if I continued onward, I would die. In a mad panic, I turned back and raced through the tunnel toward the Real World, bouncing from one wall to the next, in the darkness. When I reached the first junction in the labyrinth, I stopped short.

"Left or right?

"Oh my God! I can't remember.

"Why had I been so stupid? Everyone knows that you are supposed to trail a string when you enter a labyrinth. Why had I forgotten the string? I thought I was a careful adventurer. Now I am between the Real World and the Other World, lost in a nameless nothingness, with none of the glory of either. Why hadn't I brought Angela? She would have led me home. Where is Moolynaut? Why did she leave me?

"Stay calm," I reminded myself. "Stay calm."

Still in the dream, I sat down. But while my body remained in the labyrinth, my mind found a new clarity.

I remembered those first few moments after my avalanche when I had started to lose consciousness and the mountains began to grow fuzzy. At that moment of extreme crisis, I had willed the landscape back into focus. Now I was teetering again, trapped this time in a dream.

"I must bring myself back.

"Back?" I asked myself. "What does 'back' mean? In the Real World, time moves forward only and there is no 'back' to return to. OK. I must stop bouncing off the walls, trying to return to where I was before I ate the *mukhomor*, because I'll never get there. I started the journey, and now I can't go back. Maybe there is no light at the end of the tunnel, no shining room where Kutcha sits in state, either. But this journey has happened; I will remember it forever. So what is so bad with just being here? Now. With no past and no future."

I remained sitting. Then, as a fog dissipates, the labyrinth dissolved into nothingness—and I found myself not in the labyrinth but in Goshe's musty green easy chair. Misha was talking in the Other Room. He was in the Real World, talking to real people. Friends.

I stood on wobbly legs and walked slowly toward the lit kitchen. Lydia, Misha, and Anastasia were drinking tea and eating bread. It was 9:00 P.M.

My friends looked up and I spoke: "I was lost in the cavern. I was afraid of the Other World and returned to the Real World. May I touch someone? Just to be sure that I am in the Real World and not the Other World?"

Lydia grasped my hands in hers.

"Your hands are like ice," she commented.

"No, it is impossible. I have been running for a long time. I am tired and sweaty."

"Your hands have no blood in them. They are like ice."

"It doesn't matter. I was lost halfway between the Real World and the Other World. I saw a light. It was the Other World, but I was afraid to go there. I couldn't find my way back. There were so many paths in the labyrinth. But now, I think I have returned. Are you sure that this is the Real World?"

Lydia pulled gently on my arms and spoke softly: "Come back from that place you are in. Come back to this world. We love you. Your friends are in the kitchen drinking tea and eating bread. It is good bread. I cooked it myself. And butter. If you are lost and hungry you must eat butter. You are too skinny."

And Lydia poked me playfully in the ribs.

After what seemed like a long time, I whispered meekly, "OK, thank you. I think I understand now."

Lydia handed me a piece of soft, aromatic homemade bread, slathered thickly with butter. I took a bite and chewed slowly, rejoicing in the taste and nourishment.

Journey in This World

I must have gone to sleep, because in my next memory I was lying on my pad and morning light was streaming through the dirty window, casting a dull pastel hue to the peeling paint and dusty furniture. I awoke, confused, uncertain what world I was in, what had transpired in reality and what had occurred in the dreamworld.

Misha was snoring, so I walked outside to sort out my thoughts. The beach, the breaking waves, and the ocean beyond were familiar by now, friendly for all their ferocity. But the *mukhomor* wasn't finished with me yet. The tunnel and the light reappeared, weaker than it was last night, subliminally intertwining itself with the hissing surf.

"Why had Moolynaut brought me to this tunnel? Or had I brought myself here? I'm an outsider, a Caucasian, a journalist. Maybe I've probed too deeply into Moolynaut's world. Maybe she conjured my hallucinogenic fear to send me away, just as Amazonian aborigines posted shrunken heads in jungle rivers to warn: 'You are traveling too far. You are not welcome here. Turn back now.'

"No, I didn't believe that. The mushroom had spoken to Moolynaut, and she was simply the messenger. Don't shoot the messenger. Moolynaut healed me; she is my friend. My friend, yes, but if she is my teacher, she isn't speaking. Or if she spoke I didn't hear. I only heard the *mukhomor*—but I didn't understand it. This *mukhomor* had first spoken from the summer tundra, telling Moolynaut that it had a message for Jon Turk. Now it was talking directly to me. Had I been deaf, blind, or undeserving? Had I failed the mushroom, Moolynaut, or myself? Did Kutcha ever hear me and comprehend that I was trying to thank him?"

Troubled, I returned to the house to be with my friends. Misha was inside, drinking tea. He asked me if I was all right, and when I nodded shakily he explained that last night he had journeyed to a beautiful landscape of three-dimensional kaleidoscope colors and shapes, spinning and swirling. He had encountered no sinister overtones, no fear, and no Other World.

Lydia entered with another loaf of fresh bread and I was relieved that she didn't talk about the *mukhomor* or ask about my failed passage to the Other World. Then Oleg walked in huge and bearlike, with a broad smile on his face.

He spoke to me directly in Russian: "Let's go hunting."

His simplicity and warmth drew me away from the labyrinth and the confused thoughts. I wanted to hug him. Yes, how did he know? That's exactly what I needed: a foray onto the tundra, where I felt confident and competent, where my navigation was good and I could always find my way home.

I nodded and replied, "*Da. Ochen harasho.* [Yes. Very good.]"

Misha and Sergei were also eager to escape town, and of course Wolfchuck was ready to go. We packed food and gear for two days and carried our supplies toward the lagoon where the speedboat was moored. Winter was closing in and children were sliding across frozen puddles as their parents pushed wheelbarrows and carts to the town well.

When we reached the lagoon, Oleg removed the spark plug from his trusty Yamaha. It was dirty and clogged and I would have replaced it, but in a land with few spare parts and in a year with no fishing income he blew on it, for good luck I suppose, and threaded it back into the cylinder. Meanwhile Sergei splashed around the shoreline in his hip boots, like an overgrown youngster, breaking the thin ice that had formed overnight. We dragged the boat over driftwood logs into the water, revved up the engine, and headed inland, the aluminum hull breaking the ice with a sharp, almost melodious tinkle.

Several miles from town, Oleg cut the motor suddenly. A whiskered seal bobbed to the surface and watched us curiously. I was surprised to see a seal so far into fresh water but remained silent as Oleg reached for his shotgun. It was a long shot across open water for a 12-gauge, but Oleg's aim was good and soon we hefted a dead seal into the boat.

We continued upriver for a few hours, stopped at a *serei*, started a fire, and boiled water for tea. Sergei asked me if he looked like an American Indian.

I replied, "Yes and no. Both the Koryak and the Amerindians have similar high cheekbones, but the Koryak are different: more Asian, although that's hard to define." Then I went on to explain that both the Koryak and the Amerindians had a common origin in Central Asia, southwest of here.

Sergei shook his head. "No. This is not true. The Vyvenka River is the center of the earth. In the beginning, a long time ago, there were no people in the world. One day, Kutcha flew around for many days until he found the most wonderful place to live on the entire planet. Then he reached into the Other World and grabbed a handful of Koryak people and set them down gently, right near here, on this tundra. Kutcha chose us first and gave us the best place to live, in the center of the world.

"Kutcha then put all other people in this place. But they traveled away. You white men came from here, but you became a little stupid after you left this place."

Then he reflected for a moment, "Or maybe you left this place because you were already stupid. I don't know about these things. It happened a long time ago. Long before I was born. You must ask Lydia. She knows about these things."

After tea, we went fishing, using bits and scraps of old monofilament line, rusted hooks, and an odd assortment of lures, including one hammered out of a kitchen spoon with a hook crudely welded to the cut-off handle. Despite the strange tackle, the fish were biting and we filled a large gunnysack before retiring to the *serei* for dinner. We waited for darkness to blanket the land and then Oleg announced that we would hunt hares by flashlight. We dressed and walked into the night, sneaking through willows and trying to walk silently on crinkly, half-frozen mud. I held one flashlight and Misha held the other, probing through the thickets for a glimpse of motion, while our two friends wielded shotguns, swaying the barrels with the dancing electric beams. But after several hours, we didn't see a single hare and returned to the *serei* empty-handed.

Oleg was discouraged. "We used to eat reindeer. Now the reindeer are gone, so we hunt hares. But every year, there are fewer and fewer hares. Today there are none. Maybe next year we will eat only ptarmigan."

I was reminded, sadly, of the quote by the great Oglala Sioux chief Sitting Bull: "When the buffalo are gone, we will hunt mice, for we are hunters and we want our freedom."

I set the despair aside and tried to be positive: "But we shot a seal and we have a large bag of fish."

Oleg nodded grimly.

The next morning the fishing was slow and Oleg became despondent again. "It's the platinum mine," he lamented. "They are spilling their poisons into the small streams at the top of our sacred river, killing the fish. Now there are not so many fish anymore, and every year it is harder to find something to eat."

I had anticipated this accusation and carried a few small, clean sample bottles in my day pack. I explained that I had a geologist friend at the University of Montana who specialized in mine pollution and reclamation and that he would analyze the water for heavy metal contamination. Then I could send the results to Misha, who was a hydrogeologist. Maybe it would be impossible to fight the big mining interests, but it would be interesting, in any case, to know if the operation was polluting the water and poisoning the fish. Everyone agreed, so I collected some Vyvenka River water.

Despite a slow start, the fish began biting by mid-morning and we filled a second gunnysack by lunchtime. After the midday sun melted the overnight ice, we loaded our catch and gear into the boat and headed downstream, toward town. The motor purred, the hull planed gracefully over the mirror-smooth river, and Oleg guided us adroitly past underwater shoals. Then he cut the engine and the boat drifted with the current. A small cloud of exhaust floated away with the breeze and the tundra silence overtook us. I scanned the glassy water for another seal but saw nothing.

After a few moments Oleg looked at me. "Jon. Do you know why you were afraid to enter the Other World?"

I looked into his weather-beaten face, lined by hardships of the land and the economic and political world he lived in. Oleg was a pragmatic man, a hunter, "Duck Devil." He could keep an engine running, without spare parts, for a decade after most people would have sung its requiem, but he seldom talked about emotional or spiritual matters. He smiled softly.

"No," I answered. "I don't know why I was afraid. But the fear was real. I couldn't force myself to walk through the door into the Other World."

Oleg nodded. "I understand."

The boat drifted in the current, spun slowly in an eddy, and then caught the downstream current again. The tundra drifted by, gold and red with autumn colors.

Oleg continued, "Every person is born with a certain amount of power. The gods have given you great power to travel in the Real World. But because you have channeled so much energy in this direction, you don't have enough energy left over to travel in the Other World. You were smart not to walk through the door into the Other World. Maybe you would never have found your way home. You are a poor traveler in the Other World, like me. I am a good hunter. But I do not travel into the Other World."

I almost cried with relief. There was no plot against me, no shrunken heads warning me to retreat. I was among friends and limited only by myself.

No, I wasn't limited; I was empowered—as long as I understood my own frailty. And now quiet, taciturn Oleg, my adventure partner—not Moolynaut, Lydia, or the *mukhomor*—was the teacher I had longed for yesterday. I didn't know how to explain all this to Oleg, so I smiled, certain that he would see across the gap in our cultures and heritage and accept the heartfelt thanks in my silence.

Oleg continued, "You obviously came here because you are seeking something. But you will not find it in the *mukhomor*. Kutcha lives in the Other World, but maybe you can find him on the tundra. Wait and watch. Kutcha will understand and he will visit you in the Real World. Then you can thank him. Do you understand me?"

I nodded and Oleg continued, "You and Misha must return one more time. You must make a long, hard journey across the tundra, in the Real World. You will be hungry and tired. Then maybe, if you are lucky, you will find what you are looking for."

I was dumbstruck. I had come here ostensibly to thank Moolynaut but really driven by some subconscious quest that I felt obligated to follow, even if I didn't understand it. The *mukhomor* had led me into the labyrinth, but I had become frightened. Now I was in the Real World, where time moves in one direction only and no one runs backward. The mysterious unattainable white light still glared at me from the end of the tunnel. As I hoped it always would. Now it was so obvious; why hadn't I seen it before? I wasn't seeking a threshold leading into a blinding, gold-lined room. All of that would have been so inconsistent with all of my other experiences here on the eastern edge of the Eastern world.

Moolynaut had healed me. I assumed that she was my teacher as well, even though she had never spoon-fed me long lectures on how to live a meaningful life, as Don Juan had guided Carlos Castaneda. Words weren't the main method of communication around here. A few days ago, Moolynaut gave me the *mukhomor* and then walked out of the room. I hadn't seen her since, so language or no language, she wasn't guiding me directly. Was the lesson so obvious that she didn't need to express it? Or so complex that I wouldn't understand it? No, that was phrasing the question in my Western, left-brain logic and vocabulary. I had to remind myself that Moolynaut grew up on the tundra, in a skin tent, herding reindeer, steeped in a nonverbal reality. Conscious of what she was doing or not, she was leading me toward a right-brain-oriented gestalt, and I shouldn't expect her to use verbalization to teach me the opposite.

The lesson was right in front of me, if I would only look into the embers of Nikolai's campfire and imagine talking to wolves during a winter blizzard. Now Oleg was giving me the same message through the hunter's certainty that the land would teach me everything I needed to know.

But wait a minute. Moolynaut had given me one verbal message. She told me that I had to believe. Believe in what?

The boat drifted lazily in the current. The dead seal, blood oozing out of the bullet hole, seemed to be watching me, waiting.

Siberia is a harsh land, so you might think that it is a place where survival depends mainly on left-brain logic and pragmatism. But it was here that I learned that magic and dreams underlie strong deeds. It was here that I learned that magic flies around us all the time, waiting only to be recognized—to be realized.

I had tried to follow a hallucinogenic drug to the mysterious Other World, to thank Kutcha. And failed. Now Oleg was telling me that I could accomplish the same goal by going for a long walk. Like Moolynaut, Oleg used words sparingly. He didn't—and wouldn't—elaborate, but I intuited that, in Oleg's mind, the Other World and the Real World were part of the same concept. I could talk to the spirits—and thank Kutcha—by communicating with the land.

I felt that I was peeling away the layers of the proverbial onion; from Moolynaut, a tangible human who clearly lived in the Real World, at least most of the time; to Kutcha, the half-imagined and half-formless trickster messenger god; to the tundra, which was tangible but paradoxically formless in its immensity. I was probing—seeking. Thanking Moolynaut or Kutcha was merely the excuse I needed to convince my Western logic- and goal-oriented left-brained mind to come here. The problem was that even though I was getting closer to the answer—whatever that means—I was losing track of the question. Whoops, I was falling over my own words. Enough thinking already.

I turned to Misha. "Will you join me?"

Misha smiled broadly, a familiar warm smile of two friends who had shared great adventures together. "Of course, Oleg is right. We must do this thing. We must go to the Wild Nature. It will be like paddling to Alaska across the sea. Yes, Jon, we must do this thing. Together."

Oleg pulled the starter cord and we continued downriver beneath the broad tundra sky, listening to the hum of the outboard. After half an hour, when we were a few hundred yards from town and could watch the children playing on the beach, Oleg cut the engine again.

"Remember Dimitri?"

I recalled Dimitri's joyful enthusiasm and the fifty dollars I gave him. I remembered my soft embrace with Svetia against the rusted old bulldozer— her tears, her touch, and our tender kiss.

"*Conyeshna* [of course]," I replied.

"They found his body this summer."

"Where?" I asked.

"A few days' walk from Manily."

"How did he die?" I asked.

Oleg shrugged. "No one knows. He was traveling late in season. A bad time to travel. Dimitri was strong. He thought he was a good traveler, like you and Misha. But he died because he didn't listen to the land. Probably he died in October or November, about this time of year, when the tundra was beginning to freeze. Maybe there was a blizzard and he couldn't see. Maybe he was hungry and didn't want to stop and wait for the storm to pass when he was so close to town. Dimitri was an impatient man. They found his body near a small lake. We think he walked across thin ice in a blizzard and fell through. He swam to shore, but once he was wet he would have died quickly."

Oleg waited for all of this to sink in and then continued, "When you return to make your journey, you must listen to the land. You must be patient."

We drifted in silence and I reflected that while the tundra may be a metaphor on this strange journey, it was real as well. It could kill.

Oleg grabbed the starter cord, but before he pulled the engine back to life, he turned his head and asked, "Do you have any questions?"

I took a deep breath. Oleg was standing sideways, with one hand on his beloved engine and his head turned toward me. There was a soft smile on his face. No, I didn't have any questions. I knew about death on the land, not right up close, but close enough. We all try to listen, but the line is thin sometimes and people make mistakes. Or get unlucky.

But Oleg's query seemed open-ended. Did I have any questions about life in general? I thought for a minute and realized that I only needed to follow the example that Oleg set by his quiet, honest way of life: Love your family. Earn money when you can. Find some way to eat when you have no money. Keep your machinery running—even if you don't have any spare parts. Be patient. Don't get excited when things go wrong. Don't kick your dog.

I had no questions. "*Nyet, spaciba. Panemayoo.* [No, thank you. I understand.]"

Creation

When we returned to town, I told Lydia that Sergei had recounted the Koryak creation story. Then I asked her whether white people left Vyvenka's Eden because they were stupid or they became stupid after the exodus. She told me that Sergei had the creation story wrong:

> "*When the cosmos was new, there were no people, so Etinvin, our God, made people and placed them on earth. He started off first by making the Northern People. He gave them the best, richest, and most wonderful place on the planet, right here near Vyvenka. He put salmon in the rivers, seals in the bays, and reindeer on the tundra.*

When Etinvin finished, there were many places left on the earth with no people. But he ran out of genuine parts to make people with. He asked Kutcha what he should do and Kutcha suggested that they carve some people out of wood. So Etinvin carved people out of wood. These people became the Europeans. They are stupid because they are made of wood and not genuine parts. They fight too much and they don't think about the future of the earth. They build too many machines that destroy the earth.

When all the people were finished, Etinvin looked down and saw a woman on the tundra. She was giving birth and crying in great pain. Her husband didn't know what to do, so he tried to cut the baby out of the woman's stomach with a large knife. But that made the woman and the baby dead.

Etinvin was sad and called Kutcha: "These people are new and they don't know how to live. You must fly down from the heavens and teach the people how to live."

So Kutcha gathered the people, and explained: "Women must go to the tundra. Watch the birds and see how they give birth."

The women walked out to the tundra and watched the birds laying eggs. And then they understood. They had many healthy babies and their numbers grew. But still the people did not know how to live very well. So Etinvin called Kutcha again and told him to go back down to the earth and tell the people how to live.

And Kutcha gave the following advice:

"Ocean water is full of salt and is not good to drink. Drink water from the mountains. That is the sweetest water.

"When the sun is setting, your children must not cry. They must sit near you and you must tell them stories. After the stories, the children must sleep.

"You must wake up early in the morning, especially in the spring, when the earth is waking after the winter night.

"If a child falls down, you must say, 'Stand up. Don't cry.'

"When fish swim up the river, you must have silence near the *river. The fish will have babies, so you must be quiet to respect the children.*

"If you have a headache or stomachache or other pain, you must call Kutcha and say, 'Help me.' And Kutcha will put on his raven coat and fly down from the heavens. He will spit on the place that makes the pain. Then you must push the pain through the body with one finger. Pick up the pain on the other side of the body, grab it in your hand, and say, 'Go to your mother. She lives in the darkest place in the North.' Then you must go outside and throw the pain into the wind."

Lydia concluded, "That is what Kutcha said to the people so that they know how to live."

Kutcha Pays Me a Visit

That night we celebrated Lydia's forty-sixth birthday. The guests spanned five generations, with one generation, Moolynaut's children, missing. Moolynaut was the eldest. Oleg, Lydia, Sergei, Misha, and I represented the next generation, young enough to be her grandchildren. Oleg and Lydia's children composed the fourth generation, followed by Anastasia's infant daughter, who lay squirming and smiling in a bassinette.

I was the second oldest, behind Moolynaut. I don't often think of myself as an elder, but when I do I often reflect on my first adventure abroad. I was eighteen, broke, and hitchhiking around the Middle East. I checked into a youth hostel in Istanbul. People were smoking hash; couples were having sex. I was the youngest person in the building, observing activities I had only dreamed of. Now, thirty-nine years later, I was sitting in Goshe's kitchen, still traveling, partying with my Vyvenka friends.

We feasted on cabbage, potatoes, and onion from Lydia's outdoor garden, cucumbers from her greenhouse, seagull eggs collected in June and stored in a permafrost refrigerator, hare meat from a prior successful hunt, and precious mayonnaise from the store. The television was blaring and while everyone else seemed to ignore the electronic commotion, Moolynaut stared at the screen while she ate. I tried to imagine what she was thinking. If you look at the tundra casually, from afar, it is a bland wash of rolling hills—green, yellow, or white—beneath an overpowering sky, bringing sunshine or blizzard, warmth or near death. Beauty doesn't jump out at you, like a calendar photo of the Tetons or Yosemite Valley; it is in the details, like a freeze-dried tundra cranberry offered by Angela, or a fox lurking among the hummocks, hunting mice. Moolynaut was born on this tundra and was so attuned to it that the *mukhomor* spoke to her from among the grasses and sedges. Now these swirling, spinning, rapid-fire mélanges of color and violence were reaching their not so subtle fingers into all of our consciousness.

After dinner, I asked if we could turn off the television and play a game. When everyone agreed, I blew up some balloons and we all batted them around, to much laughing and giggling.

Lydia asked me about my father's health and I told her that he was fine, alert, and engaged.

Lydia continued, "Have you tell me before that he live in New York?"

"Not in New York, Connecticut, near New York."

"Yes, I understand, in New York, right near that big house that burned and fell down when the airplanes hit it. We saw it on the television. It was very bad. The airplane crashed into the big house and there was much fire. People were jumping. And then the whole building fell. That was very bad. We were sad and worried about your father. When we saw this thing on the television, Oleg said, 'Jon must come to live in Vyvenka. It is too crazy out there in America.'"

I smiled. "But where would I live?" I asked, as if expecting that she wouldn't have an answer.

Lydia smiled. "Maybe Gecka Bay. You know this place? About fifteen kilometers south of here. You passed it in your kayak. The water is most of the time calm. There are many seals. The fishing is good. There is an old house that you could fix and live in. And you could buy a snow machine so you could come to town whenever you wanted. It is only a half-an-hour drive on a fast snow machine. You must need a rifle and some fishing net. But you could buy this thing in Petropavlovsk before you walk to Vyvenka. It is not possible to buy a good rifle in Vyvenka. Bullets, too. You have need of many bullets for the rifle."

"And Chris?"

"Oh, of course," replied Lydia, laughing. "Chris must to come, every time."

Two years ago, Moolynaut had enjoined me to return to Vyvenka be-cause "it will be good for you." I had returned, and it had opened a new and enthralling chapter in my life. I was warmed by the open generosity of Lydia's offer, but this was a step too far that I was unwilling to take.

"Thank you, Lydia. Thank you very much. I will think about this."

It was getting late, so Misha and I walked Moolynaut home, with a gift of ten kilos of rice, pickled beets, sauerkraut, sugar, honey, and macaroni. The moon was shining through lenticular clouds; puddles had frozen, thawed, and refrozen, leaving films of ice interspersed with scattered mud. The ubiq-uitous surf reverberated and echoed against the sleeping whale. Moolynaut was more hunched over than usual, clutching her broken ribs but still walk-ing at a brisk gait. When we stopped at her door to say good-bye, she asked me to take some *mukhomor* back to Chris. I told her that I would get in trouble with the American Pogranichniki and she nodded.

Then she looked straight at me with her penetrating gaze and said, "You and Misha must come back to take this walk on the tundra. That Oleg talked to you about. Maybe I will die before this time, but you must come back."

I promised her that I would and then hugged her very gently, so as not to put pressure on her injured ribs.

The next morning, Lydia, Misha, and I returned to the top of the whale's back, where I had picked berries with Angela. Lydia carefully collected branches, rejected many for defects I couldn't see, and made two crude brooms. Lydia explained that when I returned home I was to take one broom and give the other to Chris. She instructed me to walk clockwise around the inside of the house, sweeping away evil spirits, while Chris must make a counterclockwise loop. We were to meet in the middle and then Chris must sweep the evil spirits through the center of the house and out the front door while I followed behind her beating the *boubin* and chanting, "Evil spirits, go away. Go to your mother. She lives in the darkest place in the North."

Lydia made me promise solemnly that I would do this, and I agreed. We walked down the hill, encountered Oleg on the street, and continued, together, toward home. The town's orange bulldozer came clanking down the street, pulling a monstrously heavy trailer piled with scavenged wood from the Soviet apartment buildings. The trailer had two flat tires on one side, so frayed rubber flapped noisily as the bare, bent rims churned trenches in the already-rutted street. A young boy was hanging upside down on the listing side, grinning and waving.

Oleg's horse came galloping out from between two ruined buildings. This horse had always been an enigma to me. Not just that it was fat and nearly hairless in this Siberian land of frigid winters, but that it existed at all. I once asked Oleg why he bought it and he answered, "*Normal* [it's OK; don't worry about it]." Oleg is not prone to long, complex explanations about life—a lesson in itself. I asked Lydia about the horse and she spoke lovingly about her husband's inefficiencies and idiosyncrasies, completing her comment with, "Oleg saw the horse, so he bought it." I asked Sergei about the horse and he assured me that it was very strong.

"But does anyone use it?" I asked.

"*Da.*"

Then he thought for a moment and modified his affirmation with, "*Potom* [later]."

Anyway, the "*normal, potom*" horse, who usually hung around doing nothing, dashed onto the street, kicking its heels, and ran alongside the tractor.

Oleg thought that the horse was lonely and hoped that any large moving object might be another horse. Even a female horse if he was lucky.

A six-inch-high Pekinese dog came charging out from somewhere barking in a squeaky voice. The horse neighed. Lured into action by the commotion, half a dozen rough-looking husky-and-German-shepherd mutts decided that it would be a good time to rise from their private slumbers to have a rousing dogfight.

We turned the corner and went into the house for tea.

The sheer madness of it all was a temptation to take Lydia up on her offer, buy a rifle and a fish net, and move to Gecka Bay. With a wind generator I could have abundant and reliable electricity; with a satellite hookup I could enjoy occasional, albeit expensive, access to the Internet. But the temptation only lasted an instant. I'm too old to learn fluent Russian and I would always be an outsider. Chris would never agree to leave North America, and then, after a few long, dark, lonely winters, I might end up chasing a bulldozer and a trailer, like Oleg's horse, hoping it would be a woman.

The night of October 19th, the wind blew out of the north and the temperature plummeted to well below zero. We awoke the next morning before sunrise, so we could make it back to the airport in Korpf for our flight the following day. Oleg explained that the smaller ponds on the plateau would now be frozen, so he would drive us upriver in the speedboat and we could follow the shortcut across the tundra.

There's always a seminal moment in late fall when winter reaches out and announces, "Hey, Jon, old buddy. It's me, again. How'z it goin'? Snow's on its way. No more slouching around in the sun."

And I respond with, "Whoopee ding! Let's go skiing."

But this was Siberia and the cold was intense enough to reach tendrils into my sinuses and temper my ebullience. We said our good-byes but didn't see Moolynaut and walked to the lagoon where Oleg stored his boat. Platelike flakes of ice coated the beach with a delicate crystalline whiteness and wind whipped the bay into whitecaps. Oleg turned the speedboat into the wind and accelerated. Spray froze on the windshield, on the deck, and on our parkas. Lydia had wrapped my *boubin* in protective canvas, but I didn't trust the covering, so I opened my parka and slipped the *boubin* close to my body, where it would be as warm and dry as possible, under the circumstances. But with the *boubin* close to my chest I couldn't zip my parka back up, so the damp cold reached toward my core. The sun lay behind a low hill and clearly had no intention of throwing out any warmth for the next five months. As soon as we left the brackish tidal zone and motored into freshwater, the hull lurched and crunched through a half an inch of crystal-clear ice. I wiggled my toes in my boots and clenched my fingers in my mittens to keep blood flowing. The engine sound changed abruptly, Oleg quickly hit the kill button, and the boat settled into an icy slurry. A chunk of ice had lodged in the cooling system, so we waited a few moments for residual heat from the engine to melt it. Then we started up again, drove a quarter mile, waited again, and slowly inched our way northward.

I thought, "If we had waited another day, the ice would have been too thick to motor through and still too thin to walk across, and we would have been stuck in Vyvenka until freeze-up. I would have missed the bar mitzvah."

Finally, Oleg decided that he couldn't continue any farther, so he dropped us off on the north shore and gave us directions to Korpf. After the speedboat headed south, following the channel through the ice that it had just broken, Misha and I were left alone in the quiet vastness of the tundra.

I smiled and remembered the old Soviet battle cry, which we had used when launching through the surf.

"Labor and Defend."

"Yes, Jon. Labor and Defend. Many things have happened. Now we will go home and work at our offices. We will make many papers. Away from the Wild Nature. Labor and Defend. This is our last day in the Wild Nature."

We followed the riverbank until it intersected the winter road. The road was so churned up and rutted by *visdichots* that walking was difficult, but footing was even more uncertain on the tundra where skiffs of early-season soft snow had collected between the tundra hummocks. We crested a hill, enjoying the silence, absorbing and reflecting on the events of the past week. Below us, the winter road transected a large lagoon with open water in it, so we cut eastward, toward the beach. We made rapid progress on the wind-swept hilltop but encountered thick groves of waist-high elfin cedar in the arroyos as we descended. Misha got down on his hands and knees and crawled through the bushes, but the clearance was minimal and I was afraid that I would puncture the delicate skin of the *boubin* against a sharp stob. Instead, I reasoned that the gnarled trees were so densely spaced that I could half-walk and half-squirm across the top of the thicket.

I climbed the first tree, carefully balanced on my knees, and crawled a few steps, holding the *boubin* with one hand, being careful to place my weight on the thickest concentrations of sturdy branches. Emboldened, I rose to my feet, feeling like Paul Bunyan standing triumphantly on the forest canopy, wielding his magic ax. I took a step, lost my balance, ran a few steps to try to catch my toppling center of gravity, and then slipped through a weak place where needles were unsupported by branches. I heard a sharp grunt and realized that I had almost landed on Misha, who was wiggling along on his belly through a nearly impenetrable maze of unyielding trunks.

I expected a reprimand, but instead Misha laughed.

"What's so funny?" I asked.

"You are the squirrel and I am the bear."

I tried to imitate a squirrel's chatter. "And how are you doing today, Mr. Bear?"

Misha growled.

I picked a cone and coaxed out a few precious and tasty pine nuts, hoping that all the bears had gone to sleep and that they wouldn't be prowling about, looking for the same delicacy.

Town seemed far away, daylight was passing, and a bivouac would be seriously uncomfortable. But there was no other way and Misha's strategy was about as fast as mine, so we persisted until we reached the coastal plain and the soft sand beach. We walked into town after dark and spent the night with a friend of Oleg and Lydia's.

On my return flight to Japan, I was stopped again at the customs desk in Vladivostok. This time, the officer pointed at the canvas that held my *boubin*. "What is in there?" he asked.

"A drum."

He took the instrument from its case, shook it to listen to the jangles, and struck it with the black dog foreleg.

"No, this isn't a drum."

I was surprised, "It isn't a drum?" I asked incredulously.

"No. This is a *boubin*. A *boubin* and a drum are different. You cannot take this out of Russia."

We argued and he sent me upstairs to see a white-haired officer who sat behind a large desk, dressed in a neatly pressed uniform, with ribbons and gold braid on his shoulder. His English was measured and excellent.

"Sit down, please. May I see the *boubin*?"

He struck it gently. "It has the voice of a woman."

I was shocked, remembering Lydia's comment: "This *boubin* has a woman's voice, which is good, because you are a man and you need women in your life."

I didn't say anything and the officer continued, "This is a valuable cultural artifact. Our law prohibits taking cultural and spiritual artifacts out of Russia. You cannot take this home with you."

I was devastated and didn't know how to respond.

A short silence hung between us, and he continued, "You did not buy this in a store. This is not a souvenir. Where did you get this?"

His eyes were stern and penetrating and I could clearly tell that he was career military. I thought back to the woman who had hassled me on the incoming passage and realized that the officer before me didn't have to resort to antics, pounding his fist on the table and shouting, "Don't lie to me." Perhaps he had been an interrogator for the Soviets; in any case, he had the weight of empire behind him. What did he know, this officer in the army that once pushed shamans out the doors of flying helicopters?

I took a deep breath. No, a lie wasn't going to work. So where was the story that would bring my *boubin* home? Despite the military protocol, the officer knew that this *boubin* had a woman's voice? Yes, Russia is "a riddle, wrapped in a mystery, inside an enigma." It produced both Stalin and Rasputin.

So I took a chance and told the story from the beginning, with the kayak journey, the avalanche, Moolynaut, our journey across the tundra, the healing séance, and my return to thank Moolynaut. I omitted the *mukhomor*. He listened with rapt attention, no longer as an inquisitor but as a friend, and I imagined that we were sitting across a campfire, with a bottle of vodka between us.

When I finished, he smiled. "I cannot take this *boubin* away from you. It is yours."

Then he led me back downstairs and personally escorted me past the long, slow line at the customs desk.

I returned to Tokyo, to greet Chris and many members of my family. Dan's wife, Yuki, hosted us warmly in their spare but elegant apartment. When the bar mitzvah was over, Chris and I hiked around the Japanese Alps and soaked in hot springs where genius landscape architects had "cleaned up" the natural world to make it so much more orderly and placid. Then, with winter and ski season on its way, we returned to our Montana home, nestled into the pine, spruce, and fir forest of the Bitterroot mountains.

Using the brooms that Lydia made for us, I walked clockwise around the inside of the living room while Chris made a loop counterclockwise, sweeping away any evil spirits that might have penetrated our castle. We met in the middle and, as instructed, Chris solemnly swept the evil spirits through the center of the house and out the front door while I followed behind her beating the *boubin* and chanting, "Evil spirits, go away. Go to your mother. She lives in the darkest place in the North."

Then Chris followed as I walked around the house, beating the *boubin*, giving thanks for my healing and all the wonderful adventures that had transpired. The reverberating woman's voice harmonized with Chris's silent yet palpable feminine presence.

Several years before, Chris and I had built a tower against the east end of our house. This tower rises above the roofline, almost into the forest canopy. It's a small bedroom, not much larger than a child's tree house. Most of the walls and nearly the entire ceiling are encased in glass.

We climbed the narrow staircase into the tower/bedroom and sat together on the bed, enveloped in the collected sunlight. Chris leaned gently against my shoulder, reaffirming our companionship and the sexual energy that permeated our tower. I beat the *boubin*. A raven flew to a nearby branch and cawed.

I looked up and struck the *boubin* again, chanting, "Is that you? Are you Kutcha? Did Moolynaut send you? Or Oleg? Or did you watch me in the labyrinth and come of your own accord, out of sympathy for my weakness? Or in recognition of my strengths? Or are you just any old raven that lives in this Montana forest and just happened to fly past at this moment?"

The raven cawed.

"I never made it to the Other World, Kutcha. But I tried. I'm sorry. I just got scared."

The raven cawed again.

"So now you are visiting me and I can thank you in person. Thank you for healing me. Thank you for perching here on the branch above this tower. Thank you for bridging the Other World and the Real World and showing me that they are united. I hope we can meet again."

I beat on the *boubin* as rhythmically as I could.

The raven cawed a final time and flew away.

Part 4

Across the Tundra

You have noticed that everything an Indian does is in a circle, and that is because the power of the World always works in circles . . . The sky is round and I have heard that the earth is round, like a ball . . . The wind, in its greatest power, whirls. Birds make their nests in circles, for theirs is the same religion as ours . . . Even the seasons form a great circle in their changing, and always come back again to where they were.

—Black Elk, Oglala Sioux holy man

Raven

According to the Northwest coast Tlingit mythology, Raven created the pea pod, which, in turn, gave birth to humans. According to the Haida, ravens created the oceans and routinely transform themselves into human form. In Australian mythology, Raven created death so he could make love to widowed women. While many aboriginal myths recognize that Raven may cause problems for humans, there is almost always an element of intelligence, coupled with fanciful trickery and a playful sense of humor. In one Inuit story, several young men and one beautiful woman were visiting in a large igloo. All of the men lusted after the woman, but Raven plotted his own, unique seduction:

> After all the men went to sleep, the raven melted feces and put it in the girl's pants. He woke her up and she saw that he was going to tell all the men that she had dirt in her pants. He will tell all this if she doesn't get married to him. So finally she marries Raven. Then she becomes pregnant and they had a baby boy.[1]

If you assume that the raven is an embodiment of nature, then this myth reminds us that the natural world sometimes "puts feces in our pants."

But animistic religions make it clear that lowly, puny humans shouldn't be disturbed by this mischief.

> *One day, an older Raven was flying far over the man, and dropped a walnut perfectly on the man's head. It was done on purpose and all the Ravens almost fell off their branches laughing so hard the way they do. . . .*
>
> *The man was feeling bad and was hurt by being made fun of, so he asked the Raven . . . , "Why are you all picking on me."*
>
> *The Raven stopped laughing and became very serious. "We thought you understood us, but apparently you don't. If you did you would know that we are not mocking you . . . well maybe a bit, but it is done in our way of having fun. We are 'playing' with you and that is all. It is not to be taken seriously. You should know us better."[2]*

Again the message is clear: Ravens may drop walnuts on your head, storms may batter your canoe, blizzards may scatter your reindeer, but lighten up; nature is "'playing' with you and that is all. It is not to be taken seriously." The myth doesn't offer any advice on how to control the forces of nature; instead there is a clear missive to laugh at misfortune and move on with life.

In contrast, among the Europeans, Nature, as embodied by the Raven, is often a harbinger of unmitigated foreboding. During the witch craze in medieval Europe, ravens were demons. To Edgar Allan Poe, the raven is a

> *"thing of evil!—prophet still, if bird or devil!*
> *Whether Tempter sent, or whether tempest tossed thee here ashore,*
> *Desolate yet all undaunted, on this desert land enchanted—"*

A few stanzas later, Poe begs:

> *"Get thee back into the tempest and the Night's Plutonian shore!*
> *Leave no black plume as a token of that lie thy soul hath spoken!*

Leave my loneliness unbroken!—quit the bust above my door!
Take thy beak from out my heart, and take thy form from off my door!"
Quoth the Raven, "Nevermore."

Poe wants Raven-Nature, and all the associated evil, out of his life, to "quit the bust above my door! . . . and take thy form from off my door!" He never seeks communality, never attempts to opens a spiritual connectivity with either the storm or the messenger from the tempest-tossed shore. There is no playfulness, no sense that storms, Raven, Nature, fate itself, is just playing a practical joke, which is "not to be taken seriously." Poe's poem is beautiful, but once you fear and demonize nature you open the philosophical floodgates for the bulldozer and the chain saw.

Regardless of whether you view Raven as a messenger of darkness or a playful trickster, both aboriginal and Western folklore are filled with accounts of raven intelligence. Many of these accounts even imply that ravens have a special bond with people. In one story, a hermit living in a remote forest cabin steps outside and a raven flies in his face, cawing loudly. The man looks up and sees a cougar lying in wait, about to spring on him. The man thanks the raven for saving his life.[3]

Scientists tend to discount anecdotes, but controlled laboratory experiments prove that ravens are inordinately intelligent. In one experiment, two ravens, Betty and Able, were housed in a large outdoor aviary. Scientists put food in a small bucket, which was lowered into a glass cylinder. They then placed several straight wires and one bent wire next to the cylinder. The birds flew to the edge of the cylinder and attempted to reach the food with their beaks, but it was too deep inside the cylinder. The ravens stepped back and surveyed the tools provided for them. Within a few moments, Betty picked up the bent wire, reached into the cylinder, hooked the bucket handle, and retrieved the food. The next day, Able picked up the hooked wire, flew away, and hid it from Betty. Nonplussed, Betty grasped a straight wire in her beak, held the other end under her foot, and bent the wire into a hook. Then, with her manufactured tool, she retrieved the food and feasted, without sharing any with selfish Able.[4]

This experiment illustrates not only that ravens use and even manufacture tools but also that they engage in complex social interactions, including deception—just like humans. Two raven researchers, Bernd Heinrich and Thomas Bugnyar, conclude that the intelligence of ravens "appear to be on a par with, or exceed, that of great apes," and "these tendencies may have allowed it [the raven] to become the most widely distributed bird in the world, inhabiting the same continents as humans and being at home in as many diverse habitats."[5]

In the Arctic, bears, hares, ptarmigan, and owls all camouflage themselves in white, the color of winter. But Raven, saucy, strident, and supremely confident, remains clothed in black.

When I try to explain why the raven perched above the tower at that instant in time, I collide with the same dilemma that I face when I try to understand how my pelvis was healed. Magic or coincidence? Should I just ignore the explanations and start believing? Or pretend that all these events weren't that unusual anyway?

I can't answer any of these questions, but I'm proud and happy to count Raven as one of my friends. Raven knows how to laugh, complain, joke, and play. He has created enough free time in his life to hang out on fence posts and shoot the shit with his buddies.

Fourth Journey to Vyvenka

Chris was surprised that I was intent on planning a fourth expedition. When we sat on the couch together and she asked me to explain, I told her that I felt like I was living inside a narrative and I was too curious—or fascinated—to put the book down. There were hints about the outcome, but these clues were interlaced with vagaries and innuendo and a sense that more input was needed. Clearly, I had to return to Kamchatka.

It was Oleg, the hunter, who told me that I was a lousy traveler in the spirit world, so I had to make my journey in this world. Oleg may not have known it, but he was following an ancient tradition in offering this sugges- tion. Jesus sought deprivation and enlightenment in the desert. Perhaps Oleg would more closely identify with Igjugarjuk, a Greenlandic shaman who said: ". . . solitude and suffering open the human mind, and therefore a man must seek his wisdom there. . . ."[1]

I had failed to penetrate the labyrinth and cross the portal into the Other World and had failed to thank Kutcha directly. But more than that, I never clearly understood who Kutcha was, how I would recognize or thank him, and what would happen if and when I did. But I knew how to journey across the tundra, where Misha and I would assuredly encounter what Igjugarjuk proposed: "suffering through hunger and suffering through cold." In Koryak spirituality, gods are Nature and Nature is God, so if I wanted to thank somebody for something I could speak directly with the tundra.

In the past, I had always planned expeditions with a goal in mind, some adventure hook that would convince sponsors to ante up money, airplane tickets, or gear. I'm not sure what Chris thought and don't remember exactly what she said, though she looked at me quizzically. Maybe Chris was born with the equanimity and understanding that I was so dutifully seeking. In Chris's perception of the world, skis were for sliding downhill. She had wan- dered around the tundra with me once, on snow too flat to whoopee-ding on and that was fun while it lasted, but she saw no reason to return. I could go trudge around the tundra if I wanted to; she would stay home and slide around on spring snow in our beloved mountains.

Through a few phone calls and a sporadic e-mail exchange, Misha and I decided that we should start in Vyvenka and ski north to Pevek, on the Arctic coast. The straight-line distance was seven hundred miles, but our route meandered along river valleys and through mountain passes. We had no real reason to go to Pevek, no spice islands or gold mines at the end of the rainbow. Siberia is so big that any goal is arbitrary, but I fixated on Pevek because it was the last bastion of land before the North Pole. It was also Dimitri's destination and perhaps we owed it to his memory to complete the passage.

I arrived in Kamchatka on March 14, 2004. We were scheduled to fly to Korpf/Tillichiki on March 18, but there was a warm storm to the north, bringing heavy snowfall mixed with rain, and our flight was canceled. The storm broke two days later, but a new problem arose. As Misha explained, "In Korpf, there is many ice on the road that the plane comes down to. They have not special machine to make this ice go away."

He paused. "Actually, they have this special machine, but it not working." Another pause. "Crashed. You understand?"

"I understand."

For emphasis, Misha continued, "Finished."

I understood.

The next day, Misha learned that the special machine wasn't crashed after all. But the machine operator was crashed, or gone hunting, or watching television, or distilling vodka, or whatever.

We finally flew on March 24th, after a six-day delay. As the plane touched down, I saw pools of water glistening on the runway, mud in the streets. Warmth was our enemy because we needed frozen rivers and hard snow to travel on. Oleg and Sergei were supposed to meet us with snow machines, but they hadn't arrived. The electricity was out of service in Vyvenka and the phones didn't work, so we had no communication. A toothless old woman told us that snow machines couldn't travel because the snow was too soft: "Your friends will come when the cold returns."

We had a hard freeze overnight and Sergei showed up with his snow machine in the morning. Four hours later we drove down the main street of Vyvenka and I exhaled a long, slow sigh of relief. Lydia raced out with a shovel of red-hot coals, gave me a hug and a kiss on the lips, then pulled a piece of wool from my hat and burned it in the coals, chanting a brief prayer in Koryak.

I apologized for showing up a week late and at first Lydia seemed confused by my apology. Then she giggled and assured me that there is no such concept as "being late."

She ushered us into her apartment and served borscht, boiled potatoes, and cucumber fish. Little Angela stood shyly to the side and blushed when

I thanked her for protecting me after I ate the *mukhomor* during my last visit. Lydia, who hadn't seen any visitors all winter, started talking in a fast monologue, linking news, stories, ideas, and spiritual lessons together without obvious transitions:

"Moolynaut was ill last winter. She tried to transfer all her power to me, but there were too many ideas in Moolynaut's mind and I couldn't understand or learn all of them."

I reflected, "Yes, you spent your formative years in a Soviet school, sitting on a chair, in front of a desk, lined up in a neat row inside a rectangular room, learning letters, which are just squiggles on a piece of paper—an abstract of the thing and not the thing itself. This is Stalin's enduring legacy, but it is also the background and legacy for nearly everyone who lives in the twenty-first century. Your mind was molded so Moolynaut can never transfer her power to you, and my mind was molded in the same way, and so was Misha's. When the old grandmother dies, two million years of accumulated wisdom, insight, and intuition will pass into the ground with her."

Lydia continued in a non sequitur, as if the previous thought were trivial—or too painful to dwell on. "My daughter Irene, who studies medical technology in Khabarovsk, had a dream that Kamchatka will fall into the ocean in 2012. Moolynaut agrees. She tells us that humans live on a one-million-year cycle of Utopia to Chaos. During Utopia, each person has a house, a garden, lots of family all around, plenty to eat, and abundant firewood. During times of Chaos, people fight too much. Europeans are wooden-headed people because they fight too much and they are on a low point of the cycle."

Lydia paused and added, "Maybe Chaos is creeping into the North, because a lot of people have become alcoholic and some men beat their wives."

I looked over her shoulder at a perfect pink rosebud growing in a pot near the coal-dust-streaked window. Chaos or Utopia, magic or nonsense, the rose was a tangible physical object, symbolic of Lydia's personal effort to create a happy home here in northeast Siberia, within the political and economic chaos that surrounded her.

Angela climbed onto my lap.

Lydia continued, "This was a good fishing year. The men caught three thousand tons of salmon and each person made seventy thousand rubles or more. Goshe drank vodka all winter and now he's in a treatment center in Korpf."

I heard the sound of Oleg's snow machine, recognizable by its smooth purr, and soon Oleg and his son, Volvo, burst in. Volvo was eleven years old now, traveling with the men, who had been gathering birch to make new sled runners.

Oleg greeted us with a warm smile. We had traveled together, sat through storm days in a tent, and now I had returned to Vyvenka because he had told me that I must make my travels in this world. Our friendship was cemented.

We had all spent a hard, cold day on the land, so we sat down to eat. By 7:30 it was starting to get dark and the electricity still wasn't working, so we went to bed early.

Moolynaut's House

The next morning, Lydia burned a piece of baleen in the *petchka* for good luck. Then she dipped rabbit fur in butter and threw it into the fire, for the traveling spirits. When her incantations were finished, she announced that Moolynaut would like to see us. Previously Moolynaut had come to Goshe's or Lydia's home, but for the first time she had invited us into her home. Moolynaut lived a hundred yards away, in another nondescript wood and masonry building with tar-paper siding and a corrugated metal roof.

Bright sunshine reflected off the snow, assuring us that spring was well advanced, but the seasonal cold was returning, and the mud and slush had frozen into ruts and ridges in Vyvenka's main street. As Misha, Lydia, and I walked into Moolynaut's yard, her tethered dogs looked up and wagged their tails but laid their heads back down sleepily when they realized that we didn't have any food and we weren't about to harness them for a run across the tundra. We opened the front door and stepped into an unheated, unlit vestibule. I was blinded by the sudden darkness but stimulated by pungent animal fragrances of traveling and hunting—the smell of fur clothing, dried fish, seal fat, and deer-hide harnesses. Lydia opened the inner door without knocking and ushered us into a dark cavelike room. I stopped to let my eyes and nose adjust, hoping that colors would emerge as my vision cleared. The walls consisted of gray, unpainted masonry, lit only by one small window smeared with coal dust. A wooden table, bleached white with age, was positioned next to the window, and three rickety stools, without backs, surrounded the table. A tiny open cupboard, barely larger than a shoe box, held four cups, five saucers, three plates, and a small pile of bent, twisted, pitted silverware. A few cloth bags of food were stacked in one corner and dried fish hung from a bent nail. No one had stoked the fire in the *petchka* for several hours, and it emitted only feeble warmth. I half-expected to see emaciated, broken prisoners scurrying in the corners, hunting rats. But quite to the contrary, I felt love, power, and happiness ensconced in all this poverty.

Suddenly I realized that I hardly knew Moolynaut, this woman who had healed me. Yet I had returned, and she was waiting, with the calm demeanor of an older woman who had once been a young girl who had herded reindeer.

Moolynaut was in a small room, about six feet square, off to the side, with a large south-facing window. The sunlight beamed on the old woman's face, and I felt as if I had left the gulag and entered a medieval cathedral. She was dressed in a bright red flowered shirt and scarf, kneeling on a blanket that was folded across the wooden floor. The walls had been whitewashed sometime in the distant past, but there was no furniture. Moolynaut was intently studying a small piece of intricately carved wood, about the size and shape of a cribbage board, but she quickly set it aside as soon as we entered.

"I am very glad to see you. You have come so far to visit us."

We returned her salutation and sat next to her, cross-legged on the blanket, close, intimate in the small space, warmed by dusty rays of spring sunshine.

"You are going first to the reindeer camp?" she asked. " Where you went before?"

"*Da.*"

"Ah . . . ah . . . I lived with deer all my life. My father had deer and my grandfather had many deer. But now we have none. We had eight hundred deer in Vyvenka in January . . . What year was that, Lydia?"

"Nineteen ninety-eight."

"Yes, in that year we had eight hundred deer in Vyvenka. Then in the spring, people sold meat to the Russians. Sometimes the Russians stole deer. One day wolves killed twenty-one deer. They ate only the tongues. By autumn we had only fifteen deer. Then, in early winter, a blizzard came. All the herders were drinking vodka. The deer ran away. We never found them. Now we have no deer."

She paused. "It is good that you are going to a place where there are deer. I am too old. If I were not so old, I would go with you."

She paused again. "But someday the deer will come back. They will come from the south. Maybe I will be alive on that day . . . but maybe not."

I couldn't think of anything to say, so we sat in the sunshine. I shifted my weight because my ankles were rubbing against the hard floor.

Then Moolynaut started talking, bouncing from subject to subject with the combined clarity and disjointedness of an elder. Misha translated.

"You and Misha must have no need for worry. You will be safe in your journey. The rivers will be all the time frozen. You will travel quickly.

"If you meet with a bear or a wolf, you must without fear say to him, 'You must not hurt me because I am a man and you are an animal. God looks to both you and me.'

"If you have an open fire you must put in some fat and say for Kutcha, 'You must keep us safe from wild animals.' When I was a little girl I go with our father to the tundra and meet two small bears. My father have many dogs. The dogs may kill the bears. But Father says to dogs not to kill the bears. Then Father says to bears, 'You must run away. But in the future you must remember that I did not hurt you. Now you must not hurt or kill my daughter if you see her on the tundra.' That is the way you must talk to all animals and they will not hurt you."

Moolynaut paused, as if worn out by all the memories, all the talking. Then she seemed confused.

"Where are you going?" she asked, as if we hadn't told her before.

"Ah, Chukotka. You are going to Chukotka. It is far away. One day, many years ago, my father went to Chukotka by dogsled. He took my sister and left her in Chukotka. She married a man in Chukotka and she never came back. Make this journey in memory of my sister. In memory of our ancestors."

Then Moolynaut waved her hand, as if she was tired by all the memories. She picked up her small board and rocked back and forth, singing to it or with it, I couldn't tell. Lydia motioned for us to leave.

Return to Nikolai's Camp

When we returned to Goshe's, Oleg told us that the snow, which had been soft when we arrived, was almost firm enough to support a snow machine. That night the temperature dropped to zero degrees Fahrenheit.

The next morning, three snow machines pulled up in front of Goshe's, driven by Oleg, Sergei, and another man, with a thick, bushy beard, also named Sergei. Oleg sheepishly announced that the second Sergei wanted to come and asked if I would mind feeding him and buying a little more gas. I nodded and everyone smiled, obviously relieved. The second Sergei had already gassed up and I handed him some worn ruble notes to pay for his fuel.

Misha and I walked to the edge of town and stepped into our skis. Even though Lydia had assured us that no one is ever "late," seasons progress and our travel would become much more difficult, and dangerous even, after the snow and river ice melted. Due to the storms, we were leaving later than we had planned. We had a long journey ahead of us, and therefore we were motivated to move quickly. Misha and I could expect plenty of silence and exercise on the trail to Pevek, so we asked Oleg and Sergei to tow us to Niko-lai's. I picked up the rope behind Sergei's machine. The snow had thawed and frozen until it was rock hard, and as we bounced up the first grade I absorbed the shock in my legs.

I leaned against the towrope, feeling the wind in my face and the sensa-tion of motion. For those who love to travel, motion is like a familiar place, a warm kitchen aromatic with the smell of baking bread, where the brain relaxes because this is where it wants to be.

Moolynaut grew up as a tundra nomad, crisscrossing this land by dog and reindeer sled and living in a skin *yuranga*. The tent, like almost every-thing else in her life, was made of reindeer. Skin walls spoke to her and she spoke back to them. When the Soviets severed Moolynaut's emotional and spiritual connectivity with her home, she never fully adjusted. If some Rus-sian reality-show home-improvement TV host swooped into her gulaglike kitchen with paint, potted roses, silk tablecloths, and crystal chandeliers, it wouldn't make much difference. She had left the tundra eighty years ago and decorations could never lift the lifelong exile.

My weight was centered firmly on my skis, and my body articulated painlessly on my pelvis. When we crested the hill, Sergei looked back and flashed a thumbs-up. I grinned and returned the thumbs-up, and he accel-erated until I was bouncing, occasionally airborne, over bumps and wind-driven *strastugi*.

Even though Vyvenka is a remote outpost, with few amenities, it felt urban and confined compared to the broad tundra, clothed in white, spread-ing toward infinity in all directions. The Arctic wilderness removed all boundaries, inside and out. Words flew away without hitting their intended targets, and worries had no walls to reverberate against. The cold wind in my face seemed to exorcise personality, history, past accomplishments, and fail-ures. All that was left was me and my pain-free pelvis, skiing on crusty snow.

My home in Montana is infinitely more colorful and cozy than Moolynaut's, but according to the norms of my society, I am egregiously neglectful of interior decorating. In this small way, Moolynaut and I share a commonality. For both of us, strength lies in the tundra. Maybe I couldn't understand all of her words, but that didn't matter. I had come out here to thank Kutcha, and if Kutcha didn't reveal himself, I could thank the hard, frozen, forbidding but tangible landscape. The snow spoke to me through my skis in a familiar tactile way, and I felt comforted that snow, one of my totem spirits, was right beneath my feet, where I could always find it, created and continuously altered by the cycle of the seasons. For the next month or two, my life depended on communication with the tundra and on understanding the narrative that would unfold every second in the sky, the snow, and the inexorable progressions of the seasons. Life was simultaneously precarious, complicated, and simple.

This was the first morning of the first day of a long journey across a cold and dangerous place. Dimitri had died here. Misha and I expected to encounter people, but not many, and soon our friends would return to Vyvenka and we would be totally dependent on each other.

We reached the Holy Stone in a few hours and stopped to rest and pay homage to the ancestors, the gods, and the landscape. I left a small icon I had bought during a climbing expedition in Nepal and then sat apart from the others to soak in the spring sunshine. A year ago, Simon told me that no one lived on the tundra near here or traveled across it on foot anymore and as a result, people weren't giving energy to the stone, so the stone was losing its power to heal and to protect the people. That statement was one of those mysteries I would never understand, but I knew that I had come here to experience the joy and suffering of this tundra, on a mysterious, maybe even crazy, mission to thank a Spirit Raven for healing my pelvis, whatever that meant. I wasn't going to understand or explain my healing, but through the tundra I might assimilate some element of Moolynaut's ancient wisdom and offer my energy to wild landscapes so I could draw strength from them when I needed it.

My reverie was interrupted by the sound of engines, and when I looked up, Oleg signaled that it was time to go. We traveled steadily throughout the late morning and afternoon. On exposed ridgetops, the snow was hard, crisscrossed by frozen *strastugi*, and Misha and I struggled to keep our balance as we bounced along behind the snow machines. When we dipped into hollows and creek bottoms, the snow was soft and rotten, making travel difficult. Misha and I both fell on occasion. The snow machines got stuck. There was no need for us to ask each other, "Are you all right?" "May I help you?" We were a team, traveling hard. Everyone knew the drill.

When we crossed a low pass and dropped into the next valley, most of the snow had melted or blown away in the recent storm, revealing a patchwork of bare ground. The men turned off their machines, but the memory of the roar reverberated in my eardrums and the smell of exhaust lingered in the guard hairs of my sinuses. The evening sun hung low in the southwest, beckoning us to make camp.

I stepped out of my skis and shook my legs to loosen cramped, stiff muscles. Sergei grinned, "*Oostal* [tired]?"

"*Da. Ochen oostal.* [Yes, very tired.]"

"You should be; we've gone one hundred and seventy kilometers [about one hundred miles] already."

I whistled. It was a long way to be towed behind a snow machine on hard, windblown snow. It was late and we had already traveled as far today as we traveled in eight days on our last journey. "Let's make camp and eat dinner," I said.

But for some reason, Oleg didn't want to make camp—and he *was* the captain of this expedition. Sergei started his machine. I wearily stepped back into my skis and picked up the towrope. We traveled about twenty yards across snow and then Sergei's machine bounced across bare tundra, small sticks spewing out the drive wheel of the track, as if it were a lawn mower. I was five yards behind the sled and thought, "Surely he'll slow down when my skis reach bare ground."

But he didn't. I half-sprinted, half-stumbled across the grass until we hit snow again. Sergei looked back and grinned. And so we continued into the evening. Sergei expected that every time we encountered bare ground I could draw on reserves of explosive energy and sprint like an NFL receiver, on skis, even though I had been bouncing behind the snow machine for twelve long hours. After a few miles, I crashed, landed hard, and lay on the ground, smelling sedge and willow, thinking that if I looked pitiful enough, Oleg would sympathize and make camp.

With an aura of disappointment at my obvious weakness, he finally took pity on me and told me to ride on the sled. Misha toughed it out, though, managed to stay on his feet, and continued on skis.

We pitched the tent in the dark, and during dinner the hirsute Sergei told many jokes, but no one laughed and Misha didn't bother to translate.

In the morning, I took a GPS reading and told everyone that we had traveled one degree of latitude yesterday. Oleg looked at me, deep in thought. "How many degrees is it from the South Pole to the North Pole?"

"A hundred eighty," I answered.

Oleg smiled. "I have lived my whole life in the small village of Vyvenka. I always thought that the world was very big. But it's not really. If there was enough snow, and if you bought the gas, I could travel around the whole world in one year."

We reached the geology camp at noon the following day, but tattered roofing rattled in the wind and drifts ramped to the eaves. There were no people or even comforting signs of recent habitation—wood chips on the snow, dog shit along the trail, or the smell of smoke. Gold was still locked in crystals imbedded in the rock beneath our feet, but the humans weren't here to crunch, maim, and grind it out of the earth. At 4:00 P.M. we reached Nikolai's camp, but it, too, was abandoned. No dogs barked; no friendly faces appeared; no reindeer grazed nearby. We stepped clear of the machines wearily and felt the wind blowing across the otherwise quiet landscape, rustling bits of bare grass and rattling loosened windowpanes.

Oleg appeared visibly disappointed and he must have been hungry, because he hadn't eaten all day, but he quickly regained his composure, saying "*Payette, normal*," meaning, "Fine, OK," or, by implication, "I'm accustomed to disappointment; I've learned to live with it."

The door to the herders' house was latched with a string and a stick, so we let ourselves in and built a fire. The building was dark and cold, smelling of furs, with frost clinging to walls and ceiling. Kitchenware was neatly stacked on a few wooden shelves, and the table and stools were arranged as if someone expected to return. We dug into a snowbank to find a firewood stash and stoked the sheet-metal stove until it glowed red.

Sergei cooked a huge dinner of noodles and kielbasa. After the meal, we relaxed with tea and the hirsute Sergei broke the silence with one of his stories.

"Early in the morning, a few months ago, one of the men in our village was walking on the tundra with his dog. The sun had just risen and was still low on the horizon. There was a bear between the man and the sun. Bears are smart; they know how to hunt. The bear stalked the man because he knew that the man was blinded by the sun. When the man heard footsteps in the snow, he turned, but it was too late. The bear swatted him in the chest, breaking several ribs and knocking him down. The bear lunged and the man struck back, using his rifle as a club. Before the bear could strike a second blow, the man's dog bit the bear in the hind leg. The bear wheeled, giving the man enough time to chamber a bullet and shoot.

"When the man returned home, he was in great pain because of his ribs, but he had no money to buy vodka, so he shot the dog and sold its skin to buy vodka."

I waited for the narrative to continue, that was the end.

"Is this true?" I asked.

Oleg nodded. "Yes, it is. Vodka is very bad for our people."

Misha explained in English, "Most of the times, we visit in Vyvenka with Moolynaut, Lydia, Oleg, and Sergei. They are happy. But many bad things happen in Vyvenka. Many people drink vodka. Sometimes men and women kill themselves. This is very bad. This man who kills at his dog, he is not a bad man, but bad things comes to this man because he wants so much the vodka. Vodka is bad for all of Russia."

Oleg interrupted in Russian and the two men talked. Then Misha continued, "Oleg tell at me that it is not good to talk about this things. We have many difficultness ahead. Many long traveling. We must think about the tundra and about Kutcha. Maybe now we sleep."

Evening with the Herders

The morning sun hung low and red on the southern horizon, as if reluctant to crawl out of its cozy sleeping bag, face the cold, and go outside for a pee. The three Koryak men gassed up their machines to return to Vyvenka. We said a casual good-bye, as if parting for a day of fishing, and then the machines roared off. Misha and I waited for the exhaust and noise to dissipate into the vastness. In one sense we were "behind schedule" due to the storms and the delayed airplane and therefore "in a hurry" to reach Pevek before the snow and river ice melted. Those terms were poignant with respect to the success of our expedition and even to our survival, but emotionally they held no weight right now.

We drank another cup of tea, and then, when we couldn't procrastinate any longer, we loaded our sleds, strapped the sled harnesses around our waists and shoulders, and clasped hands briefly as a sign of solidarity. I swung forward at the waist to break the sled free and then took my first few steps. The sled pulled easily over a firm crust that scratched under my skis. A fierce headwind blew from the north, bringing cold air from the North Pole and the Arctic Ocean. My eyes shed tears in the wind, so I stopped and put on goggles.

Instantly all those mini-adventures, delays, and inconveniences morphed into a series of paltry trifles contrasted with the task ahead. Soon I would dream of the opulence of my economy Aeroflot seat, with the scrumptious meals, the silent camaraderie of the fat man, snoring and the relaxing, familiar cadence of *Pirates of the Caribbean*.

I was on a crazy mission either to ski to a small Arctic port that few people had ever heard of or to thank Kutcha the messenger, who glided on black outstretched wings between the Real World and the Other World— or something like that. I half-hoped that he would swoop over us and say hello, but that was too much to ask, so I refused to be disappointed when he failed to show up. Right now, it didn't matter where I was going or why I was out here; both my physical and spiritual survival hinged on the three attributes of my new mantra: mindfulness, curiosity, and observation. Even though the landscape appeared monotonous, I must live within the wondrous complexity of its subtle changes. Remember Dimitri. No hubris. Don't get wet. Don't do anything stupid.

After a mile, Misha and I dropped into another willow-infested creek bottom and the sleds bogged down in soft wind-deposited snow. The traces tangled in the dense brush and my sled tipped over as I impatiently jerked it across a log. It took us half an hour to progress a hundred yards, but we resumed normal walking speed as soon as we regained the exposed, wind-blown tundra. Grasses and sedges poked through the thin snowpack, forming splotches of yellow against white. On the horizon, these bare patches were foreshortened so they seemed to stack together and it appeared as if there were no snow at all. The sun rose and snow melted along the edge of the vegetation. This was bad. We needed snow to slide across. I understood the folly of my white man's propensity to count and measure, but we were, indeed, "behind schedule" and "in a hurry" to travel north.

That afternoon, we followed faint ski tracks to a small *serei*, aromatic with the pungency of reindeer skin, meat, and fat. The camp belonged to the clan we had visited in 2001 and whose house we stayed in last night. The brigadier, Nikolai, who had befriended us, was now in Manily, leaving the deer and only four adult herders in the camp. A young woman cooked while cradling her young baby.

In 2001 we had felt a vibrancy and enthusiasm in camp. At that time there were 800 deer and the tribe hoped to increase the herd to 2,000. But now, three years later, there were only 840 deer. One of the herders, Vladimir, explained that they were caught in a vicious, negative spiral. At best, herding is hard work for little money. Increasingly the young people leave the camps and seek easier, higher-paying jobs in the cities and on the fishing boats. But then there aren't enough herders to care for the deer properly. Right now, with the birthing season imminent, they had only two young men to guard the animals. With them short staffed, it was impossible to protect the reindeer from marauding wolves, who ate up most of the potential profits. So they were poor. So young men had no incentive to join the brigade and herd reindeer.

Vladimir concluded despondently, "The brigade is dying. No money. It's a boring life. No dancing, no music, no women. No doctors. It's almost time for spring festival. My grandparents tell me that in the olden days the whole tribe would go to the Holy Stone, where they would meet with other tribes. There would be partying, romance, excitement, companionship, wrestling, dogsled and reindeer races. Now we are the last herding brigade in the area. There is no gathering at the Holy Stone. The Holy Stone is dying. We are alone and dying."

Sergei the elder smoked a pipe and listened quietly to Vladimir's complaints. Then Sergei asked about our expedition. I felt a little embarrassed, even on the edge of being crazy, when I tried to verbalize what we were doing. It was OK to talk about this venture with Misha and my friends in Vyvenka, who were partners in crime, so to speak, but even my dear wife, Chris, had raised her eyebrows when I tried to explain what I was up to. This man was a perfect stranger. I took a deep breath and told him that Moolynaut had healed my pelvis in 2001 and we were making this journey to understand the nature of her power and to thank Kutcha for his part in the healing.

Sergei puffed on his pipe thoughtfully. "It is hard to understand where power comes from. You will not find the answer, but you are looking in the right place."

After a pause, he continued, "Oleg is right; ultimately power comes from the tundra. When the Soviets took our young people away from the tundra and forced them to forget the old language and the old ways and live in Russian schools, we lost our way. I know this. I spent my childhood in a

Russian school. Maybe, now, Moolynaut is the only Koryak left alive who has real power.

"A few years ago, there were three very old Koryak women who had grown up on the tundra, before the Soviets, and still remembered the healing of the old ways. One lived in Manily and she died quietly a few years ago. Another lived in Magadan, farther south. Before she died, she tried to pass her power on to someone else. No one could learn because no one had grown up on the tundra. When this woman was very old and sick, she walked out into the forest and put her hands around a tree. She said, 'My power came from the land and I return it to the land. Tree, take my power.' And the power went out of the woman and into the tree. The tree exploded and the woman died. Now Moolynaut is the only one left."

We all sat in silence until Sergei broke the reverie by asking me what I did for a living. I explained that I was a writer. Sergei asked if I would write about my experiences here in Kamchatka and I said that I planned to, if the Koryak people didn't object.

Sergei responded, "No, we don't object. That is good. It is good if people in your land learn about the Koryak on this land."

I nodded because I knew he was right.

Journey to Talovka

The next morning the temperature was twenty below Fahrenheit and the north wind raged. We donned goggles, pulled our hoods tightly around our faces, and headed toward Pevek. In some ideal but nonexistent never-never land of Arctic travel, there must be a smooth, undulating field of spring-hardened snow, where sleds slide effortlessly across the vastness. But here we never encountered joyous, unfettered travel, muscles stretching in long strides, the mind drifting in the vastness because it wasn't needed in the practiced repetition of walking. Instead, we bashed through shoulder-high thickets of willow and elfin cedar and then scraped our sleds across exposed grass, dirt, and rocks. It was impossible to talk because the wind blew the words back into our throats and then chased them down our alveoli, like a junkyard dog making sure they'd never climb over the fence. Misha and I walked side by side, close but isolated, each nesting inside the few centimeters of tenuous warmth that lay between our bodies and our clothing.

We were headed toward the Arctic Ocean or toward a rendezvous with Kutcha—both destinations seemed about equally obtuse.

A whirlwind swept snow into a small funnel cloud that washed our faces in swirling whiteness before it raced off, dancing erratically across the empty plain. The spindrift melted against my face, carrying some of my urban, left-brain rationality off to that distant land where urban left-brain rationality resides. Whatever happened, or didn't happen, because of Moolynaut, I saw a glimmer of the potential of an unencumbered right brain. I saw it again in the labyrinth, and I had seen it in the avalanche—roiling in the mayhem between life and death. Those experiences changed my life, forever, and for the better. Now I was out here—ostensibly to thank Kutcha but really to open my mind by "suffering through hunger and suffering through cold." But that wasn't really right, either. It seems strange that in an urban world, with a warm house and the assurance that there will be food on the table tomorrow, I frequently fill my head with worry. Out here on the tundra, where life is so fragile, surrounded by cold, hardship, hunger, and immensity of space, I find it easy to sweep the cobwebs out of the brain with Lydia's magic broom and exorcise them with her incantation: "Evil spirits, go away. Go to your mother. She lives in the darkest place in the North." And when the fur-clad, hunched-over evil spirits trudge off through the snow, what is left is a peaceful oneness with all that space.

Many of my Koryak friends had assured me that I could never experience the world as Moolynaut does, because I hadn't grown up on the tundra. But insight isn't binary, on or off. Moolynaut's gift wasn't merely healing my pelvis. Maybe her largest gift was bringing me back repeatedly to Vyvenka, where I learned to accept, cherish, and follow that right-brain, nonverbal voice that was always inside. And now, as I shivered against the cold and the sled harness chafed against my shoulders, I was reaching for a power within me that is released by wild landscapes—even though I was absolutely certain I would never grasp it as firmly as Moolynaut had.

We followed a narrow streambed into the mountains and then climbed a U-shaped swale leading toward a low pass. Late in the afternoon, we stood at the summit looking northward at a broad system of river valleys and swamps that stretched largely unbroken for 350 miles until it collided with mountains that guarded the Arctic Ocean. Our bodies were vibrating in the intense wind, like twigs and grasses poking out of the snow, waiting for summer.

The landscape below us was glorious in its immensity but sobering in the details. Wind had blown almost all the snow off the tundra, leaving a broad, dun-colored plain. There was no way we could drag our sleds over bare dirt.

But, with no other alternative, we turned our sleds around and lowered them, stern first, down a steep brushy hillside to a tributary of the Talovka River. It was nearly dark. Wind-deposited snow had collected in the lee of the riverbank, so we dug a cozy nook into the drift and pitched our tent.

The next morning, we loaded our sleds and climbed the bank to plot a course toward the town of Talovka. For the next few hundred yards, there was no snow on the tundra. None. Zero, zip, zilch. Wind rustled two-inch-tall birch trees and shook the freeze-dried seed pods that clung tenuously to the grasses and sedges. Frostbite nipped my chin and cheeks. The tundra was snow covered to the west, against the mountains, and I suggested that we make a long detour to find easy traveling. Misha shook his head: "That is not the Russian way. In Russia we go straight. We do not travel west just to find an easy way. You are in Russia now." It seemed silly to me, skiing over bare ground, pulling a reluctant sled, in a wintry wind. But I was in Russia now.

The sleds scraped over rocks and caught on every twig. Pulling the sled was like trying to coax my dog from the car into the hated veterinarian clinic. At every step, all four paws, claws out, reached forward, scratching, digging, holding on, yielding distance reluctantly. I tried not to think that the sled was alive, angry, and uncooperative. This was an expedition; we were experiencing a bad break in the weather. It would snow soon, covering the tundra with glorious, slippery white. "Stop whining," I told myself, "even internally."

I was grumpy anyway. By midday I told Misha that we were losing too many forces and not going very far. As an alternative, I suggested we follow an ice- and snow-covered river, but the river meandered around the valley like a cut snake. Even though we traveled quickly, we were looping back and forth, without getting much closer to Talovka. Finally, when the river took a large swing to the south, Misha rebelled. We hauled our sleds back onto the naked tundra and pulled a few feet into the wind. Then, like identical twins who think identical thoughts at the same time, we silently turned back into the shelter of the riverbank, built a huge fire, and boiled water for tea to recharge our forces.

The next day was a repeat of the previous. If I couldn't will myself into a Buddhist state of calm, at least I could tell myself a story that would embarrass me into continuing. Four years ago, Misha and I had paddled across the North Pacific to follow a maritime branch of the ancient migration that carried Stone Age people from Asia to North America. While some of these early migrants paddled across the sea, others made the incredibly difficult journey over land, on foot, passing close to where we were now. I imagined wandering around out here, in the cold wind, with my pregnant wife, baby, and grandparents. I kept my eye alert for a crippled mammoth or an abandoned calf, which I could poke to death using a long stick with a piece of bone tied to the end. I felt a deep awe for the power of my ancestors as well as an embarrassment about my own frailty.

When wind blows across the ocean, it piles the water into waves that rise, grow steeper, and then collapse to produce white foam that hisses down the blue-green face. After the storm passes and the winds calm, the waves recede, leaving gentle swells that sing a soothing reminder of yesterday's tribulations. In contrast, when a blizzard screeches across the tundra, it drives the snow into waves that lock into place, crystal compressed into crystal, as if time itself had stopped. Thus the snow becomes the memory of the gale, accurately preserving the intensity of every puff and eddy, waiting only for the passage of springtime before it would release its hold on itself, molecule by molecule, and flow back toward the sea.

About every fifty yards, my sled smashed to a halt against one of these frozen drifts and I had to unbuckle my harness, walk back, lift the sled over the obstacle, return to my harness, and buckle up again. Misha tried to jerk his sled over one obstacle, and the sled broke. Neither of us said anything. We bridged the edges of the broken plastic with birch sticks and lashed the joint together. But the plastic was slippery, the ropes stiff, the birch gnarled and twisted, and our fingers were desperately cold. One sequence of knots didn't seem sufficient, so we added another layer of knots and sticks, and then a third. All the ropes tangled. I poured water on the mess to freeze everything together, figuring that when the ice melted, our fingers would be warm enough to do a better job.

A few hours later, my sled broke. We fixed it, working together, silently, in the howling wind. We reached the bank of the Talovka River, but the willows were so thick that they were virtually impenetrable. I took out my saw and cut a trail, one branch at a time. Two hours of hard work to travel fifty yards. We camped.

The Talovka River was a hundred yards wide, covered with crystal-clear ice, about three feet thick. The winter cold had expanded the ice until it pressed against the riverbanks, bulged, and cracked. Cracks and bubbles crisscrossed the river ice like a map of time, outlining alternating moments of joy and destruction within a matrix of clarity. The ice surface looked like a huge lens and I imagined that it was magnifying mysteries, if I was only wise enough to interpret them. The sleds pulled easily across the smooth ice, but our skis found no traction and we slipped over the wavy surface, wishing for skates. We wanted to head northeast, but when the river swung to the southwest we followed it reluctantly, knowing from the map that it would swing back eventually. Even though we were in Russia, we went the wrong way so we could go the right way. This expedition had morphed from a heroic dash to Pevek into a jaunt of curious origin, unknown objective, and uncertain future.

At 3:30 we rounded a bend and were surprised to see a cargo scow, frozen into the ice and secured with heavy lines to the shore. The ship's log, scribbled on a piece of cardboard that was crammed against a light fixture above the wheel, told us: "Went aground, Sept. 15, 2003. Moored to the beach. Will return at high water after breakup." The cargo was gone. Someone else's misfortune was our bonanza. Misha and I built a fire in the cast-iron stove, relaxed on sagging bunks, and dried our clothing and gear.

We walked through the wind for two more days without talking much. Misha was nonexistent but everywhere, inside to give me strength, outside to save my life if something bad happened. After a while, everything was like that. I felt that Chris was far away, like the light at the end of the labyrinth—mysterious, out of reach—across the tundra and the ocean. But she was within me as well, just as Moolynaut and Kutcha were, all part of the endless landscape that stretched all the way to the North Pole. Misha and I had kayaked across the Pacific Ocean, and that journey had forever defined space and distance in terms of human muscle power. Yes, I would lie in bed with Chris again, in our tower in the pine forest, but first I must walk across this frigid windblown tundra. Then the kaleidoscope turned and Chris was cuddled up next to me. The wind stopped and stars twinkled and her naked body was soft and warm beneath the down comforter in our unheated bedroom.

Once time and space entered the dreamworld, everything became simultaneously ephemeral and tangible. That willow that I just brushed against was a foot away, or an infinity, disappearing in the swirling images of Kutcha's Other World.

Out there on the tundra, pulling my sled over bare dirt and *strastugi* alongside Misha, I felt something leave and something enter until the inside and the outside got all mixed up and became indistinguishable. But because nature had become part of me without bringing any words or stories along— only the present—I lost the baggage of the past and the worries of the future. Then, even though I was cold as hell and my fingers ached, I understand why Oleg, or Moolynaut, or Kutcha had sent me out here.

After a few days, and for no particular reason—no struggle with the Devil or judgmental balance of karmic consequence—Kutcha switched off the wind and stoked the fire inside the April sun. The temperature rose above freezing and the river valley narrowed into a canyon that cut between rolling hills. The canyon walls provided a windbreak, allowing a lush forest to grow. Soft snow covered the ground. Gray and white sparrows flitted from branch to branch, building nests and singing love songs. We shed our outer parkas and continued onward, dressed in light pile jackets that allowed our bodies to breathe.

Early in the afternoon, we saw a snow machine parked on the ice. A dog barked. Smoke curled through the forest. A man in a bright orange jump-suit and intricately beaded dog-fur hat walked out of the bushes, waited silently till we arrived, and introduced himself as Vischyslav. A fur-clad woman, in her fifties, was sitting on reindeer skins in the middle of the river, fishing through a hole in the ice. We greeted her, but she barely responded. I remembered that when we first met Moolynaut she was cleaning fish and seemed marginally interested in us. When Koryak women are catching or processing fish, they aren't easily distracted.

We followed Vischyslav to the campfire. He was Koryak, in his late twenties or early thirties, with a broad, cheery face. A gulag-thin Russian, obviously drunk, sat cross-legged on a reindeer skin by the fire, dressed in ragged pants and a *kuchlanka* that was trimmed elegantly with polar bear fur but now stained with fish oil and snow-machine grease. Big lips. Standard-issue bad teeth. Wild unwashed hair. He glanced at us without interest or recognition, as if we had jostled against each other in the New York subway at rush hour. I never learned his name.

Vischyslav asked about our journey but was guarded, barely hospitable, as if we could be dangerous. Within a few moments, the woman burst through the bushes, like a water buffalo, admonishing, taking control.

"Have you forgotten your manners?" she shouted, arms waving. "There's food in the sled. The travelers are hungry. Why are you hiding the food? Are you stingy?"

She yanked the tarp off their sled and grabbed fry bread, butter, and a can of pale meat-sort-of-stuff. Then she stomped back to her fishing hole. Apparently, for Koryak women hospitality is one of the few things more important than fishing. Vischyslav, sufficiently chastised, became gracious and spread out a snack. He explained that we weren't the first travelers to come through here. In fact, lots of visitors came by, all the time. Two in his lifetime. There was Dimitri. Had we heard about Dimitri?

"Yes, we knew about Dimitri."

Vischyslav reminded us that Dimitri had been exceptionally strong but had died because he didn't respect the dangers that lurked on the tundra. After Dimitri, a "delegation" came from Colorado. "Delegation" sounded like an official word. As near as I could understand, a group of people from somewhere near Telluride, Colorado, was interested in indigenous hallucinogens and descended on Talovka by helicopter. They ate the mushrooms. Vischyslav took them fishing.

Vischyslav scratched his chin and stared into the fire. Then he looked directly at me. "You are a white man from America. I am glad you came. I have a question. I have been thinking about this question for a year. You Americans are very strange. But maybe you can help me."

He continued, "The American woman caught a large fish. A beautiful fish. But before anyone could do anything about it, she let it off the hook—on purpose—and it swam away."

Vischyslav shook his head in disbelief. "I was very angry. It was a beautiful fish; we all wanted to eat it. I was very angry. Do you know why she let the fish go?"

The drunk Russian looked up, alert to the conversation for the first time.

I took a deep breath. We were all about to have a cross-cultural experience. "They call it catch-and-release fishing."

Misha didn't bother to translate; they wanted an explanation, not an incomprehensible title.

"OK. That's the way people fish in Colorado. If you let the fish go, you can't eat it."

I held one finger in the air, speaking slowly, full of faux gravity.

"But you can catch it twice."

This sent both men into howls of laughter. The Russian's laughter was hoarse, through a throat repeatedly desiccated by cigarettes and vodka. He tried to stand but toppled forward, pitching out of control until he was about to fall into the fire. Vischyslav, reacting quickly, like a tuned athlete, hit him with a cross-body block that deflected his trajectory away from the fire. Both men fell in the snow giggling like schoolchildren.

Now we were buddies. The Russian wobbled to his feet and pulled a flask of vodka from his boot.

After we ate and got a little drunk, Vischyslav drew a map in the snow, showing us the route to town. He would meet us there tomorrow.

As we shouldered our day packs and clipped into our harnesses, the drunk Russian handed me a small homemade fishing lure. It looked like a crayfish, artfully crafted from a brass bolt, filed and bent with a hole drilled in one end and a hook brazed inside.

"Here, take this back to America. But if you catch any fish with it, you must eat them."

Marina

Misha and I skied for another few hours, made camp, and then followed a well-traveled winter road the following morning. Talovka appears in my *National Geographic Atlas of the World*, right where we found it, at 62° 2.7' north latitude (four degrees south of the Arctic Circle) and 164° 39.4' east longitude (almost halfway around the world from Greenwich, England). If you imagine the Kamchatka Peninsula fused onto the huge continental mass of Siberia, Talovka lies right on the suture joint, a geographical border town. The town was linked to the port of Manily, two hundred meandering miles downriver, by cargo scows, when they didn't go aground, by a telephone line, when it worked, by a government mail helicopter, when it showed up, and by a winter road passable for five months of the year by *visdichots* and sometimes by eight-wheel-drive army trucks.

Talovka was born on May Day 1944, when a couple of cargo scows loaded with bulldozers, cement, rebar, and lumber motored up the river and dropped anchor. In my fantasy, I see a fur-capped Russian engineer step off the scow onto the broad tundra, like Magellan on the beach in the Philippines, and plant a bright hammer-and-sickle flag into a piece of ground that a few seconds before had been wild reindeer tundra. A band plays. The crew stands at attention. Unseen, Kutcha flies overhead, tilting his wingtips, cawing softly to himself. The engineer makes a long-winded speech about the glory of the motherland. No one listens. Then he graciously beckons: "Welcome to the great village of Talovka."

To put this forgotten event in historic perspective, World War II still raged. The Russians had endured a million civilian casualties during the German siege of Leningrad that ended a mere three months earlier. Now the blitzkrieg had been halted and Hitler was on the defensive. But the German Luftwaffe was still incinerating babies in London while the Americans and British were incinerating babies all across Germany. Allied forces were massing in Britain for the D-day landing that would occur a month later.

Incredibly, amid this whirlwind of mayhem, war, and death Stalin and his minions had the time, energy, and inclination to build a town out here in nowhere land, to civilize the Koryak, to wrest the children from their homes and the people from their gods—so that everyone in the world's largest empire would become Soviet.

Snow gave way to frozen mud, so we took off our skis and scraped our sleds into town. A few curious onlookers gawked. The main street was a wide frost-cracked concrete boulevard with a deteriorating central promenade. A pedestal rose in the town square, but the Lenin statue was gone. A large administration building had caught fire a week ago and now it lay charred and smoking, exuding the acrid smell of still-vaporizing plastic.

Vischyslav was the municipal constable and offered us accommodation in a smaller government building, with central heating and electricity. The following morning a boy came by and told us that the woman who was fishing when we met Vischyslav, Marina, had invited us to lunch.

Marina greeted us in her home with a smile so broad that her cheeks bulged. Lines extended from her nose to the outer edges of her mouth, giving the impression that her smile curved around in a big circle, so her whole face radiated. She was my age, fifty-eight, not as short as Moolynaut but still barely over five feet. Marina wore a red and purple scarf and a blue shirt, with an embroidered palm tree, three jaunty sailing canoes, and rows of stylized waves.

On a modest table in an impoverished kitchen, Marina had laid out an elaborate buffet, combining the best local foods with the most expensive store-bought delicacies available: dried reindeer meat, fresh reindeer tongue, two kinds of dried fish, onions, potatoes, fry bread, cheese, wine, and apples from a faraway orchard.

We sat on stools and she knelt on the floor, leaning back to sit on her heels. She looked at us with an intense gaze and boundless energy: "You men are travelers. Moving is life. If you will sit, you will very fast old. You must keep moving. You must know about all the nature around you."

Numerous artistically beaded deerskin dresses and boots were hanging throughout the kitchen and an adjacent room behind us. Marina explained that she was a seamstress who made dance costumes for a troupe from Talovka. This troupe traveled all over the region to perform at ceremonial functions. Marina decided that it was time to open the wine, but no one had a corkscrew. She tried using a fork, but the tines broke. She gouged away with a knife, and after considerable effort and some nervous giggling we drank a surprisingly delicious wine from Georgia, with only a few bits of cork in it.

"Can you tell me stories of your own childhood?" I asked.

"Ah . . . ah . . . ," Marina began, just as Moolynaut would preface a story that involved looking into the past. "My mother married when she was very young. I don't remember exactly because I wasn't born yet, but people tell me that she was just a girl. She was pregnant and it was winter, and we were between camps, traveling with the herd, carrying all of our things and our *yurangas* bundled up on several reindeer sleds. It was snowing. Then, without warning, I was born, out there in the blizzard. My mother cut the sleeve off her *kuchlanka* and wrapped me inside it and kept walking to keep up with the herd and the tribe. Then all the people worked together to set up the *yurangas*. Then they could build a fire and warm themselves and she could nurse me.

"Let me tell you about fire," Marina continued. "Fire is food, warmth, and protection from bears. Fire is life. Always speak to fire. All things you can know if you speak with fire. If a bad voice comes from fire, put fat on the fire and say to it, 'Help me please from this bad thing.' Don't put water on fire more than once or twice a year because fire is your friend and it doesn't like water. Only put fat on fire."

Marina stood up, walked into a dark corner, and came back with a stick, almost like a war club, adorned with bits of fur, a rusted, bent length of chain, beads, and a very dried-up red fox hanging from its left hind foot and staring outward.

She stood in front of me.

"Have people told you how we lost our reindeer?" she asked, shaking the club almost threateningly.

"Yes. People told me that the Koryak lost their deer due to poaching, loss of markets, predation, and vodka."

"Ah, they told you what happened but not why it happened."

I waited, meeting her intense stare. The smile had gone out of her face and she was suddenly a stern warrior.

"We lost our reindeer because we threw away our medicine sticks. Like this one. With this medicine stick a small family can manage two to three thousand deer. No problem. Without this stick, you cannot do this thing.

"Let me explain. There are devils on the tundra. Wolf devils. People devils. They move like a herd, clustered close together. Everyone knows that devils walk across the tundra like reindeer."

Marina seemed to grow taller and larger before me. She closed her eyes, chanting in Koryak, shaking the stick. She opened her eyes and held my gaze again. I was almost frightened.

"Sometimes devils live like people. Sometimes they live like wolves. The shaman must go to the devils' house and make pain for the devils by hitting them with this stick."

Marina just about clunked me over the head. I almost ducked but held still, holding her gaze. Marina raised the medicine stick so the fox's eyes were looking into mine. Through those eyes, I tried to imagine the tundra as it was in Marina's youth, with tens of thousands of reindeer, children playing, girl-mothers giving birth in the snow.

But before I could journey far into my reverie, Marina continued, "The Koryak people lost their magic first. They lost their beliefs. They lost their shamans. They forgot that everything has magic. Everything. Do you hear me? They threw their magic sticks away. If you lose the magic in your life, then you lose your power. That is why our people lost their reindeer. You must write this in your book. You must promise."

I had been transcribing her words into my notebook. She stopped talking and I looked up. Then my eye turned again to the page and I underlined the sentence: "If you lose the magic in your life, then you lose your power."

"I promise."

Marina relaxed, chanted a few stanzas in Koryak, and smiled, no longer the fearsome devil warrior.

We finished the wine and talked late into the afternoon. As we stood to go, Marina lamented, "The people in Talovka have a harder life than the people in any other Koryak village. Bad roads, bad river. It is difficult to bring food and fuel from the outside world. But then . . ." She paused and smiled. "Who knows that live good, live good.

"*Dosvedanya* [good-bye]."

Kielbasa on the Tundra

Vischyslav showed up the next morning, accompanied by five weathered men dressed in furs and ragged canvas army fatigues. Some wore reindeer-skin boots while others had rubber hip waders, folded down below their knees. Vischyslav entered the room and sat on a stool while the men stood solemnly in the doorway, like a Greek chorus.

Vischyslav spoke, looking back and forth between Misha and me: "We ask you, please. Do not try to ski to Pevek." He smiled nervously.

I knew what he was going to say but waited for him to continue. "There is no snow on the tundra. Your travel will be slow. With no snow, the ground will absorb the sun's heat. Spring will come early. The rivers will melt. The tundra will melt. You will not be able to cross the rivers. There will be many rivers. You will die."

The Greek chorus nodded and murmured in agreement.

"We don't speak lightly. I talked to you before about Dimitri. I think you understand."

Every time I've traveled, people have warned me of sea serpents and monsters beyond the horizon. An adventurer has to ignore local superstitions if he is to complete long passages. But at the same time, you have to trust local knowledge as well. So every piece of advice must be weighed. I looked at Vischyslav and the weathered men behind him; they were right. Misha nodded reluctantly. Given the gear we carried and our overall strategy, it would be suicidal to continue. I felt only a slight pang of defeat and regret. We had encountered bad luck with the weather. We were alive, well fed, and happy.

Vischyslav suggested that we visit Talovka's remaining reindeer herd, and when we agreed he drew a simple map on a piece of scrap paper. The reindeer were to the east, in the mountains, where there was more snow. After spending a few days with the herd, we could ski over the mountains, return to the airport at Korpf/Tillichiki, and fly home. The chorus nodded in unison and dispersed. Left alone, Misha and I bought food in the local store and packed our sleds. Marina walked briskly down the frozen street, smiling broadly. With a hug and a kiss, she gave me a beaded deerskin hat with dog-fur trim.

About five miles out of town, we came to a small river, about twenty yards wide. Water was flowing against the far bank—a clear indication that Vischyslav's warning had been prescient. A week ago, Misha and I had walked on thick ice on the Talovka River, but during the past few days the warm afternoon sun had begun to release the landscape from winter's icy grasp. I shuddered to think of what would have happened to us if we had tried to continue toward Pevek.

Our grand and ambitious expedition had imploded and we were just two friends, wandering around, in a great void, once again looking for a bunch of reindeer. I thought back to the day when Moolynaut had healed me and to the more recent encounter with Marina and her medicine stick. What did I know for sure? Oleg was right; I was a lousy traveler in the spirit world. But I could cross a river covered with thin ice. I knew with absolute certainty that tundra, mountains, deserts, and oceans had opened a window for me. And every time I peered through that window I took one tiny step closer to Moolynaut and Marina's world—a perception I would never quite attain. But I didn't need to "get there" any more than I needed to "get to Pevek." Every infinitesimal step along the way brought me closer to that mysterious, unattainable light at the end of the labyrinth, to thanking Kutcha in person, to heeding Marina's stern admonishment not to lose sight of the magic around and within me.

The next day, as we were eating lunch before another river crossing, the sound of wind in the bushes was broken by the sputtering groan of a large, ailing diesel engine. Soon a dull rust red Stalinistic steel-tracked tractor clanked into view, pulling a large sled made of gray, weathered four-by-twelve wooden beams. Eight logs were bolted vertically to the sled, and heavy siding was nailed to the verticals, forming a wooden house, without a roof—the Russian version of an all-weather, all terrain, over-the-snow RV. This whole monstrously heavy contraption was hauling no cargo, just three men and the driver, which in terms of fuel efficiency was analogous to driving your pet poodle to the hairstylist in a military tank. They were in a hurry, if "hurry" can be used to describe the speed of the tractor, because they had consumed all their vodka and were racing to town to get drunk.

Apparently, and incredibly, the reindeer herd we were going to visit was a *sovcholtz*, a business that was operated, financed, and controlled by the Supreme Soviet. But the Soviet Union had collapsed fifteen years ago. I asked Misha how the *sovcholtz* could continue to exist, clinging tenaciously to the jugular of the tundra herders, after its head had been chopped off— but Misha didn't seem to understand the question. *Sovcholtzes* had always existed—this was Russia after all.

But if I couldn't understand the economic and political underpinnings of this predacious entity, at least I could understand its activities and impact. When it was time to butcher deer, the *sovcholtz* administrators took all of the meat, sold it, and paid their own salaries. Then, every once in a while, they got a little food and a lot of diesel fuel and vodka together, revved up their tractor, and crunched across the tundra to make sure that the reindeer herders were doing their job. By the time the administrators reached the herd, they had managed to spend so much money that, with drunken apologies, they announced that nothing remained for the herders' salaries: "Maybe next year."

The driver was in his twenties or thirties, but the other three men ranged from fifty to one old-timer who was wrinkled enough to be in his late sixties or early seventies. All were dressed in beaded Koryak hats and the now-familiar assortment of canvas and deerskin clothing. I'm sure that the old-timer had been a herder once and I wondered whether his drunkenness was the result or the cause of his transition from worker to parasite.

After the tractor rumbled off, we crossed the river and climbed a hill. In the distance, two figures, a man and a boy, were silhouetted against a snowy ridge. We waved; they waved back and then sat to wait for us. The man had a plain oval face, weather-beaten skin, trimmed moustache, and narrow, squinty eyes. When we were still twenty yards away, he pointed to me and called out, "Marina made that hat. How did you get that hat?"

Misha replied for me, in Russian, across the narrowing distance between us, "We visited with her and she gave it to Jon."

We skied close enough to shake hands. "Marina is my sister. If you are Marina's friend, you are my friend. My name is George, and this is Nikolai. You will have dinner with us."

Nikolai, who was about twelve, shuffled shyly and looked at the ground.

George picked up the harness to his ultra-light homemade sled, made of steam-bent birch lashed together with rawhide straps, and commanded, "Follow me!" Then he took off at a slow jog across the hard snow of the windblown tundra. We couldn't maintain George's pace, so we followed the barely perceptible tracks until we reached his camp. George was setting up their canvas wall tent and Nikolai was cutting firewood with a dull, wide-bladed hatchet that looked like a medieval beheading tool. Misha helped George, and I took out our saw to help Nikolai. George watched me intently, as if he was about to criticize, then shrugged and resumed his task. After we had completed the camp chores, we slipped into the tent, out of the wind, made a fire in the sheet-metal stove, and boiled water for tea. George sat quietly with his head in his hands. Last night he had gotten drunk with the tractor crew and now he was hungover.

Eventually he regained enough composure to explain that the Alexei, the brigade leader, had gradually increased the herd to sixteen hundred animals. Now they had diverted four hundred to start a second brigade, which George had joined. His new comrades were driving these reindeer down the valley. Tomorrow his job was to stop the animals and have a camp ready when the others arrived.

The valley was a mile or more wide, bounded by gentle hills that a reindeer could easily climb. Numerous thickets made visibility difficult, yet, this middle-aged man and young boy—without horses, dogs, or machinery—were confident that they could find the herd and communicate to them that they should stop walking, congregate, and graze.

George stared into his steaming hot tea. "When the Soviets were in charge, reindeer herding was a good life. The Soviets sailed a ship to Bukta Natalia [Natalia Bay] every year. We would have a big slaughter and sell deer to the men on the ship. Then they would sell the meat in PK and Vladivostok. Now, after perestroika, there is no ship and no one to sell deer to. The past is just a romantic memory of a fallen civilization." He paused. "And I am part of that romantic memory because reindeer herding is all I know."

George got up and walked outside the tent into the evening light and we followed. He rummaged through my sled, pulling out all my gear and scattering it on the snow. "Look at this tent! This is a lousy tent. It is too light. It will blow away in the wind. Look at these sleeping bags. They are too heavy. Didn't anyone tell you that it is springtime? Next he pointed to my plastic ski boots and started to laugh. And those boots, maybe they would be good for beating a bear to death, but they are no good for walking. And not only that, you cut firewood with a saw. How do you two know-nothing guys stay alive out here with all those foolish ideas and lousy gear?"

I quietly rummaged through my pile of useless gear and gave him three treble hooks and a fishing lure. George beamed.

We returned to the tent and chatted as George boiled a pot of noodles for dinner. I noticed that he tilted his face sideways toward the conversation. It's unusual for people who live in quiet societies to be hard of hearing, so I asked if he had been injured and become deaf in one ear.

George laughed. "Not injured exactly. Once, a long time ago, we ran out of vodka, so I binged a little on a bottle of eau de cologne." George grinned sheepishly, like an errant teenager. "This ear has never worked well again." He waved off the infirmity with a smile and stirred the noodles, apologizing that we had no meat because he had been drunk the night before and forgotten to bring meat. I slipped out of the tent, returned with some kielbasa and handed it to him. George looked at it and screwed up his face quizzically.

"What do I do with this?"

"Cut it up and add it to the noodles."

George laughed as if this were the funniest joke he had every heard. "*There is lots of free meat on the tundra. Kielbasa costs money. You guys are too funny. This is the first time I ever heard of anyone taking kielbasa to the tundra. You cut firewood with a saw, live in a too-small tent, walk around with boots you could kill a bear with, and eat kielbasa on the tundra. You guys are too funny."*

I decided to add to the joke, so went back outside and returned with a can of corn. Even though it was heavy, we had taken it to share with someone as a special treat. George was neutral about the corn but excited about the can.

"Could I have the can?" he asked. "I have many uses for it."

I smiled and went back out to our sleds, returning this time with our sugar, which we kept in a plastic jar with a screw-on lid. I poured the sugar into a Ziploc and handed George the jar.

George beamed, stood ceremoniously, and took it gingerly from my outstretched arms. After screwing the lid on and off several times, he put one hand over his heart. "This is a good jar," he announced. "I will carry sugar in it, just like you did. I will take care of this jar. I will carry it with me for the rest of my life. Like my teapot. My teapot and my sugar jar. For the rest of my life."

After dinner, we laid out our sleeping bags and dozed off. Sometime in the middle of the night, Nikolai got up to stoke the fire. There were holes in the rusted stove and flue pipe, so tiny orange spotlights danced on the inside of the canvas.

To Grandmother's House We Go

In the morning, George told Misha and me to continue up the valley to an old babuska's house, spend the night, and then walk another day to meet Alexei and his herd of reindeer. After our visit, we could retrace our steps to George's camp and spend another night together. Then we could follow a low pass south to Korpf/Tillichiki, where we would find the airplane that would take us to the distant and incomprehensible world beyond the tundra.

As we shook hands good-bye, he said, "People from Talovka usually visit a few times a year, and we always get very drunk. You came from a lot farther away. We just talked. You two are a little strange, but you're fun and interesting. When you come back, the deer will be here and I will have meat for you. I very much wait your return."

We stepped out of the warm tent into a gray predawn with the temperature hovering near zero degrees, slipped into our harnesses, and started dragging our sleds north. The river had cut a small meandering canyon into the tundra, about a hundred feet deep and a few hundred yards wide. A dense thicket of willows and cottonwood trees grew in the canyon, but everywhere else incessant wind had stunted the vegetation. We skied over an endless mottled kaleidoscope of wind ripples, *strastugi*, and low-lying grass. My skis slipped on the wind-hardened snow, and when I tried to maintain balance even the sharpened tips of the ski poles couldn't penetrate the rock-hard surface. It was April 10th and the temperature rose quickly with the mid-morning sun. But the north wind accelerated, so I put on goggles, pulled down my hat, donned a neck gaiter, and tightened my hood.

This was George's world, his whole world. There was nothing else. To me, it represented hardship, and we had come here as a part of a great undertaking. But to George, and so many other people across the northern rim of this vast continent, it was everyday life. Today the reindeer would mosey down the valley, munching grass, moss, and sedge, and George would step out and stop them. Then he would sit down and watch the deer chew their cuds, antlers waving in the wind, as he had watched for so many days and decades in the past. Somewhere, on the other side of a distant ridge, a pack of wolves might be lurking. Spring was bringing warmth to the land. Soon the snow would melt and the mosquitoes would hatch. As a writer, I fabricate a narrative by linking events together. Thus any story can be a comedy or a tragedy, depending on how I interpret the events and the connections between them. But now what happens if I delete the links altogether? Then there's no story anymore and I'm left with the tundra: broad, infinite, mysterious. If I accepted Moolynaut's healing and abandoned the idea of making any sort of connection to another thing I could grasp, I was opening myself to the tundra, which, in its wordlessness, is the greatest healer of all.

Misha and I dropped down into a willow thicket that bordered a tributary creek. Hundreds of round indentations in the snow told us that the deer had bedded here last night. Delicate hairs still clung to twigs and branches. The deer tracks veered south, toward the main river, and we continued northward, following the road as it rose back into the wind. A short while later, we met a man silently gliding toward us on a sled that was pulled by a single reindeer. As he approached, the only sound was the scratch of runners on the hard snow and the measured breathing of the deer. We greeted each other, exchanged news, and passed on. Over the last few days, Misha and I had seen seven people and numerous reindeer tracks. Compared with our passage to Talovka, we were in the midst of populous rush-hour traffic.

Eight hours after leaving George's, Misha and I crested a low rise and saw a weathered wooden *serei*, with rusted tin roof and tar-paper siding, surrounded by a woodshed and a few shacks, slowly losing their grip on verticality.

A dog barked. The door opened and an old woman emerged, bent over, walking without a cane but looking like she needed one. She was dressed in a patched, gray-brown, baggy, hand-sewn one-piece reindeer-skin suit with a gray wool scarf tied over her head. Scraggly unwashed jet-black hair hung to her neck. Long, thin strands of white and blue beads dangled from her ears, providing a sinuous line of color that stood out dramatically against the earth tones of her body and clothing.

Wordlessly she ushered us into the house, which consisted of a single square room, about twenty feet on a side. A huge brick *petchka* dominated the middle of the room, but otherwise it contained only a low table, a crude counter made of old planks, a water barrel, and a saggy bed in the far, dark corner. Opaque glass windows, covered with filthy plastic, let in a faint glimmer of diffuse daylight. Wires and long-useless lightbulbs were evidence that there was a generator here in bygone, Soviet times.

The babushka boiled water for tea but didn't ask questions, tell us her name, or engage in any conversation. She sat sideways to us and looked toward the far corner of the darkened room. We sipped our tea in a silence that was at first awkward and then relaxing. We were introducing ourselves by our presence, rather than through words. Misha offered some dry fish, which we munched on with our tea. After a prolonged silence, I showed her photos of my life back home. She was uninterested in my possessions, such as the house and pickup truck, but cooed gently over photos of my grandchildren. She asked if my father was still alive, and when I nodded in the affirmative she asked how old he was. I told her he was eighty-five and then asked how old she was. She didn't know. She had a passport and people who knew how to read reported that it had a date on it, but she had forgotten the date and everyone told her it was wrong anyway.

That was enough talking for a while. She walked into the shadows, to a large canvas wall tent that was stretched out flat on the floor. She teased apart an old piece of rope, twisted the fibers into thread, and began sewing patches into the worn cotton, which had been grown long ago in some warmer climate.

She spoke slowly, in a low monologue, from the darkness, where I could only see the shadow of her face and hunched body. A man named Ivan was headed by reindeer sled to George's. Another man was due to arrive from Talovka to help during the birthing. And so on. I realized that she was both an innkeeper and a central dispatch. She had a World War II–era hand-cranked radio in one corner of the room and could contact either Talovka or Alexei, who lived up the valley. If Misha and I failed to arrive at our next destination, she would know and people would track us down—literally. This tribe of herders was strung out over the whole valley and at first it seemed disjointed, but now I understood that each person, from young Nikolai to the aging babushka, was essential to the amorphous whole.

After about fifteen minutes, she looked up: "You can sleep here tonight." Then she returned to her careful stitching.

I picked up my journal and wrote: "I've expressed a lot of grandiose goals for this expedition—or walkabout—whatever you want to call it—but now my only agenda is to watch spring arrive, and maybe to lie down on warm grass, and feel the sun's heat. If I'm really lucky, a flock of geese will fly overhead, but I shouldn't ask for too much."

I shut the book, listened to the sound of the wind outside and the gentle rumble of the fire, and smelled the aroma of reindeer skins and meat. Misha asked if we could help with any chores and the old woman gave us some buckets and an ax and asked us to fetch water. We followed a footpath for about a hundred yards, past the well-stocked woodshed, to the river. Someone had cut a hole in the ice over a deep eddy, but new ice had filmed across the opening. We fractured the new ice with the ax and filled the buckets, using a dipper that was hanging from a bush. When we returned, she instructed us to pour the water into the large barrel in one corner of the room. Misha surmised that whenever travelers passed this place they would help her with chores. Since it was uncertain when the next person would visit, we returned to the creek and hauled a second load of water to fill her barrel to the top. When we finished and removed our parkas, the babushka silently fetched frozen reindeer meat from an outside cold box, spread a sheet of plastic on the floor, and cut the meat up with the ax. She tossed the meat into a large pot of boiling water, added a few handfuls of noodles, and we sat by the fire to wait.

After the water came to a boil, she stirred it with a long, hand-carved wooden spoon. Then she looked up: "Where did you come from?"

Misha replied, "Vyvenka," and I noted that he didn't say something incomprehensible like "Montana" or "PK."

She answered, thoughtfully, "Ahhh." After a pause, she asked how big Vyvenka was, as compared with Talovka, and when Misha described the town she again replied, "Ahhh."

Misha and I sat on reindeer skins by a knee-high table while the babushka ladled hot, fatty soup into bowls and put a loaf of bread on the table. She soaked her bread in tea and sipped her soup carefully, because she had no teeth. I felt restored by the warm food and glad to be out of the wind.

After dinner, she told us about herself, in short, cropped sentences, ending each one with a low, guttural, "Ahhh," accompanied, I assume, by a long string of memories.

"I had eight children. Ahhh.

"Three are dead. Ahhh.

"I used to go to Bukta Natalia every year with the brigade and the deer. It took two months to walk to Bukta Natalia. We would slaughter deer, sell the meat to the Soviets, and have a party. Then we would walk back here, to our home. Another two months. Now no ships come to Bukta Natalia. Ahhh."

Extra-long silence.

She explained that many of her grandchildren had moved to villages and small cities throughout the region. Several were trying to persuade her to move into Talovka, where life would be easier and medical attention available. But she wasn't interested. She maintained this house as a way station for herders who traveled up and down the valley, and in turn people brought her food and helped by cutting firewood and hauling water. Apparently, she preferred to live out here, alone, still useful and close to the herd, rather than move to the relative security and comfort of the village. She had lived on the tundra all her life and planned to die in this place, when the time came.

Alexei

Misha and I had no map, just the old woman's vague route description, which relied heavily on the words "here," "there," "near," and "far," interspersed with the phrases "where they usually camp" and "near the place where the deer ran away that time." Through all the confusion, she made it clear that we were supposed to follow the river upstream and then turn right where two nearly equal tributaries joined, near the "Magic Mountain."

Mid-morning, we reached a junction of valleys adjacent to a low mountain. Was this the Magic Mountain or just any old mountain? We reasoned that the Magic Mountain would have some unique characteristic and this one seemed mundane, so we continued up the larger, left-hand fork of the river. A little while later, we came to another junction and another mountain, which again seemed normal, so we again stayed to our left. Morning morphed into afternoon, the afternoon sun waned slowly, and we began to wonder if we were hopelessly lost.

My sled was heavy, we had no idea if we were going in the right direction, and I became angry at the wind as if it were alive, conscious, and malicious, blowing in *my* face, as if Nature had nothing better to do than to annoy *me*.

"Whoa! Hang on!"

I had come here to thank the tundra for my healing, but right now I was pissed off at the cold headwinds, *strastugi*, insufficient snow. Time to stop, take a rest, and eat a snack.

We sat on our sleds and ate shriveled dried cucumber fish. Then I quietly asked Kutcha for forgiveness, slipped back into my harness, and we continued onward.

Late afternoon, we saw a mountain, a little higher than the others, with a rooster comb of exposed rock on the summit. It wasn't the Grand Teton or El Capitan, but it was the most distinct landform we had seen in a week. Beyond that, the river forked into two almost equal tributaries. I almost expected some sign: a quiet thunderstorm rumbling in the distance or a cyclonic whirlwind speeding across the tundra, showing us the way. But even though there were no voices, Misha and I decided that this must be our junction. We skied up the right-hand fork and half an hour later we reached a narrow constriction where a rock cliff and a thick patch of willows blocked most of the wind. This looked like a perfect place for a winter camp, but we didn't see any recent signs of people. We must have made a wrong turn somewhere, so, discouraged, we decided to camp for the night and continue our search in the morning.

Then we smelled smoke. A dog barked. Peering through the willows, we saw a large skin tent, a hundred yards away, well camouflaged because it was the color of reindeer, dun brown like the earth, mixed with the white of snow. We quietly smiled at each other, with a warm mixture of friendship and fatigue. Then we carefully approached the camp.

A young, strong-looking man with close-cropped hair, in his early thirties, appeared. He smiled and, without faltering or showing signs of surprise, greeted us with familiarity, "Misha. Jon. We meet again. It is so good to see you."

I drew a blank, turned to Misha, and asked in English, "Who is this man and where have we seen him before?"

"Don't you remember?" Misha admonished, impatient at my forgetfulness, "This is Leonid. We met him at Bukta Natalia, when we were kayaking."

I reached back into my distant memory. Bukta Natalia. A place I had been hearing so much of lately. Of course! But that encounter was four years ago, along the coast, 160 miles from here as the crow flies and much farther if you followed a reindeer herd through the mountain passes.

When we were paddling along the Kamchatka coast, we had camped in Bukta Natalia, unaware that people slaughtered and sold their reindeer there during Soviet times. After dinner, as we sat by the fire, heating water for our evening tea, we saw a man in the distance—Leonid—purposefully walking across the tundra, carrying a rifle and a crude spear made of a stick, tipped with a rusted piece of metal, crudely bashed into a point. Leonid asked us if we had any rice, flour, sugar, or tea to trade for reindeer meat. We explained that our kayaks were small and we had no surplus food. He examined our boats silently, nodded, and sat down by the fire. I broke out an extra Snickers bar from our goodie stash.

Leonid explained that his people had traded meat here with the Soviets since he was a little boy and then one year, he didn't remember exactly when, the Soviets inexplicably failed to appear. Vaguely his people had heard about Gorbachev, perestroika, and capitalism, but they still posted a lookout to watch for the ship every summer. "It was better in Soviet times," Leonid lamented, "when we had someone to sell our meat to. Maybe they will return someday, and since we don't want to miss them, we still post a lookout. I saw the two of you, but no *ship*, which was curious, but I came down anyway to talk."

Then he asked us if we had any cartridges for his World War I British Enfield rifle. No, we didn't. He was carrying the heavy weapon, rendered useless because he had no bullets, on the essentially impossible hope that he would randomly bump into someone in an unpopulated wilderness who was carrying a surplus of live ammunition for his ninety-year-old rifle. And if he didn't find any bullets, he planned to use the spear as his only defense against potentially aggressive grizzly bears.

Now, four years later, Leonid showed no surprise that Misha and I had walked into his camp. A second man, Sergei, who was slimmer but about the same age, came out to meet us, and the two men invited us into their tent for tea.

Most Koryak tents are *yurangas*, which are circular, close cousins to the yurts of the Central Asian steppes. Yurts and *yurangas* are built with an internal frame according to a structural and aesthetic design that is consistent over much of Asia. But Leonid and Sergei's tent was square and high sided, similar to a wall tent, about twelve feet on a side. Two external A-frames supported a ridgepole. An inside frame was constructed of poles that were tied together with no discernible pattern or engineering foresight. It had the appearance of my grandkids' tree house, where sticks were lashed together haphazardly until the structure seems "strong enough" or the kids ran out of wood or enthusiasm. The fabric of Leonid and Sergei's tent consisted of reindeer skins, of all ages and shapes, colored dun and white, sewn together into a kaleidoscope that was chaotic yet beautiful, like a Jackson Pollock painting. A rusted metal flue projected out of the top.

We pushed aside the reindeer-skin door, walked counterclockwise around the sheet-metal wood-burning stove, as is customary throughout all of Asia, and sat cross-legged on soft reindeer skins. A gentle wind blew outside, the tent poles swayed, and the lashings creaked, like a boat at sea. Light filtered darkly and diffusely through the skins. The pungent aroma of home-tanned reindeer hide and fresh meat mixed with the smokiness of the fire. We all waited silently for the water to boil. After serving tea, Leonid told us stories of his world, using the now-familiar disjointed sentences and images, with few adjectives and little embellishment, followed by long pauses so the listener could fill in the details with imagination.

"This year there is little snow on the tundra. . . .

"The rivers will melt and spring is coming early. . . .

"Wolves killed two deer last night. The deer were weak and strayed too far from the herd."

Leonid explained that after the recent formation of a second brigade, his group now owned twelve hundred reindeer. They expected to lose about fifteen a year to wolves, but 550 healthy babies would be born with the birthing season just starting. Leonid told us proudly that their predation losses were low because they were vigilant and maintained sentries continuously, day and night, good weather and bad, all year. One day last year the people in nearby Slautna relaxed their vigil for just one night, during an intense blizzard and the wolves killed forty deer.

After a short while, the dog barked joyfully and wagged his tail. Alexei entered with his grandson, eight-year-old Bagdan. Alexei was sixty-three, wrinkled by winter blizzards and summer sun but with eyes that remained alert and intense. He had black curly unwashed hair, streaked with gray, which hung halfway between his ears and his shoulders. Bagdan was a stocky, sparkling boy, with rounded cheeks and red lips. He watched us with such innocent curiosity that I wanted to pick him up as if he were a baby. The fifth and final member of their tiny tribe was guarding the herd. There were no girls or marriageable women, and without them the valley felt lonely and forlorn.

Alexei asked about our journey and why we had ended up in this place. Everyone sat in rapt attention as Misha told about Moolynaut, the healing, Kutcha, our intended passage to Pevek, the headwinds and the lack of snow, and our decision to return to Vyvenka, with a detour to this camp.

Alexei chuckled softly. "And why was it so important that you find Pevek? You white men have never learned that the world is round. Oh, maybe you know this, but anyway you have never learned it. You are always trying to move in a straight line, toward a goal, as if you might find someplace that is better than the place you left."

He paused and sipped his tea. "The world is round. We must all travel in circles. Like the deer, who circle from one pasture to the next, between the mountains and the ocean. And back again. Like the sun. Like the seasons.

Your friend Kutcha, the Raven, he is a great trickster. He was laughing at you when you were trying to ski to Pevek. Maybe you saw him, maybe you didn't, but he was laughing. Kutcha loves a good joke. He blew wind in your face. He blew the snow away. Just like we herd the reindeer, Kutcha herded you. He herded you to this place, so you would come full circle, so you would see Leonid again, so we could drink tea together."

Alexei held one finger in the air to indicate that he had more to say. After a pause, he continued, "I think the old babushka in Vyvenka—what is her name? Oh yes. Moolynaut. I think Moolynaut forgot to tell you something. Or maybe she told you, but you didn't listen. Or you didn't understand.

"Kutcha is only a messenger god. He is not the highest God. Our God is the whole tundra. You must understand that God lives in every rock, lichen, ptarmigan, and sedge.

"*Tak* [so]," he continued with a smile, "you are offering thanks for your healing simply by skiing across windblown snow and frozen rivers. The tundra is listening to you. If you listen back, it will talk to you."

In the silence that followed, I thought, "Why should it be so hard to learn that there are no starting points and finish lines?" I wanted to thank Alexei but didn't know how to express myself across languages and cultures. Sometimes silence is the best thanks.

Leonid started cooking a large pot of meat and noodles for dinner.

Alexei asked me about my life. I told him that I lived in a big forest and wrote books. My office was in a small *serei* near the house. Every morning I walked down the hill, sawed some firewood, warmed the *serei*, turned on the computer, and wrote my books.

"You will write about us?" he asked.

"If you want me to, I will. If you ask me not to, I'll honor your feelings."

"No one in the world knows about the five of us living here, alone, on the tundra. Someone should tell the world about us. And you walked here. You walked past the Magic Mountain. So you are the only person who can tell our story. Yes, please write about us. That is your job. Tell the world about our lives, that we are here, in this tent, watching our deer. Tell them all those things."

After another silence, Alexei asked, "Did you feel the magic of our mountain when you walked past it?"

I answered truthfully that we had not and Alexei chuckled again. "Sometimes there is magic in the air, but you don't listen hard enough to hear it. You were not listening carefully enough. That is OK; maybe the magic went inside you anyway. Maybe you will find it when you need it."

I asked what kind of magic he felt from the mountain.

Alexei shook his head slowly. "Some things we do not talk about. I told you, the magic will come to you when you need it. Maybe that is why Kutcha herded you to this place, so you would walk past the Magic Mountain, because you will need this power one day."

I couldn't tell whether this was a calm assurance or a warning, but somehow I felt that an oracle had spoken. I resolved to try to talk to the mountain when we left this camp and returned back down the valley.

Bagdan, who had been listening intently, added, "Sometimes when a reindeer is lost, you can ask the mountain and it will tell you where to look for the deer."

I chuckled softly to myself. Who would have thought when I stood in front of five distinguished professors, arguing quantum mechanics to defend my Ph.D. thesis, that thirty-four years later I would sit around a fire in a house made of animal skins and calmly discuss soliciting the advice of the Magic Mountain to locate lost reindeer? If I stepped into my old self, this Koryak belief system all seemed too crazy, but aren't all belief systems crazy if you dissect them with a cynical eye? Anyway, my old self wasn't me anymore. The current me was exhausted from a long trek, with sore feet from wearing boots that you could kill a grizzly bear with, relaxing on a warm reindeer hide, drinking tea.

It all seemed so normal now, surrounded by Koryak friends who were absolutely convinced that if you took the time to seek, believe in, hold on to, and appreciate the magic that surrounds us, all the time, you would be a lot better off than if you passed the Magic Mountains of your life without taking a moment to touch—and be touched by—them.

I had asked Alexei what kind of magic he derived from the mountain, and he hadn't answered me. Of course I'll never know the depths and wonder of his thoughts, but I do know that in Soviet times there were eight brigades on the tundra. Alexei's alone survived. Wasn't that magic enough?

We ate dinner, spread reindeer skins across the floor, and prepared for sleep. As we slipped into our bags, Alexei asked, "I have heard that people can talk to the world through their computers. Can you talk to the world through your computer?"

"Yes, I can."

"Ahh. Every year, more of our people move to Talovka. Young men and women move to the cities far away. There are no women living with the herd. Our tribe gets smaller every year. On long winter nights in this tent, I sometimes feel alone. I would like one of these computers so I could talk to the world."

The following morning, Alexei instructed Bagdan to show us the herd, which was about a mile away. Normally, I can keep up with an eight-year-old, but Bagdan took off with a fast gait, half run, half walk, his standard mode of travel. We crossed a snowfield and then continued over hummocky tundra. I slowed down, but Bagdan seemed to float over the hummocks, with short legs and a catlike crouch. When we reached the herd, we sat and watched. One deer had a twisted leg. Many cows were swollen with young. One cow was lying on a small dry patch of grass, convulsing with birth contractions. A few tiny calves wobbled about. Alexei joined us and we all sat together. The cow in labor must have felt nervous at our proximity, because she stood up and slowly hobbled to the privacy of a thicket.

That afternoon, Bagdan and Sergei wanted to go fishing, but there was only one five-foot-long frayed, knotted piece of fishing line in the camp. I walked out to my sled and returned with 250 yards of new high–tensile strength, extra-supple, UV-resistant monofilament line, six treble hooks, and one lure, which I presented to Alexei. The old man examined the gear, then carefully cut two short pieces of line, tied a hook on each, and handed one to Bagdan and the other to Sergei. He stood silently, walked to the side of the tent, and returned with an embroidered reindeer-skin bag, about the size of a woman's purse. After rearranging his passport, a small wad of worn ruble notes, a sewing kit, and a bundle of carefully folded official-looking papers, he added the remaining fishing gear. Finally, Alexei softly thanked me. I almost began to cry.

I walked back outside and returned this time with a small Swiss Army knife, which I gave to Badgan. Bagdan imitated his elder, accepting the gift quietly, without apparent emotion. He carefully opened each blade and asked about its function. Alexei cut a piece of rawhide so Bagdan could wear the knife around his neck, because "young boys lose things, you know."

Sergei and Bagdan raced off to go fishing, but Alexei called them back sharply and ordered them to cook lunch. "No one goes hungry in this camp," he admonished. "You can go fishing after your guests have eaten."

Alexei asked me why my beard was gray, and when I told him I was fifty-eight he smiled. "I am sixty-three; I have told you this before. Do you sometimes find that your legs are not as strong as they used to be?"

I nodded.

Alexei explained that in September, after the brigade returned from their migration, nutrient-rich mushrooms bloom on the tundra. The deer race about, half-crazed, to gorge on this critical pre-winter bounty. In turn, the herders must run all day to keep the animals from straying too far. If a deer escapes and lives by itself for one or two days, it will become wild and will never return to the domestic herd.

Alexei continued, "Every year my legs are a little slower when I chase the deer." Then he stared at me. His eyes were still alert, but he seemed tired. "What will you and I do when our legs are too slow and we can no longer run after the deer?"

Alexei, who had been teaching me for these past two days, was now asking.

"You know the answer," I replied. "You already told me. If we can't run anymore, we'll walk. On the tundra. In circles."

Kutcha and a *Visдichot*

During the night, the temperature barely dropped below freezing, so the next morning Misha and I dressed lightly, said good-bye to Alexei and his clan, and skied down-valley, heading toward the airport in Korpf/Tillichiki. Over the next six days, travel was slow, due to alternating periods of hot sun and snowfall. On April 18th, as I was breaking trail through deep drifts, the sun suddenly peered through splotchy clouds, casting a bluish tint over the tundra, the mountains, and the sky. The foreground melded into the background; clouds became ethereal extensions of the mountains. Snow-flakes scattered orange rays, filling our universe with minuscule rainbows that drifted, rotated, and crisscrossed one another.

"Misha, we've been traveling for many days and I've never seen lighting so subtle, so glowing, so much like the Other World. I need to stop and look. Maybe I'll take a photo."

Misha smiled. "You are correctly, Jon. We must stop to see at the Wild Nature."

By the time I got my camera out, a cloud covered the sun, the rainbows disappeared, and the lighting changed, subtly but enough to alter the magic. I shot a few frames anyway and put the camera away.

In the distance we heard the unmistakable rumble of tired machinery. A *visdichot*. No sense starting up now. We sat on our sleds to wait.

In North America, vehicles, even trucks, aren't merely machines; they're expressions of style, small mobile enclosures designed to offer real or imag-ined elegance, to impress our friends and business associates, and to pamper and coddle our bodies. The *visdichot* offers no such pretensions. Its exterior is made of armored steel plate, like a tank, without the gun turret. The sides are sloping to deflect enemy bullets and the windows are tiny slits to reduce the chance that a sniper will blow the driver's brains out. Inside, a huge diesel engine sits raw and naked between the driver and person who rides shotgun, extending backward into the oily, gloomy rear passenger or cargo compartment. The exposed manifold and exhaust pipe snake through the cabin, shimmering with heat, ready to burn and maim anyone who moves a few inches in the wrong direction. The inside noise is so oppressive that most drivers open the window and stick their heads outside, even in the dead of Arctic winter, and drive with a back-wrenching, contorted twist, sitting half-sideways and operating the accelerator with the inside edge of their right foot. The beast has no steering wheel but turns when the driver pushes or pulls on two bare steel "sticks" that control the speed of the tracks. If the right track moves faster than the left, the armored steel contraption turns a jerky, kidney-jarring, robotlike left.

The *visdichot* rumbled closer, cranked a sharp turn, and headed straight toward us, as if we were Nazi commandos. The uneven roar of the engine and the strident clank of the tracks rent apart the Arctic serenity, and thick, black smoke drifted into the pastel blues that had enchanted our sensitivities just a few moments before.

The machine clanked to a halt a few feet from us and the engine coughed and sputtered into uneasy silence. The driver was a large, rough-looking man with a long-ago-broken nose and grease stains on hands, face, and ragged camouflage clothing.

He stared down at us from the safety of his armored perch. "Who are you? Where are you coming from? What are you doing out here?"

He reached his hand out the window and introduced himself as Valodia. Misha told our story and Valodia explained, in essence, that he was an Arctic road-warrior trader, headed to the port in Korpf/Tillichiki because a ship was due to arrive and he wanted to buy supplies to sell in Talovka and the more distant city of Manily. I imagined that he had a large wad of worn, greasy ruble notes sequestered somewhere in the bowels of the monster. He offered to take us to town.

The passenger-side door squeaked open and the driver's guard, companion, and mechanic, all bundled into one smiling, greasy young man, emerged from the armor, blinked in the bright light of the tundra, stretched cramped legs, and walked over to shake our hands.

Valodia stayed inside as if reluctant to separate himself from the machine and approach us with the fragility of an ordinary human.

I hesitated to accept the offer of a ride, uncertain whether I was ready to reenter civilization so rudely.

Valodia sensed my reluctance. "Over the next pass, on the coastal side of the mountains, there is almost no snow. For long stretches the road is raw gravel and exposed mud. The ice is starting to walk, and you will have to wade through frigid, waist-deep water whenever you need to cross a river."

I felt that I was a Stone Age hunter, lying on a hillside, looking down at a small farm. Do I accept this technology or reject it? Well, as I was headed to an airport, I would be accepting internal combustion machines sooner or later. Misha and I exchanged glances, shrugged, and hefted our sleds onto the cold armored steel of the overland battleship.

Valodia ducked inside and reappeared with half a loaf of stale bread, a small plastic bag of peeled, boiled potatoes, another bag of greasy, deep-fat-fried cucumber fish, two large, warm, slimy herrings, which smelled pungently of diesel, and a bottle of vodka.

"Time for breakfast," he announced.

For weeks, Misha and I had eaten our meals while sitting on our sleds or lounging on Therm-a-Rests or reindeer skins spread over grass or snow. Valodia had no such connectivity with the tundra. We climbed onto the frigid metal of the *visdichot*, which extracted heat from our tired bodies and dispersed it, like a radiator, into the cosmos, and spread out our picnic between grease stains and rust.

As we ate, I watched the lighting change on the ice blue mountains, realizing that our expedition had come to a sudden, clanking, diesel-belching finale. I turned my head to absorb the entire 360-degree panorama.

From the north, from the land of Alexei and Bagdan, a large bird was flying up the valley. In the starkness of light and shadow, I couldn't discern its coloration, but it seemed to be flying with the steady, powerful wing beat of a raptor. I tapped Misha on the shoulder. "Look at that bird. Do you think it's a Steller's sea eagle?"

Misha squinted into the distance as the bird grew closer, larger, and more distinct. "No. It's a raven."

Just a few days ago, I had remarked that even though Kutcha had launched this expedition, Misha and I had seen only one or two ravens during our entire journey.

The raven flew deliberately, beating its wings steadily, like a metronome, flying purposefully, unwaveringly, toward us. I watched, transfixed, as it approached until it was directly overhead. Then it hovered and rocked its wings up and down, in a motion that is inefficient for flying but a universal signal among aviators. It is the same flying motion that an Alaskan bush pilot uses to signal a friendly, "Hello down there. I see you. How's it going?"

The raven waved at us. Its black wing feathers were stretched apart, like fingers, shiny and jagged against the pale blueness of the tundra sky.

Still waving, it dropped downward, like a helicopter, until it was a few arm lengths above our heads. I stared up and it stared down, and we looked into each other's eyes.

"Such a tiny head, such a tiny brain," I thought. "How can it fly, eat, make love, care for its young, have friends, lie, cheat, share, even fabricate tools, with such a tiny brain?"

It cawed: once, twice, three times. Like a friend calling a greeting. Like Kutcha the Raven God acknowledging that I had come to thank the tundra for my healing. Like my totem spirit accepting me for all my strengths and weaknesses. Like my good buddy saying, "*Spaciba* and *shasliva* [thank you and good luck]."

I waved my hand and replied "*Pajalusta* [you're welcome]. *Spaciba* and *shasliva*."

And then the bird flew away.

Part 5

Spring and Autumn

Not forever on earth; only a little while here.

Be it jade, it shatters.

Be it gold, it breaks.

Be it a quetzal feather, it tears apart.

Not forever on earth; only a little while here.

—Nezahualcoyotl,
   a Native American poet from central Mexico,
   who lived from 1402 to 1472

Avalanche

Every year in mid-November, Chris would wake up in the middle of the night and fidget. I would reach out my hand groggily until it brushed against whatever part of her body I touched first and ask, "What's the matter, sweetie?"

And she would say, "Oh, nothing?"

When our marriage was new, I would follow with annoying, probing questions, but eventually I learned that she was just impatient for ski season to start. So I'd mutter something incomprehensible, roll over, and fall back asleep. Soon the covers would rustle and Chris would step into the night. She was just too energized by the onset of winter to sleep. Sometimes she'd crawl back into bed and snuggle up during the gray light of predawn, but usually I'd find her in the morning sound asleep on the couch, book fallen onto her chest, reading light still on.

Chris joined me for only one of the four expeditions to Kamchatka and Vyvenka, but this fact might give a misleading picture of our closeness. We were married for twenty-four years, eleven months. During that time, I spent four seasons as a commercial fisherman and participated in nine expeditions without her. Altogether, we were apart for 26 out of 299 months.

During the remaining 91 percent of our marriage, we were together virtually all the time. We both worked at home, ate, and slept together. But more important, we played together. We climbed and skied in the great mountain ranges of the world, sea-kayaked through ice-choked Arctic waters and coral-studded tropical oceans, and mountain-biked across the Mongolian Gobi. On expeditions, she was always tough and uncomplaining, yet she never fixated on completion of a goal as a worthwhile achievement in itself. She would climb a mountain because she enjoyed being on the mountain, not because she felt any inherent value in gaining the summit. She was my best friend, partner, ski buddy, teacher, and lover.

In March 2005 Chris and I left our winter home in Fernie, British Columbia, with two friends, Mark Cunnane and Jonny Walsh, and drove to Bishop, California, to ski spring snow. Bishop is situated in the Owens River Valley, between the Sierra Nevada mountains to the west and the lower, desert dry White Mountains to the east. To the north, out of sight, lie the imposing granite walls of Yosemite National Park, and to the south Mount Whitney rises 14,495 feet above sea level, the highest peak in the continental United States. From downtown Bishop, if your eyes drift beyond the pink Baskin-Robbins ice-cream sign, they will probably linger on the east face of Mount Tom.

Mountains speak to us through our relationship with them. Photographers might see a perfect calendar shot. Hikers view probable hiking routes, and climbers focus on exposed rock. If you're a serious backcountry skier, you can't look at Mount Tom without placing yourself in the middle of that face, careening downslope, knees driving steel edges into the snow, crystals flying, wind in your face. From town, the east face looks nearly vertical, but this perspective is foreshortened and the slope angle itself is only about forty degrees, steep enough but entirely manageable.

One warm, sunny morning at the end of March, Mark, Jonny, Chris, and I joined three locals, Darla Heil, Bob Harrington, and Will Crljenko, to ski this mountain. Bob and Darla were good friends; we had never met Will before. Shortly after noon, Mark broke trail up a short headwall to gain an arête that led to the summit ridge. Halfway up the headwall, the snow emitted a soft, hollow *woomph*—like a rattlesnake shaking its tail before biting. The snow dropped only about half an inch, but for that brief instant Mark felt as if he was falling helplessly though space.

It is a common cliché that every snowflake is unique. But for a skier, it is more important to know that every snowstorm has a unique signature. If the snow is cold, then fluffy flakes poof into the winter air like fairy dust. Alternately, warm temperatures create a dense, wet snowpack, suitable for building snowmen. But the storm itself is only the beginning. Snow changes as soon as it stops falling. Crystals settle and interlock. Depending on the temperature, the crystals melt or sublime and water molecules refreeze. In addition, wind drives delicate crystals into dense drifts or even *strastugi*, as we experienced on the tundra near Talovka. Due to the differences in each snowstorm and the effect of continuous metamorphosis, mountain snowpack is always layered, like a cake or an onion. Each layer has its own distinct density and tensile strength.

The snow settled and woomphed under Mark's skis because a relatively dense layer of surface snow was perched above a less dense, structurally weak layer beneath. The *woomph* told all of us that there was an instability in the snowpack—and that the avalanche danger was high. Suddenly a cheery outing among friends had turned sinister, potentially deadly. We grouped on top of the headwall and discussed the danger. I looked into people's faces: my wife, four of my best friends, a man I hardly knew. Then my gaze wandered across the peaks and ridges of the high Sierra—snow, rock, jagged ridgelines against a desert blue sky. We were so powerless and the mountain was reluctant to reveal its secrets.

Avalanche prediction combines the precision of physics with the guesswork and intuition of understanding nature, for all its wonder and chaos. Every day, backcountry skiers reduce a lifetime of experience to one simple and absolute question: "Can I ski this slope safely?" The question demands a yes-or-no answer. No maybes, no nuance, no shades of gray. Yes: I can point my skis downhill and fall into the soft, welcoming embrace of gravity. No: if I venture into the danger zone, the mountain will avalanche and perhaps kill me.

The margin of error here is uncompromising. An all-star baseball player connects with a hit once out of every three times at bat and an NBA basketball player draws a multi-million-dollar salary if he hits 50 percent from the floor. In contrast, I've logged two thousand days on snow and I've made two critical mistakes. Batting average 0.999. Not nearly good enough.

Several large storms had blanketed the Sierras over the previous few weeks. At lower elevations, the snow had settled and stabilized under the influence of warm spring temperatures. But here on the arête, the quiet, low-frequency *woomph* reverberated in my ears like the warning of a sow grizzly bear protecting her cub.

Without comment, Will started to break trail up the arête. I hung back, afraid, wondering what to do. For some reason that I'll never understand, Chris didn't seem as nervous as I was, but she generously offered, "If you want to ski back down now, Jon, I'll go with you." I looked into her face and all the years and adventures we had shared. Then I looked below me. We could have skied down the headwall that we had just climbed, but that was exactly where we had detected unstable snow. Alternately, we could have skied directly into the gully, but that involved dropping over a very steep, potentially dangerous convexity in the slope angle. A few hundred feet above, Will was nearly on the summit ridge.

Fear is an inconsistent spokesperson. You can be afraid when no danger exists or exude confidence even as you perch on the brink of disaster. I was afraid, but I was trying to analyze the situation logically, without the burden of excessive emotions. I reasoned, perhaps incorrectly in retrospect, that since we were high on the mountain and there was no safe way down, anyway, the next few hundred feet wouldn't materially increase our risk. The mountain was quiet, peaceful, and calm between the white-cold snow and the hot spring sun. Mark stopped to take a picture of Chris, with her Diva pack, light shell pants, a thin long-sleeve shirt, and a sun hat, smiling happily into the camera.

We followed Will. Chris was in a buoyant mood and climbed quickly. She was always stronger at altitude than I was, so I struggled to keep up, breathing laboriously in the high mountain air. When I reached the ridge, she was chatting cheerily with Darla, enjoying the vast panorama of mountains that spread out to the west, seemingly forever, as if Los Angeles, San Francisco, and the rest of coastal California were an insignificant sliver of concrete and steel between the mountains and the sea. Brightly colored metamorphic intrusions reflected the immense heat and pressure that lifted these mountains deep in the recesses of geologic time. Normally, I would have skied over and enjoyed the views with Chris, my best buddy, but on this day I was scared out of my wits, and even a little angry, perhaps, that she was so cavalier. Some dark devil deep inside me wanted to growl, "Would you shut the fuck up and think about the terribly dangerous situation that we're in?" But it was a wondrously sunny day among friends and I didn't want to drop the monkey into the teapot, especially because I might have been paranoid about a perfectly benign situation.

I tried to calm myself but couldn't. I'm embarrassed to admit that for a brief instant I thought about taking her aside, putting my arm around her shoulder, and saying, "I'm really scared, dear. Someone could die out here today. Let's be sure it's not you or me. Let's hang back and go last, after others have skied the slope. If an avalanche is going to happen, I'd just as soon let someone else get caught."

Then I hated myself for that thought. How could I smile innocently at one of my best buddies and lie, "You want first tracks? My pleasure," when I had a premonition that first tracks could be a death sentence? In the mountains, someone always has to take the dangerous lead. Perhaps to seek absolution for my silent heresy, I felt the responsibility to shoulder that risk.

I argued with myself.

"Maybe I'm making all this up. Maybe there is no danger."

"No, this snow has spoken, and when the snow speaks, you listen."

Enveloped in my own turmoil, I forgot all about social interactions. For me, death was potentially in the air, and I concentrated on the snow. Below us, the mountain folded into ridges, arêtes, and gullies. I reasoned that over the past few days the intense spring sun had repeatedly melted the surface snow on the left, south-facing side of the gully. Then this wet snow had frozen during the cold alpine nights. As a result, the south-facing snow had consolidated and stabilized somewhat, while the shaded, north-facing aspects remained loosely unconsolidated and therefore much more dangerous. I saw a line, which I thought would be safe, over crusty snow on the left edge of the gully.

I was staking my life on a thought process that seemed reasonable, but . . . I looked around. We were high on the mountain and I felt that my choice, tenuous as it seemed, was the safest way down.

I thought about going over to Chris and explaining my reasoning, but she was busy talking and I was scared and at the same time annoyed that she was not paying attention to the snow. I thought she understood. She must have understood. She heard the snow speak; how could she ignore it? I saw the profile of her face, tanned, wrinkled, smiling. I didn't go talk to her. I've regretted my omission until I can regret no more.

Mark was standing aside and I skied over to him.

"I guess I'll go first."

He nodded wordlessly.

"I'll stay to the left side of the gully."

We looked into each other's eyes.

Safety lay a half a mile and a thousand vertical feet beneath me. The space in between was filled with sparkling crystal whiteness, a mysterious blanket hiding so many secrets.

I stepped into the fall line and my skis started to move, so slowly at first, like a ponderous freight train pulling a load of iron ore, then faster, as a blues guitarist would sing about the hobo life.

I made a few tentative turns, trying to carve lightly on my edges, as I headed toward the convexity that was the most dangerous trigger point for an avalanche. I made a turn just before the change in slope angle and then tried to float over the steep transition, so I would transmit the minimal force on the most sensitive part of the snowpack. My mind was hyper-alert, my whole body tensed to detect any minuscule instability in the snowpack. I looked down the gully as I had looked down thousands of ski runs before—a smooth, undulating cloak over the naked rock and talus beneath. My skis scratched over the sun-crusted snow as I muscled awkwardly through the next turn.

"Awkward is OK. Don't fall. Don't stop. Speed and consistency are your best friends right now."

A few moments later I raced through the narrow neck of the gully, feeling like I was in the crosshairs of a rifle sight, but then suddenly I was on lower-angle snow, letting my skis run in the bright sunshine. Heart pounding, I slid out of the gully to a safe vantage behind a small rock outcrop. No avalanche. Maybe I had been too nervous all day. In any case, I had led the pitch, as I should have. The others would surely understand my line, and soon we would all be laughing, heading home to cook a big pot of spaghetti. I set down my pack, took out an apple, and relaxed to watch the others.

Jonny skied second, a little to the right of my line, also without mishap. Then Will cut across the top of the gully. He reached the north-facing aspect of the gully, turned into the fall line, and began carving turns through fluffy dry, light powder. When Will was ten turns into the run, Chris followed his traverse and started to ski.

One of the most elementary and easy-to-follow rules of avalanche safety is to ski a dangerous slope one person at a time. That way, the load is minimized and, if an avalanche does occur, the consequences are also minimized. But on that day Chris chose to ski a big, dangerous mountain while Will was clearly still in the danger zone.

Chris was a beautiful skier. I can visualize the graceful dance that was her signature, passion, and love: shoulders pointing straight downslope, knees rolling seamlessly from one smoothly linked turn to another.

A tiny crack radiated from the tips of Will's skis. They say that the fracture of a slab avalanche propagates at 200 miles per hour. In my recollection, the fracture paused for an incomprehensibly long time.

"It's a warning," I rationalized—or hoped. "The snow is talking to us. But it's not *the thing* itself."

The crack arced upward. Two hundred miles an hour? In my memory, it stopped in mid-motion again, as if it took the time to consider whether to continue its uphill path and engulf Chris or take a right-hand turn, across the slope, and spare her.

The surface of the snowy couloir crinkled above Chris until the smooth, rolling contours of crystalline whiteness fractured into a jigsaw puzzle of discordant chunks, separated by dark, menacing lines of blackness. Chris lost her rhythm and balance and rocked vertiginously onto one ski as the other hung uncharacteristically in the air. Then the chunks started to move, chaotically, crashing into one another, tumbling over one another, breaking into ever smaller pieces, replacing the Mother Nature of stability and harmony with that of storm and terror. From my perspective on the slope below, all this happened silently, because sound was traveling so much slower than the event itself. This silence lent a dreamlike quality to the moment—a dream that I only vaguely had time to comprehend.

An instant later an uncanny roar seemed to shake the sleeping mountain as the sound wave caught up with the speeding light. The huge slab avalanche gained speed and size, breaking more snow loose, in a branching chain reaction, like a nuclear explosion. Will and Chris disappeared into a rising cloud of airborne crystals that danced and sparkled in the sun.

The Next Few Hours

I was standing quietly beneath the rock outcrop, out of the avalanche path, as the big white cloud raced down the mountainside, obliterating the sun, the peaks, the landscape, and my thoughts. Inside that cloud, chunks of snow were churning. Chris and Will were tumbling within that snow, terrified, maybe hurt, but almost certainly still alive.

"Please," I willed to both of them, "keep your wits about you. Fight for your lives. Swim toward that spot of light."

I felt the apple in my hand, as if it were an alien object that had no right to exist, and dropped it absentmindedly into the snow. Then I grabbed my pack, so I would be ready for action.

In less than a minute, the avalanche reached the bottom of the slope and oozed to a stop. The noise subsided. Airborne snow spread a thin veneer of dust on my parka. The sun came out again. The air was still and quiet, as if nothing had happened. But the gully was filled with basketball- to refrigerator-sized chunks of snow all jumbled together, replacing that smooth cloak of crystalline whiteness that had sparkled just moments ago. I searched for a glimmer of colored clothing, a ski tip, the edge of a pack, a hand, or a foot. Nothing but the fractured, desolate moonscape before me.

In most avalanches, buried victims remain alive for twelve to fifteen minutes, so every moment counted, and I was the closest person to initiate the rescue. Backcountry skiers wear radio transceivers that broadcast their exact position in the event that they are buried. I immediately turned my transceiver from "transmit" to "receive" and watched the small digital readout as red dots blinked, an arrow materialized and then a number. Ten meters.

It looked like just any old flicker on a video game, a few LEDs blinking in a culture of ubiquitous LEDs, but this wasn't a video game. These tiny flickers of light told me that a human being, maybe Will or maybe Chris, was ten meters away, trapped in an icy tomb, compressed under blocks of snow, breathing impossible, waiting desperately for the impact of a shovel, the removal of snow, the vision of blue sky. I could reach that person in a few seconds.

Calming myself to move methodically and not make any hasty mistakes, I followed the directional arrow, watching the numbers steadily decrease. Hope welled. I was now three meters away and less than a minute had passed. Surely I could dig the person out in time.

Jonny yelled. I couldn't make out the words, but I heard terror in his voice and looked up with horror to see a second white cloud roaring down the mountain. During the first avalanche I was standing out of harm's way, but now I had skied into the gully, right in the avalanche path, to dig for my buried friend or loved one. Instinctively I jumped, rotated ninety degrees in the air, and pointed my skis straight downslope. In the time that had transpired since the first avalanche had stopped, the chunky snow had hardened. My transceiver was now set to "receive," so if I was buried, no one would find me till summer. As I accelerated, one ski smashed into an icy block and I launched into the air, landing unevenly on the other ski, arms flailing, knowing that if I fell, I would die beneath the second avalanche. After a few endless and terrifying seconds, I gained enough speed to ski up and out of the gully. A wave of compressed air hit me on the back of my head, and in my peripheral vision I half-saw and half-sensed the second deadly wall of snow race past me.

Surely in all that chaos and power I should have tweaked a knee, wrenched my back, been buried, mashed, mushed, broken, or rent apart. But no, I was just Jon Turk, surreally alive, in the sun, dusted with snow again, with all the bones and ligaments still attached, almost as they were when I was born, pink and damp, in that hospital room so long ago.

I grabbed my transceiver, now flapping loosely around my neck. All the numbers were wrong. The arrow was wrong. I screamed to myself, in panic for the first time, "The stupid fucking thing just broke on me!"

Then I collected my senses and looked up. "Oh shit."

The landscape was once again covered with jumbled avalanche debris, but the world had changed. Buoyant hope vaporized into the thin mountain air. In escaping the second avalanche, I had skied two hundred yards downslope from the original transceiver signal.

I desperately tried to sidestep back up, but that was too slow. Painfully aware of time ticking past, I stopped, removed my skis, and slapped climbing skins on the bottoms. People were shouting. Mark had been carried down in the second slide. Apparently he was OK. Fear and trepidation tried to overtake my brain, but I had no time or patience for those emotions. I had to locate that signal—again—and dig.

As I raced back uphill, I detected a second signal. Mark and Jonny were already digging in the vicinity of the first, so I honed in on this tiny beam of radio waves, silent to my ears, discernable only to the sensitive instrument that was strapped around my neck. The second avalanche had piled a lot of snow on top of the first and my transceiver told me that the victim was over six feet beneath the surface. I dug as fast as I could, willing myself with every shovelful to dig faster, angry at my arms for moving so painfully slowly, shouting down at the nerves and muscles to get with the program, knowing that I had already lost too many minutes. Too many precious minutes.

I excavated a straight, narrow shaft and my shovel descended into the white-blue bowels of the crumpled snow. But soon the hole grew deeper than my shovel handle. I lay on my belly and continued digging, peering into the shaft, as if I had laser eyes that could melt the snow and reveal a speck of cloth, a patch of skin or hair. But the shovel handle bumped against the side of the hole and I could no longer remove any snow. I shoved my transceiver into the hole and learned, with horror, that I was still over three feet from the victim, the body, the human being who was lying down there, under the compression of all this weight. I stood up and widened the shaft. More precious time ticked away.

People who have passed close to the portal of death and returned almost universally report that the last few moments of consciousness are infused with a peaceful disconnect, as the brain chatter dissipates, exposing a blissful, unfettered awareness. I hope so.

I was a survivor, and in an odd mental parallel my brain chatter suspended as well, leaving nothing but the nonverbal sense that I was alive, aware, sun still beating down on me, wet from sweat and digging in the snow.

Everyone blessed with a long life must eventually face the loss of loved ones. The blessing and the curse are inseparable. I surmise that over the 2 million years of hominid evolution we've developed a self-protective emotional response to death. Instantaneous, accidental death is too huge to simultaneously comprehend and cope with all at once. So the mind dulls. You comprehend only a minuscule fraction of what happened. You cope with that fraction. Then, over time, you comprehend a little more, and you cope with that. And so on.

We dug Chris and Will free of their snowy graves and laid them on the snow. I took a last look at Chris's face and gave her a brief, cold, hug, but the lack of response was too terrifying, so I didn't linger.

I understood intellectually that they were both dead. But I didn't comprehend. It seems contradictory that the mind can know something—absolutely, positively, without question—and yet not know it, but the mind does things like that. I knew I didn't comprehend, and I didn't want to. I was protecting myself, because I had to.

The five survivors congregated on the snow, surrounded by the eerie stillness and omnipresent beauty of high peaks and rock buttresses. Bob, Jonny, and I were physically unhurt. Mark had tweaked his knee in the second slide but could still ski. Darla had also been knocked off her feet in the second slide and now felt a sharp pain in her leg. (It turned out later that she had a hairline fracture in her fibula.) We decided that Mark and Jonny should ski out and call the sheriff while Bob and I would help Darla to the car.

Darla couldn't ski because the rotational moment of the ski created too great a force on her cracked fibula, but she could walk, bravely. I took off my skis and broke trail, trying to punch the snow with my boots, to give Darla even footing, while Bob supported his wife.

As I walked slowly down the mountain, carefully stomping short footsteps, my mind was engulfed in the battle between comprehension and denial. The enormity of what had happened hovered. I don't remember much of what I thought during our slow descent; I guess it was a protective blankness—until we were near the car, almost off the mountain.

The day had passed and evening was closing in around us; my eyes stopped registering colors. The snow was now firm and Darla was hobbling under her own power, toward the parking lot, with city lights twinkling in the valley, far below.

The change of light was Chris's favorite time of day. So many times, when we were skiing in the short days of northern winters, we'd return home in the twilight. I often felt a sense of urgency to reach the trailhead before true blackness descended, but Chris would put a gloved hand on my elbow and ask me to slow down, watch the colors dissipate, and feel the peacefulness of night.

This was Chris's final entry into the night and I stopped to feel her spirit within the spirit of the mountain—the spirit of all mountains that we had climbed together and skied for the twenty-five years we lived together. I wanted to say a prayer but didn't have any words, so I tried to open my mind as the light was turning off. I needed to unlock one emotion, even as I continued to protect myself from all emotions. I needed a single image to penetrate the massive wall of brain defense, one image to make this moment tactile yet bearable—so even now, as the darkness was descending, I could begin living again.

I took a deep breath. OK. I would open the floodgates and allow one uncensored thought to penetrate the defenses. One thought. One image. And please, let me be kind to myself.

Through the chaos, grief, and darkness, I saw Alexei's kindly face, with his dark curly hair protruding from beneath his beaded dog-fur hat. I heard his guttural, Koryak-infused Russian and Misha's translation: "The magic will come to you when you need it. Maybe that is why Kutcha herded you to this place, so you would walk past the Magic Mountain, because you will need this power one day."

At the time, I only half-believed Alexei, as I only half-believed all of the magic in that Koryak world. My deeply ingrained suburban Connecticut childhood prejudices were tenacious, after all. But I hadn't dismissed the magic, either. Now I turned to look at the red alpenglow high on the ghost-like east face of Mount Tom. My mind superimposed the Koryak Magic Mountain on top of the real mountain. In the center of that tapestry, I saw that tiny spot of light again: the blue sky that gave me hope as I was tumbling down the mountain in my own avalanche, the Other World in the dream labyrinth, Moolynaut's perception of the world, the village of Vyvenka. I needed the magic now. I had to see Moolynaut again.

Coping

When Chris and I lived in our house in the deep forest near Darby, some-times I wouldn't go to town for a week or more at a time, and on many days Chris was the only person I saw or talked to. During the rare times when we were apart, usually because I was away on an expedition, I would often count the hours between the present and the time when we would be re-united. One month is only 720 hours. Not too bad, really. Now the hours were infinite—in this lifetime at least.

I knew immediately that I had to continue living, so I tried to force my-self not to grieve. I reasoned that death is a natural component of life's cycles, so it couldn't be all that bad. Maybe in retrospect, I "should have" stopped for longer to feel and accept the pain, but the phrase "should have" has no meaning. I can only tell you what I did.

I tried to arrange the memorial, but some people couldn't come on one day and others couldn't make it on another. The dates weren't convenient. I wanted to scream, "I understand that this is not convenient!" Then I meekly set the memorial for a month later.

My second book, *In the Wake of the Jomon*, was released a few weeks after the tragedy and I had already booked an aggressive speaking tour. My agent, editor, and publicist all offered to cancel these engagements, but I had made a promise to myself and to the people who had placed their faith in me, and I couldn't break that trust and return to our half-empty home to cry, alone, on the couch. I needed to grieve and I also needed to continue living—both at the same time.

I thought back to the day on the Vyvenka River, drifting in the current in Oleg's aluminum speedboat beneath the vast tundra sky. I remembered Oleg's broad face and his simple, gentle smile: "You are a poor traveler in the Other World . . . You must make a long, hard journey . . . in the Real World. You will be hungry and tired. Then maybe, if you are lucky, you will find what you are looking for."

I couldn't struggle against myself. I threw some camping gear, books, my computer, and my mountain bike in the back of the pickup truck, drove down my long dirt driveway, with spring grass rising between the tire tracks, and turned out onto the highway.

My younger daughter, Noey, had been in France at the time of the accident, working as a volunteer on an organic farm amid medieval buildings. When she heard the news, she immediately stuffed her belongings into her tattered green backpack, jumped on the train to Paris, and stayed on airplanes or in airports until we met in Missoula.

Noey and I, father and daughter, headed onto the freeway, westward, across the mountains. We crested the summit of Lookout Pass, crossed the narrow panhandle of Idaho, and then I clicked on cruise control and let the truck drive itself onto the broad, semiarid rolling wheat fields of eastern Washington. Noey fell asleep and I clicked the cruise control off, to keep myself awake through a subtle kinesthetic connection between foot and accelerator. The wheat was sprouting in vibrant green under the spring sun. In a half-dream state, I felt that I was such an improbable coincidence of one sperm meeting one egg, of all the zillions of sperms and eggs floating about the cosmos, yet this incredibly random event had produced me, alive and conscious. A few weeks ago, Chris was a similar sentient being. We had joined together. Now she had completed her long passage from ancestor, to human, to spirit guardian, which is the ancestor of all of us. And I was continuing my journey alone, through a world that is alternately blessed and buffeted by events, some defined by our own actions, others dictated by the decisions of others, or by luck, or by fate. Faced with tragedy, I had to find the essence of me, untethered to anyone or anything else. In an effort to accept that change is a part of life and tragedy is a form of change, I repeated an old cliché, over and over again: in life, pain is guaranteed, but suffering is optional.

Was I alive today because I had accurately analyzed the snowpack, or was all that analysis just a rationalization and I was alive simply because the fates had smiled at me? Had Chris and Will suffered from lack of judgment, or had the Big Guy in the sky decided that their time was up? I don't know. For those of us who were left behind, maybe it's important to temper our last image of our loved ones and to conclude that no mistakes were made. Perhaps. Too many unsolvable mysteries hang in the air about that day. But more directly germane to events that we have control over, I asked myself, "Should I tweak the odds in my favor, stop skiing avalanche-prone slopes, and live a more secure life in town?" No, I couldn't do that. I could and would resolve to be more careful, but I wasn't willing to become a new person.

My first speaking engagement was on April 16th, three weeks after the avalanche, at a sea kayak symposium in Port Angeles, on the Olympic Peninsula. Noey and I stopped at a convenience store and asked two hippies if they knew of a place to camp. After some hemming and hawing, they invited us to stay in a wooden, yurtlike structure in the rain forest that served as their guest bedroom. We got high in a cluttered room with tie-dye tapestries, and in the morning I walked through an unkempt garden with a pink plastic flamingo eyeing me from its perch on a cracked toilet bowl that was nestled into the greenery.

At the sea kayak symposium, I stood up in front of the audience, looked into all those faces, and started to cry. Then I composed myself and talked about my adventure and the central theme of the Jomon book, that some people have an inherent genetic, irresistible urge to seek danger, to explore cold, lonely places. I cried again.

The next day, Noey and I hiked up a mountain in the pouring rain until we ran into too-deep snow. I thought about Chris all of the time and none of the time. Images formulated and dissipated. Noey and I got cold and wet and then we bathed in a natural hot springs. We camped in the rain at a state park campground. Young college students shared cheap hot dogs and bad beer with us and asked us if we were carnival people or craft-fair people or what?

"No, I'm a wandering storyteller."

"Yeah, we could tell you were something like that. Want another beer?"

We held a memorial for Chris in Darby. I decided to let the party organize itself in some ill-defined organic way, and my good friend Nina Maclean, who lived down the road, took charge.

It was a warm, sunny day in the Montana forest, with our small green excuse for a lawn as the only clearing nestled into a cluttered, untended stand of second-growth pine, spruce, and Douglas fir. Suddenly there were people all over the place, representing the two and a half decades of my life with Chris and the five and a half decades of Chris's tenure on this planet. I tried to connect with everyone but found the effort more exhausting than I could imagine.

I wanted to be surrounded by my friends, but at the same time I didn't have anything to say to anyone. People were standing, chatting, and their collective voices melded into a composite hum. I sat down in the middle of the crowd so I would become invisible, but I wasn't invisible, only sad, forlorn, and feeling silly. I stood and put on my funeral face.

"Yes, thanks for coming.

"Thanks for the condolences.

"How are you doing, Barstow? Good to see you." Unspoken between us were all those days when Chris and I lived at John's house and skied the Wasatch Range together. Snow, ski lines, fresh powder. Chris's favorite mountain range. Many laughs. "Yup, I'm fine, hanging in there."

"Hey, Gray, good to see you." Gray and I were coauthors, climbing partners, best friends. Several years ago, Gray, his wife, Eloise, Chris, and I had paddled a turbulent river in the Northwest Territories and then we had pulled the canoes to shore and hiked into the mountains. Gray and I had scaled a vertical granite wall, completing the ascent in thirty hours of continuous climbing, as the first snowstorm of an Arctic winter pushed across the landscape. So much history lay between us, but now Gray had little to say and I had no reply. "Thanks for coming," as if there were any possibility that Gray and Eloise would not come.

Needing to be alone, I escaped into the forest and sat by the tiny creek that gurgles over rocks and logs a hundred yards from our house. No, not our house anymore, my house now.

"The magic will come to you when you need it. Maybe that is why Kutcha herded you to this place, so you would walk past the Magic Mountain, because you will need this power one day."

I didn't always need a gnarly mountain, or a Magic Mountain, or a blizzard raging across the Siberian tundra. The Magic Mountain was here in spirit, as was Kutcha, even though he didn't fly overhead as he had when Misha and I sat on the *visdichot*. Right now I could draw my solace from this tiny creek, swollen from spring snowmelt. My granddaughter, Cleo, sat with me and we shared a glass of fresh, cold water from a tin cup that was hanging on a willow. I think that she felt embarrassed because she didn't know what to say, so she shyly excused herself and returned to the party. Cleo, you didn't need to say anything. I had nothing to say to you; your presence alone reminded me of youth, the continuity of life, and that thought alone brought so much healing.

When the memorial was over, I kayaked the Selway, a technically difficult wilderness river, so I could face Nature's glory and danger once again, in the company of friends.

I pulled into the eddy above Ladle, the most dangerous rapid on the river, slipped out of the cockpit, and walked downstream to scout a narrow, sinuous line through the mayhem of rock and roiling water. Oleg's words came back to me again.

"Every person is born with a certain amount of power. The gods have given you great power to travel in the Real World. But because you have channeled so much energy in this direction, you don't have enough energy left over to travel in the Other World."

Maybe grief is a journey to the Other World. Maybe that's why I didn't know how to grieve. But there had to be a balance here. One of these days, I needed to slow down and allow myself to fall utterly and completely into the abyss. Yes, but for now, nature was my teacher. This rapid was absolute and in the present, without thought. My paddle strokes and the angle of my hips, alone, would control my fate. Hard times are a given. Turbulence is a given. There is no place to hide.

I walked back upstream, tightened the chinstrap on my helmet, and grasped my paddle, familiar and comfortable in my hand. I did a quick Eskimo roll to wet my face and activate familiar nerve-muscle pathways and then peeled out of the eddy, feeling the current rotate my bow.

"You obviously came here because you are seeking something. . . . Kutcha lives in the Other World, but maybe you can find him on the tundra. Wait and watch. Kutcha will understand and he will visit you in the Real World. Then you can thank him. Do you understand me?"

I found the tongue of green water in the middle of the river, paddled left past a partly submerged rock, and dug deeply to make the critical move along a subtle pillow of water that snaked first left and then hard right.

I'm not really sure what it means to grieve. Maybe it's feeling the pain until you feel nothing else, no past, no future, just the agony of the moment, like you feel joy when you are making love, like you feel excitement when you are skiing. Maybe grieving is about letting go so completely that you fall until you can't fall any further. And then you take a big breath, shake yourself off, evaluate your injuries, and hobble back upward, into the world of trees, flowers, good beer, and loving friends.

I tried to avoid the abyss but fell anyway, often when I least expected to. One day, during my long road trip, I pulled off the freeway to get gas, coffee, and a sandwich and then, swinging back toward the on-ramp, I picked up two hitchhikers. They were a young couple, obviously in love and, in my imagination, unscathed, as yet, by tragedy. We made small talk and then I started to cry, violently and uncontrollably. They looked worried, as if they had just gotten a ride with a madman. I tried to explain. . . .

Through many similar incidents, slowly, inevitably, I was healing. As the months passed, I cried less and dared to think about the future. I was almost sixty years old and lived a strange, nomadic life, bridged between two countries. Surely no woman would adapt to my idiosyncrasies for long and I wasn't ready to change, so I reasoned that I would live the rest of my life alone. Then, I fell in love with Marion, a dear friend from decades ago. I tentatively moved to Boulder, Colorado, to her peaceful house and Zen gardens on the flanks of Sugarloaf Mountain. But my chaotic restlessness lurked beneath us, like a gnome under the bridge.

A month later, I met Gray in the Wind River Range, in Wyoming. Gray asked how I was doing.

I answered, "Not too well. Mostly I'm living out of my pickup and spinning my wheels."

Gray smiled. "And what's wrong with living out of your pickup and spinning your wheels?"

We hiked into the mountains and rock-climbed on spires of speckled gray granite. I drove back to Boulder, Colorado, to Marion's house, but the book tour continued to call. In quick succession, I traveled to New York, Salt Lake, and Portland, Oregon.

Two avalanches. Was I cursed or careless? Maybe I was too unobservant to call myself a mountaineer. When I was hurt in my avalanche, eight years previously, I woke up from my surgery with eight tubes shunting fluids into or out of my body. A day later, I asked the doctor for a pair of light dumbbells so I could begin working out, so my muscles wouldn't atrophy, so I could become whole again. Now I had endured my second traumatic avalanche, but there were no dumbbells; there was no rehab that would coax my life back to what it was.

I wanted to wrap my arms around Chris, stroke her forehead, and ask forgiveness for a lifetime of transgressions. Transgressions, failures, inadequacies. In some way, I blame myself for Chris's death. We had talked about the danger that day, as we climbed the arête, just before she died. But then, in those final fateful moments, Chris was chatting away, and I said nothing. I skied over to Mark and then I dropped my skis into the fall line.

I "should have" said something to Chris. If I paid $150 an hour to see a counselor, he or she would tell me not to blame myself. I don't feel like spending the money and sitting in some stuffy room, with a dumb photo of a waterfall on the wall and a box of Kleenix perched strategically by my chair, so I keep reminding myself, over and over, as if repetition will convince me: "There is no 'should have.'"

My friend Conrad Anker called. He had lost a dear friend in an avalanche and gently told me not to torture myself with survivor guilt. The mountain had spoken. Mistakes were made or not made.

Somehow I needed to grieve without dwelling in the past, without self-blame.

I drove fifteen thousand miles that summer. Rolling across the eastern Montana prairie, in the middle of the night, wired on a near-toxic combination truck-stop coffee, NoDoz, and Red Bull, I pulled off on a dark, abandoned ranch exit to pee. When I stepped out of the cab, my whole body shook with the caffeine overdose. I knew that I was dangerous to myself and to others, but then I got back behind the wheel, cranked up the sixties station on my satellite radio, and drove back onto the highway. Mick Jagger sang "Street Fighting Man." What was I thinking? I was thinking, "I better not smash this pickup into the guardrail."

No, that's a lie. That's what I tried to think about. I tried to create so much movement that I would be encapsulated in a protective whirlwind, to deflect memories and images. But under that smokescreen, I thought about Chris, all the time.

Our first date, twenty-five years ago, was a two-week jaunt into the Utah desert. We spent the summer together in the small ghost town of Southern Cross. That fall, we moved to Bozeman, where Chris was finishing her degree in soil science at Montana State University. Two of my three children, Nathan and Noey, came to live with us. Every morning I played "Oh, How I Hate to Get Up in the Morning" on the kazoo to wake the kids and they grumbled. After breakfast they rode to town on the yellow school bus while I stayed home and wrote and Chris pedaled her bike to the campus.

But all that was just the story of my past, and now I had to create a meaningful present. I returned repeatedly to Marion's home in Boulder, perched peacefully on Sugarloaf Mountain above the city bustle. Marion worked in her immaculately orderly studio, designing homes, and I created a messy office on the second floor of the main house. We met for coffee and lunch, walked in her gardens and on nearby trails, and she continued to sooth me. We talked about books and ideas, art and chaos, enhanced by memories of the good times we had shared when we were in our twenties, trying to structure a future together.

And all the while, I was trying to comprehend, cope, comprehend a little more, cope again, find myself, define myself, and accept myself.

In the late nineteenth century, my grandparents escaped from the pogroms in Eastern Europe and migrated to North America. Then for two generations my family sought stability and domesticity. I was schooled at some of the best institutions in the world: Andover, Brown, and the University of Colorado. But I passed up an opportunity to become an academic and wandered around, hodgepodging an economic existence together and living alternately in the woods in Montana, a nondescript apartment in Fernie, my pickup truck, and a tent.

I ran away from my religion, my profession, and the dreams of my family, and I kept running. And what's wrong with living out of your pickup and spinning your wheels?

That's what I was trying to figure out. Chris had been a steady, gentle, soothing presence for half of my life, and now that she was gone, I wasn't merely fighting to cope with her death; maybe I was finally learning to cope with myself.

Comprehend, cope; comprehend some more, cope some more. On walks through the forest near Marion's house, across hillsides clothed in ponderosa pine and speckled with granite boulders, I reviewed the events of The Day over and over again, and then I linked the tragedy with the larger journey or journeys that I had been following for the past five years—or five decades. But the connections were fuzzy. All I knew was that I was beaten down. Bereaved. Desperately trying to stop long enough to grieve and at the same time fighting to move so fast that grief couldn't catch up with me. I needed a string to help me find my path through this new twist in the labyrinth.

I knew that I had to follow my blink instinct; the first concrete thought that came to mind after Chris's and Will's deaths. I had to see Moolynaut. I walked through Marion's lovingly tended gardens, stepped into my battered pickup, with a cracked front windshield from too many gravel roads, and drove down Sugarloaf Mountain into the churning traffic chaos of Boulder. Then I walked into a quiet air-conditioned travel agency and bought a ticket to Kamchatka.

A Bear and a Raven

Grieving is a selfish activity. For months, my mind was filled with concerns about myself. How was I coping? How would I define my life? Manage the loneliness? Was I in some way culpable for the accident, and if so, how could I accept the guilt? Through all this emotional chaos, I spent relatively little time thinking about and caring for Chris's wandering, displaced spirit.

In my own bumbling manner, I was coping—just fine. Yet Chris was dead, returned to dust, and some voice inside me yearned to reach beyond my own survival—to speak to her one more time. We needed one last day together—in the mountains.

Before I got on a plane and flew to Vyvenka, I had to spread Chris's ashes.

Chris lived and died as a skier, so clearly I had to lay her to rest on the top of a classic ski line. The signature mountain rising above our winter home in Fernie is a massif of three closely spaced peaks, called the Three Sisters. As I write this chapter, on a bitter cold January day, the Three Sisters are bathed in wintry sunshine against a deep, cloudless blue sky. The rock is 370-million-year-old limestone, deposited on a shallow seafloor that was later thrust over the younger, coal-bearing shale. The central peak is composed of horizontally bedded strata while, just to the south, a two-thousand-foot ramp of tilted rock dips at about thirty-five degrees. The best ski line drops right off the highest peak, down a broad ramp that flows past exposed limestone buttresses. You take a left turn at the first bench, ski a headwall into a small cirque invisible from town, and then descend a steep gully cut straight through exposed rock. In this portion of the run, you feel as if you are skiing into the bowels of the earth, feet planted firmly on snow, headed inexorably into a netherworld.

You need perfect conditions to ski the Sisters. Most of the year, you wouldn't dare enter the avalanche run-out of the lower gully. However, when the avalanche conditions are stable the top of the peak is usually blown bare by high winds. As a result, while Chris and I skied the Three

Sisters several times during our twelve years in Fernie, we made the journey less than once a year. Every descent is etched vividly in my brain. When Chris and I were excited and a little scared by the mountains, we didn't talk much. At the base of the climb, in the frosty early morning, we'd adjust our clothing, affix our climbing skins, and perhaps take a drink of water, all with little chatter. On the high ridge, often the wind would blow words away, or if there was no wind, most of our conversation would revolve around small route-finding decisions, discussions of snowpack, attempts to memorize the shape of small rock outcrops that would outline the best ski line during the descent. But what I remember best is the image of Chris skiing, an improbable spot of humanity flowing down the mountainside like a river, like it belonged, like all things eventually flow down the mountain. My wife, my best friend, my lover.

In August 2005, four and a half months after the accident, I drove north to Fernie to climb the mountain and spread Chris's ashes. I contemplated inviting a group of friends, but the social complexity would detract from my communication with Chris. Then I considered making the long trek alone, but I felt selfish, so I finally asked Chris's sister, Karen, and her brother, Karl, to join me. Karl didn't feel that he could make the climb, due to a bad back.

As adults, Chris and Karen had been almost as close as twins, even though Karen was two years older. Before I met Chris, the two had lived, worked, and ski-bummed in Alta, Utah. They were sometimes called the Seizure Sisters, a playful distortion of their last name, Seashore. Decades later, people who didn't know them well would confuse the two. Frequently I would have to explain, "No, I'm married to the shorter one, whose hair is less blond, and her name is Chris, not Karen." Whenever Chris needed solace that I couldn't provide, she would hop in her car and make the five-hour drive to Sandpoint, Idaho, to join her sister for a week. They relaxed in each other's intimacy, played a word game called Royalty, knitted hats, and, I suppose, traded secrets, confidences, and concerns about their husbands.

I had spent a third of a year grieving at my own loss; now I needed to concentrate on Chris, to somehow transmit love to my cheery wife, who had exuded such joy and happiness, whose peace and calmness had quelled, or at least subdued, my personal chaos for a quarter of a century.

In midwinter, the mountain snowpack near Fernie is six to twelve feet deep. This blanket of heavy whiteness creates a smooth, undulating surface over an otherwise tangled, junglelike thicket of slide alder and devil's club. In the summer, when the snow melts, the mountain changes character as it changes coat, from sparkling whiteness to a deep, almost threatening cloak of green.

Karen and I drove for almost an hour on a rough dirt road. When the road forked, I downshifted the pickup into four-wheel drive and we bounced along a rutty track to reach the trailhead. We stuffed lunch, water, and extra clothes in our day packs, and then I picked up the canister containing the ashes.

"It's time to go, Chrissy," I announced, as if making a plan with someone who was alive. I wailed and sobbed uncontrollably. After all our adventures in the mountains together, this was our last walk, a walk that would be shared in an odd way, bereft of laughter.

In the early-morning dampness, dew brushed off the alders onto our clothing, sparkling in the sunlight that occasionally penetrated the tangled, interwoven arms of foliage. The trail ascended and we scrambled over gnarled roots and up crude ladders to reach a six-foot-diameter cavern where fresh, cool spring water gushed from its hidden streambed sandwiched between layers of subterranean limestone.

Karen and I barely spoke, each lost in our own thoughts. I tried to reach out to Chris's spirit or soul, to thank her for being my best buddy, my lover, and my teacher, the companion who held me up when I faltered, who brought stability to my life, without sacrificing adventure.

The trail continued around a flank of the mountain to a much larger cavern, several times higher than I am tall, and Karen and I walked out of the sunlight, into the echoed darkness, with only the sounds of a small gurgling stream and the crunch of our footsteps over the weathered particles of this ancient underwater reef. In many religions, the underground is the home of the Devil, where evil people are sentenced to a lifetime of fire and brimstone, but I found no such foreboding here. Instead, I felt the great expanse of time, as salts in Devonian seawater were slowly converted to rock, which then churned skyward into a mountain, to dissolve again in water and wash back into the timeless ocean. Change and death seem less tragic within the bowels of geologic time. Yes, of course, death is inevitable, but Chris's timing was a bit premature.

Karen and I climbed back into the daylight and followed the trail as it switchbacked above the cavern, to a crude log bridge across a steep gully. If you were strolling along, chatting with friends, unfamiliar with the trail, you might walk past without noticing that the log had been carefully cut by human hands and lashed artfully into place. This trail is the Zen-inspired project of Heiko Socher, one of Fernie's legendary residents, who built it when he was in his mid-seventies. Chris helped Heiko muscle this log into place, with ropes, pulleys, and levers. It was her small contribution to the trail, the town, and the mountaineering community that had taken us into its heart. I stopped and remembered the day. I had been working below the cavern and hiked up around noon so we could eat lunch together. As I approached, Chris and Heiko were bent over, backs toward me, speaking in slow, quiet tones, gently coaxing the heavy log into position, careful not to slip and let it roll, out of control, down the steep mountainside.

I told Karen the story of the bridge and she listened wordlessly, her face strained with emotion. Later Karen told me that even though she was close to Chris, they had lived apart for a quarter of a century. Karen knew that this mountain was significant to her sister, but she hadn't appreciated the physical intimacy of that relationship until she saw the bridge. Crossing the bridge was a physical and metaphysical passage across the gully into Chris's life.

The trail zigzagged steeply above the bridge, then leveled out again, passing through dense, almost foreboding, head-high alders and lower huckleberry bushes. As Karen and I were about to turn a corner, I heard a deep, threatening, guttural growl, followed by a sharp, distinct, Woof, woof! emanating from the sound box of a large animal.

Karen asked, "Is that a moose?"

I turned to look at her and then quickly focused attention back at the sound. "No, that's a grizzly bear," I answered, still concentrating on the thick brush, wondering if a bear would soon charge through the greenery, with deadly, torpedo-like speed and efficiency.

Woof, woof!

The grizzly bear is the largest and most dangerous animal in the Canadian Rockies and also in Kamchatka. Throughout the Pacific Rim, aboriginal people have respected the grizzly bear as a powerful physical totem. Watch it move through the forest, across the tundra, or along the seacoast and you, too, will feel its low rumbling power, its rippling shagginess, the innate beauty of raw efficiency wrapped in a coat that looks like an oversized pair of baggy pajamas. In the Koryak worldview, people revere this animal that kills.

Was it Chris's spirit returning in bear form from the Other World to say the good-bye that she had never had the chance to utter?

Or the Spirit Bear paying homage to Chris, to acknowledge her deep love of wild places?

Or a reminder that I, too, should revere and accept everything in nature, even bears and avalanches, danger and tragedy.

Or was it just any plain old bear who decided to warn rather than eat us, for reasons known only to the bear?

Woof, woof!

Karen and I inched slowly backward and sat on a log.

Which explanation would you choose?

A left-brain world of logic, wrapped in a statistical analysis of the probability of running into a grizzly bear on any given day?

Or a right-brain world where magic flies around all the time, waiting to be plucked out of the sky?

I like to think of that moment as a wondrous gift, because within intensity and fear the past and future were forgotten, death and tragedy dissipated. The Real World, the spirit world, and the Dream World became indistinguishable. The bear woofed.

At the same time, I knew that both spirit and real bears are dangerous and must be treated with respect. I was overjoyed but scared. I had encountered many grizzly bears in the wild, over decades of passages through shared landscapes. For me, it was a familiar, manageable fear—forever inseparable from the steep ski lines, tumultuous kayak passages, and long rock climbs that defined my life. Long ago, I had accepted the simple reality that mountains are dangerous. That truth was all too obvious today with Chris's ashes in my day pack. Now there was a grizzly bear in our path and I must act with the calm self-assurance of a dominant bear. But basically the bear—nature—was in charge right now. Either it would eat us or it wouldn't. So be it.

We heard a faint rustling in the bushes, followed by silence. The bear was walking away.

Karen and I rested, shared a snack. The only noise was a gentle breeze in the foliage. Clouds scudded across the sky, blocking out the sun and enveloping the mountain in a summer coat of gray.

"Shall we proceed?" I asked.

"We have to," she answered. So we shouldered our packs and continued onward. Chris's ashes pressed against my back. The sky darkened and the clouds thickened. In the mountains of southern British Columbia, alders proliferate to about fifty-five hundred feet and then the ecosystem abruptly opens up into spacious parks of spruce and balsam fir. Above seven thousand feet the forest surrenders to alpine tundra—a low bed of grasses and mosses rooted tenaciously among the rocks, with a few bushes and an occasional hardy tree.

As Karen and I climbed the headwall to a high pass, rain fell and blew horizontally in the intensifying wind. Clouds bunched and collided, rumbled over one another, and fought to pummel the high peaks. I put on my parka and then donned my woolen hat, which Chris had lovingly knitted for me, with patterns of pink and green cats walking in opposite directions among yellow, green, and blue flowers.

At first I was disappointed that this special day was "marred" by a storm. Then I realized that I was blind to the beauty around me. Nature never guarantees sunny days and blue skies. There was no one out here with a leaf

blower to tidy things up, no thermostat to control the temperature, no embroidered shroud to cover death. I thought about all the storm-swept ridges
Chris and I had shared and saw her face in the foggy wetness, wrapped
tightly in her hood, determined, content, and happy to be in the mountains.

Energized, I scrambled quickly over wet, slippery rock until I gained the
summit ridge. Below me, Karen was laboring up the faint trail. She glanced
furtively at the steep slope below and then looked up at me, breathing heavily, as if the ridgetop seemed impossibly far away.

I could have sat down in the shelter of a rock outcrop to wait, but instead
I stood on the crest, fully exposed to the wind and the rain, where I could
peer through the clouds at all the neighboring peaks and the ski lines that
Chris and I had loved so dearly. I imagined a blanket of snow covering the
slope below me and watched Chris ski down, as she had done so many
times in life. Oh, my love, my lover. Her pole reached out; her body rotated;
her skis turned; snow flew into the air, leaving snaky tracks of perfect turns
behind her.

And then a raven appeared, flying at waist level alongside Chris, skiing
down the hill, cawing. Wait a minute. What was real and what was imaginary? I closed my eyes, put my wet hands over my face, and took a deep
breath. There was no snow. Chris was dead. We weren't skiing. I was carrying her ashes through this storm to the mountaintop. I took my hands away
and opened my eyes. The wondrous snow dream was gone just as the bear
had disappeared into the bushes. Chris was nowhere in sight and the weight
of her ashes suddenly felt heavy on my back. But a real raven was flying
downslope, waist high off the talus, rocking its wings as if it were skiing.

The raven almost disappeared into a tiny black dot at the valley bottom.
Then it tilted its wings and rose on an updraft—lifting my tired spirit as if I,
too, were flying. In the violent, chaotic winds of the August storm, the shiny
black bird flew back upslope, directly toward me, rocking and shaking in
the turbulence. A gray-white cloud folded like water over the summit of the
mountain and dropped down into the valley as if it, too, were skiing. The
raven flew until it was directly over my head and then hovered and cawed,
barely an arm's length above me. Drops of water glistened from its jet-black

wingtips and mingled with the raindrops. As I cried, the fresh, clean rain mingled with my salty tears.

The raven swooped in front of me, and for a fraction of a second it was so large that the landscape disappeared, replaced by black wings and body, orange beak, and one beady eye looking straight at me. And then the bird skied down the mountain again, rolling its wings, just as Chris would roll her knees with the rhythm of her skis, disappearing toward the tree line two thousand feet below. When it reached the valley, it rose and with steady wing beats climbed through the storm until it was overhead again. Was this Kutcha, who had hovered overhead when Misha and I were eating slimy herring on the *visdichot*, who made the long, arduous, and perhaps dangerous journey through the Other World for me, to talk with the Old Woman Who Lives on the Top of the Highest Mountain, to heal my pelvis?

And now we all skied together, Chris, Kutcha, and me. I felt the compression of the turn in my knees, in my outstretched wings. We carved figure eights together, crossing one another's paths, separating, then drawn back together by life's dance. Crystals sparkled and washed over my face. I felt the snow melt on my moustache. Then the dream faded and the rain fell in sheets, spattering on the rocky talus.

When Raven finished its second run, it flew back, hovered above my head a third time, and then caught an upwelling of air and disappeared into the sky.

A bear and a raven. Magic moments integrated with the greatest sadness, preaching acceptance. My animal friends were teaching me to heal by finding wonder within tragedy.

Karen caught up to me and I asked, just to be sure I wasn't hallucinating, "Did you see the raven?"

"Yes, of course."

Probably we exchanged more words, maybe we didn't; I can't remember.

But I do remember that we completed the last steps to the summit together. Between labored breaths, I recalled the white light at the end of the labyrinth, the portal to the Other World that I had never reached.

Moolynaut spit on my pubic hair as I balanced on one leg with an out-stretched arm. Now I took confident steps on a healed pelvis and stepped onto the broad horizontal summit platform.

Karen and I opened the urn and tossed the ashes into the wind. Chris's body swirled into the sky to join Raven, to return to Earth, to continue its mysterious journey from dust to dust.

I had spent four years teetering between the Real, the dream-, and the spirit worlds trying to explain life's mysteries—my healing, the labyrinth, and now the bear and the raven. I no longer had any need to analyze or explain the wonders and tragedies that had embraced and buffeted me in their whirlwinds, like the storm clouds that danced across the heavens. Why would anyone want an explanation, anyway?

Oleg had understood that the Real World and the Other World are the same, so he sent Misha and me into the tactile, tangible tundra to thank the transcendental spirit bird. Anytime I want to talk to Chris or need solace and support to find my own way, I can climb this mountain, or any other mountain, or go to sea in my kayak. Or I can sit by a quiet mountain stream as I had on the day of the memorial and sip some cool water from a tin cup hanging on a willow. I don't need to be visited by a bear or a raven every time, because I've been honored enough to know that they have already visited me. They visited me on the day I carried Chris up the mountain to her final resting place and dusted her ashes into the storm.

This Time You Must Not Visit the Other World

I drove back to Boulder, but I always knew in my heart that I had to return to Vyvenka in the fall and then spend the ski season in Fernie.

My daughter Noey once told me that she feels as if she lives in a small box and every once in a while some giant picks up the box and shakes it. She gets dizzy and disoriented and all her things get scattered around. Then she sets her flowered china cups and silver spoons back on the table and invites her friends over for tea and crumpets.

I was returning to Vyvenka because some giant had shaken up my box in a major way. Moolynaut would have no surprising, epiphanous wisdom that could be summarized in a few pithy words, but I needed a moment of reflection before I could put the teacups back on the table, most probably haphazardly and certainly not in a magically pleasing Japanese arrangement.

At 4:00 A.M. on October 11th, six and a half months after the avalanche, I drove down Sugarloaf Mountain again, through the city of Boulder, toward the Denver airport. A marauding skunk flashed in my headlights. I thought that it would be a hell of an insult to my fellow passengers if the skunk sprayed me just before I embarked on a forty-three-hour journey, in airports and airplanes, across nineteen time zones, over three-quarters of the way around the world. I slowed down and the skunk slipped unobtrusively into the bushes.

I endured the flight and cleared customs in PK. Once again I climbed the dank, dingy stairs of Misha and Nina's gray concrete Soviet-era apartment building and stepped into their brightly lit, immaculately clean, cozy home. Ainu, the dog, raced to the door with a friendly bark and vigorous tail wagging until I felt certain that she remembered me. I stuffed my long legs into the cramped space beneath the kitchen table, careful not to spill a tray of wild rose hips drying in front of me. I felt that I was home, because I was among the dearest of friends, and reflected that I am blessed because I have many homes.

Anastasia was attending music college in PK. Even though she was small physically, she was maturing into a poised young woman, and when she played the piano her strong fingers created a sound that filled the room with vibrancy and energy. Maria was a svelte fifteen-year-old, with sensuous, almost pouty lips and quick darting eyes. Nina was quiet and steady, as always, bustling about the kitchen to be sure that I had enough tea, bread, butter, and jam after my long flight. Misha explained that a year ago the fishing conglomerate that had financed the construction of his bottling plant had executed a hostile takeover and fired him and all his friends. The tight group of old Soviet geologists, now out of work, had started a new company, with inadequate capitalization and inferior equipment. They lost money in their first year, but now, with Misha as CEO, they began to show a profit and pay down their debt.

Misha explained, "There are only two problems in Russia: foolish men and bad roads."

I knew by the proverb and the look on his face that business was difficult, so I asked him if he could afford a week off to visit Vyvenka.

Misha looked at me, smiled, and said emphatically, "Jon, as always, it is *schto percent* [100 percent] necessary."

After a pause, he continued, "*Schto percent* necessary for my head," and he held his hand on top of his head as if he had a migraine about to blow his skull apart and spatter gray matter all over the ceiling, "and my heart," and he held his hand over his heart and bowed a moment in prayer.

I rested a few days with the Petrov family. Because this journey was a search for peace after Chris's death, I thought about Svetia, who had also lost a spouse. I asked around and learned that she had remarried and had recently given birth to a baby boy. I thought about visiting her but wasn't sure if she'd be embarrassed or not, so I let the opportunity slide.

Once again, Misha and I flew to Korpf/Tillichiki, that run-down frontier town of half-frozen mud; diesel-belching *visdichots*; rusting hulks of moribund machinery; decrepit, tilted, unpainted apartment buildings; tall smokestacks billowing blackness; old tires; and small hopeful gardens fenced in with scrap metal and driftwood.

As we stood at the edge of the tarmac, Misha explained, "The Soviets dreamed of world revolution." Then, after a pause, he continued, "That was a really bad idea."

Word got out that an American and his Russian buddy were walking to Vyvenka. Soon a Russian official named Volodia and his Koryak sidekick, Bill, showed up in a government pickup truck, with government gas, on government time, and offered to drive Misha and me several miles to the end of the spit for five hundred rubles (about twenty dollars). As we bounced along the potholed dirt road, with a calm ocean lapping against the sand beside us, I asked Bill how he got his name and he explained that he was born with a Koryak name but after watching American westerns he wanted to be called Bill.

Volodia shifted into four-wheel drive when the potholed road deteriorated into a track. Then, even though we were traveling on a level plane, he downshifted into low range to spin slowly through wet sand. Finally, we reached a small river, swollen by high tide and bounded by thin films of ice. We had stopped at this same place three years ago, when Misha and I were visiting Vyvenka to thank Moolynaut for my healing. Volodia continued forward until the front tires rested precariously on the edge of the eroding bank. Then he turned off the motor and chatted idly with Misha, who didn't bother to translate because, I assumed, they were engaged in small talk. It was 4:30 on an autumn afternoon, in northeast Siberia. Our packs were loaded with gifts for our friends, but we had no tent, stove, or sleeping bags. I was wearing light hiking shoes and we had twenty-five miles to walk and several rivers to cross before we reached Vyvenka. I thought about suggesting that we hurry, but I was in Russia now.

After saying good-bye and paying our money, Misha and I stepped into the soft pastel light of a high-latitude evening. The river was only knee-deep, but as we waded across, the icy water jarred me out of the somnambulism of airplanes and civilizations. Now, why hadn't we brought rubber boots, or neoprene socks, or any reasonable footwear? Misha must have been contemplating similar thoughts, but instead of expressing concern, he giggled like an eight-year-old telling dirty jokes.

I ran a best- and worst-case scenario through my mind. If we reached the coal mine before or shortly after dark, we'd find a warm place to sleep. And if we didn't, the temperature wasn't that far below freezing and we would spend the night close to a cheery fire of brush and driftwood, our wet socks steaming as we held them close to the blaze. So I pushed my circumspection aside and relaxed in the simple joy of walking down a lonely beach, with the sun nearly setting into a calm sea, the smell of kelp, and the sound of gentle surf only a few yards away.

I had come a long way to experience these moments of reflection. Maybe an absurdly long way. I could have hiked into the wilderness that extends from my house in Darby, westward across the Rocky Mountains, and northward all the way to the Beaufort Sea. But instead, I stepped as far away from my normal life as I could. I'm biased because I'm a wanderer at heart, but I felt an undeniable need to see Moolynaut and to immerse myself, once again, in the Koryak culture.

Wilderness speaks to my subconscious and Siberia is one of the deepest wildernesses on this planet. Shamans and saints from steamy rain forests to Arctic wastelands have sought privation as a path to ecstasy, to jolt the mind beyond the reality that the mind creates for itself. Of course, some people can travel great distances through meditation, without a laborious and consumptive airplane trip. Without freezing their feet in a Siberian river. I was just following a path that works best for me. It's not how we seek self-awareness; it's whether we take the time and energy to make the journey.

I strained to match stride for stride with Misha, to walk, silently now, shoulder to shoulder with him. I thought about his boyhood under the Soviet yoke and the even greater oppression endured by the people of Vyvenka whom we were about to visit. I had lived a privileged life in a politically stable, economically opulent society. Faced with the death of my beloved Chris, I needed to laugh with people who had experienced more suffering than I could imagine.

After an hour, Misha and I heard the sound of an outboard motor behind us. The boat, carrying two Koryak men from Vyvenka, veered toward the beach.

"You want a ride to town?" one man shouted.

Misha and I looked at each other. Of course a ride would be convenient, but I was enjoying the walk and even half-wishing for a long, cold, uncomfortable bivouac to clear the cobwebs. Without waiting for an answer, as if a "no, thank you," was inconceivable, the driver hit the throttle and the boat bounced through the surf. Waves broke over the stern, and if Misha and I dallied on the beach to discuss our options the craft would broach and fill with water. We sloshed recklessly through the frigid water, clambered over the ice-encrusted front deck, and dropped into the cockpit. The driver immediately clicked the outboard into reverse, backed into deep water, and then continued south, toward Vyvenka.

I was dressed lightly, for vigorous walking, and had gotten soaked in the surf. Now we were bouncing along, drenched in freezing spray. The boat jarred over the ocean swell and the aluminum hull sucked any residual warmth out my body. I quickly donned my windproof shell, but I was already hopelessly wet and chilled. Lonely. Missing Chris. Uncertain of the future.

How could I have forgotten so quickly that I was on a pilgrimage?

Misha, who was similarly wet and lightly dressed, was smiling and chatting amiably with the men above the roar of the engine. I concentrated on the sunset, the pastel red glow reflecting off the waves, and the vast tundra beyond, housing memories of our journeys, of all journeys, from the beginning of time. Darkness descended, the dim lights of the village appeared, and we surfed across a sandbar, into the mirror-still lagoon. Vyvenka was even more decrepit than Korpf/Tillichiki, but it felt homey as we walked down the familiar main street. A young boy raced ahead with the news that we had arrived and Lydia met us at the doorway with a shovel full of red-hot coals, to perform her ritual greeting, plucking threads from our clothing and burning them in the embers. Then she gave Misha and me big hugs and warm kisses on the lips and invited us into the house.

Oleg, Goshe, and Lydia's sister, Vera, were waiting for us. We sat in Goshe's living room and Oleg filed us in with the news of the fishing season—how many fish were caught, the boats that sank, and the men who drowned. With the subject of death already introduced, Misha told the story of Chris's avalanche. Oleg looked at me and nodded slowly. We had traveled on the tundra and endured blizzards together. He had seen death on the sea. He said nothing, but I felt his powerful, gentle condolences.

Lydia sat next to me and put her arm around my shoulder. "Jon, Chris is by the side of you. Very near. She want you to be strong and happy for her because she love you at all time."

When I started to cry, Lydia gently wiped a tear from my cheek and instructed me, again, to be strong.

I composed myself. "Thank you, Lydia." I explained that I had been feeling lost these past months. I needed to back up and get a running start before I could resume my life. So I had stepped out of my life and backed up until I arrived in Vyvenka.

Lydia hugged me tighter. "This is the right place to come at. This is good. You need to clean himself. Have you playing at your *boubin*?"

"No, I haven't been home much." I didn't go into details about the book tour and Marion.

Goshe chimed in that after his wife died he couldn't live in his house for six months, until her ghost finally journeyed to the Other World—and stayed there.

Lydia added, "You must go home and must be playing at the *boubin*. And sing." With the seriousness of a doctor ordering a prescription, Lydia repeated, "You must sing at one hour in all days."

It sounded like a good idea, but I knew that I wasn't going to play the *boubin* for an hour every day. Maybe if we had shared a common culture and language, we could have discussed different forms of meditation and healing, but in Vyvenka verbal communication was always a bit cloudy. Cloudy? Or was real communication enhanced by the lack of language? Like a blind person compensating for lack of sight with increased senses of smell, hearing, and touch, maybe our limited ability to converse led to a nonverbal intercourse that was deeper than anything we could accomplish through chitchat. My repeated visits to Vyvenka had changed me. I was listening better. I hoped I was more open to the mysteries and the dream-world that surrounded me. Maybe I had experienced miracles. Or a skeptic might argue that I was inventing them. It didn't matter anymore. On the mountain, that day with Karen, the grizzly bear woofed and the raven skied down the mountain. Now Lydia held me tightly. Within that hug, I knew that the giant had stopped shaking my box and when I got home I could start rearranging the teacups.

Soon we moved into the kitchen, where Lydia served potatoes, ptarmigan, fried eggs, bread, butter, and smoked fish.

As we ate, Lydia announced, "Our grandmother has *mukhomor* for us. But you must rest at sleeping first. Think good thoughts at sleeping. And tomorrow you must not go to the Other World to look for Chris. You must promise."

I promised wholeheartedly, remembering vividly the terrifying hallucinogenic journey to escape from the labyrinth.

"Maybe Chris will come at you. That will to be good. But you must not to look for her. If you look for her, you will walk in the Other World a long time. Too long. If you walk in the Other World too long, you will be dead."

Vera added for emphasis, "Turn blue and be dead."

Then Lydia told a convoluted story about someone who had eaten *mukhomor* and spent too long in the Other World looking for a deceased relative. The searcher lost his way, turned blue, and died. Friends carried his body outside so they could cremate it later. But the relative who had died previously told the blue and partially frozen man that he was being rather silly to wander through the Other World before his time. So the man apologized and got up and walked back inside to surprise all his friends.

Lydia and Vera pantomimed expressions of surprise to be sure I understood.

The town generator faltered and the lights flickered off and on, creating a Halloween-like backdrop to the story. Oleg raced outside to start a Honda generator he had recently acquired, while Goshe switched bare wires and fuses, until the lights flickered back on. Lydia broke off the story of the dead man to tell us that there were two advantages to no electricity. First, snowy surfaces are much brighter and more beautiful under ambient starlight and moonlight than they are when there is electricity, so people are more inclined to take nighttime walks. Then, holding her hand over her small round mouth and giggling, Lydia told me that when the lights go off, people get to make more babies.

A Short Walk in the Snow

That night, Chris came to me in a dream. She was a young girl and had the lead role in an elementary school play. I was busy and didn't have time to attend. She suddenly morphed into her adult face and asked, "Jon, why didn't you come and listen to me sing?"

This was the first time since her death that she had spoken to me. Yet the dream was sad, and it almost brings tears to my eyes three years later, as I think about it. In real life, did I fail to listen to her sing? I prefer an alternate interpretation, that she was singing now in the Other World and, if I took the time and energy, I could hear her.

I sat up in my sleeping bag and reflected that Chris had waited until I returned to Vyvenka and was amid my Koryak friends to visit me. Or perhaps I had waited until this moment to listen. Morning light filtered through the dirty windows, but Misha was still asleep, so I dressed quietly and walked to the beach. Lydia had reminded me never to think about Chris as if she were dead. Instead, I must think of her as if she was at my side. Because she is.

The wind was howling out of the north, and cold rain slanted obliquely from scudding clouds. The sea, relatively calm yesterday, now reared into multiple lines of surf. It's tempting to use the expression "angry surf" or some similar cliché. But there's nothing angry, or happy, or sad about the ocean. Surf is simply the sea pushed into mounds by the wind colliding with the shore. As always, I mentally sat in my kayak in the middle of the rearing white chaos. This surf was manageable technically but raw and cold in the sunless October air. I didn't want to be out there but at the same time felt thrilled by the surge of power. I reached out with an imaginary paddle, which is forever hardwired directly to my endocrine system.

When I returned inside, Lydia poked me in the stomach and told me that I was way too skinny. Then she raced off to prepare a breakfast of bread and cucumber fish, served with copious amounts of butter.

As we were eating, the door opened and Moolynaut stepped in out of the storm. I hadn't seen her for a year and a half and was shocked at her frailness. She was probably one hundred years old now and she walked with a limp. Her left arm dangled uselessly and she was unable to remove her coat without assistance. Lydia explained that Moolynaut had been sick in August. Some people suggested that they bring her to the medical clinic in Korpf/Tillichiki, but instead Lydia and Oleg took her upriver in the speedboat, to fish camp. Surrounded by sun, tundra, and fresh salmon, Moolynaut recovered, but her left leg became partially paralyzed and her arm almost completely so.

Despite her infirmity, she greeted me with a warm smile and her customary cheeriness. As I expected, she didn't speak about the avalanche or give any direct advice on how to cope with Chris's death. Instead, she reminisced about the past fishing season. She asked if I had stored enough food in my Montana home for the winter. I assume that this simple query was her way of telling me that life moves onward, even in the face of death.

After only ten minutes, Moolynaut explained that she was tired and couldn't stay long. She asked if we would like to eat *mukhomor* again tomorrow. I remembered my panic in the labyrinth and the terror-stricken flight down darkened corridors but resolved to follow the drug to a happier place this time and agreed. Misha smiled and nodded quietly.

Moolynaut told us that last July, on her deceased son's birthday, she ate *mukhomor* and danced energetically across the tundra with her dead son, returning home long after everyone had started to worry about her. She explained that our deceased loved ones live in a parallel world, which she had been privileged to enter with the help of the red mushroom. Her story contradicted Lydia's admonition to me not to seek Chris in the Other World. But Moolynaut was blessed with sufficient power to make the passage—and return.

Moolynaut looked at me forlornly and explained that she hadn't regained her strength after the illness. Now she felt old and was afraid that the dance with her son had been her last return trip to the Other World. She held me with a gentle gaze: "I wouldn't have the strength to heal you, if you were injured again. I no longer have enough power to cross back and forth between the Real World and the Other World. Tomorrow, you and Misha must eat the *mukhomor,* but I cannot."

I reached out and put my hand on her shoulder. "You healed me once and that was enough. You changed my life forever and I thank you."

In the Russian way, I put my hand over my heart and continued, "But there is something more. You taught me how to reach for magic, how to believe in dreams, to find hope, and to heal myself. My first illness was physical. Now I am injured emotionally. But, because of you, I am finding my way."

Then I told her about the bear and the raven on the day Karen and I carried Chris's ashes up the mountain. I choked back a few tears and couldn't find a concluding sentence. I didn't need one.

When I finished, Moolynaut took my hand in hers and studied my palm, without commenting. I didn't want to know the future, even if such knowledge were possible, so I asked no questions. After a few moments of silence, with my hand resting easily in hers, and warm energy flowing between us, Moolynaut asked, simply, if I would walk her home. I put on my coat, grasped her elbow, and guided her out the door and into the storm. With the wind rustling her kerchief, she shook free of my hand and limped briskly down the street. After about fifty yards, she faltered, leaned against a fence, and took several short, shallow breaths. I approached to assist her, but she shook her head *nyet,* and warned me away with her eyes. She regained composure and continued, proudly and unaided, to her house.

I returned to Goshe's kitchen, drank another pot of tea with my friends, and then excused myself and walked outside. The rain turned to wet snow that melted against my face. On the beach, four boys had propped a rusted fifty-five-gallon drum precariously on a haphazard stand of twisted sheet metal. One boy stood on the drum, silhouetted against the stormy sky, like a bowsprit on a ship. The tide rose, waves washed against the drum, snow swirled, sand eroded, and the tower tilted. Finally a large wave smashed against the base of the tower, pushing it past the critical threshold between balance and gravity. The boy jumped free and raced up the beach as the rusted drum rolled into the surf.

I continued along the beach, passed south of town, and scrambled up a half-frozen bank, grasping protruding roots, as snowflakes accumulated on my jacket, hat, and moustache. When I reached the tundra, gray clouds softened the already-low-angle autumn sunlight. It was the first snowfall of the season and fresh whiteness encapsulated every tiny twig and blade of grass individually. The snow was wet and sticky enough so these delicate crystalline tubes swayed in the breeze. Soon real winter would descend, with interminable cold and darkness followed by short interludes when a reluctant sun would perch weakly above the southern horizon. Ferocious blizzards would sweep across the landscape, and near Nikolai's camp wolves would creep through the night, sniffing the musty scent of deer.

I was overcome by the miracle of survival and sustainability—that people had hunted and herded in this frigid landscape for thousands of years, that both the hunters and the tundra had survived. Without understanding the mechanism exactly, I felt certain that the miracle of this sustainability was inexorably linked with the magic of Marina's war club and Moolynaut's healing chants.

Moolynaut spoke to me because I paddled across the ocean to visit her. Alexei told me, "You walked here. You walked past the Magic Mountain. So you are the only person who can tell our story." The shaman in Magadan transferred her power to the tree and the tree exploded into a zillion splinters that scattered into nothingness across the forest floor. And then the old woman passed on. Snow fell and covered the splinters. The next autumn, falling leaves covered the splinters again, this time with a wet blanket that hastened their disintegration into dust.

I had a job to do, a book to write.

What did Alexei and Moolynaut want me to tell the people in my world? I'll never know for certain, but I think I can gather the pieces together. In all those moments, when I was standing on one leg in front of Moolynaut, or in the trance of the *mukhomor*, or again in the longer, tactile trance of cold, hunger, and fatigue on the tundra, in the voice of the *boubin*, in my conversations with the ravens and the bear, my conscious, rational, technologically oriented mind had switched off. And once that chatter had dissipated, I found healing, I saw the world as magical, and I found hope after Chris's death.

Moolynaut's magic hadn't averted tragedy in my life—it couldn't have; it wasn't supposed to; that's not the point.

Healing, magic, and hope. Acceptance.

I think I know, now, the meaning of the promise I made to Moolynaut on that day as I balanced before her, teetering between the world of the Koryak and the world of my upbringing. I promised to believe that magic is flying around us all the time, even during the deepest sorrow. To follow my dreams into a reality defined by intuition. I promised to understand that if a person is too cynical, busy, egotistical, or preoccupied to reach out and grasp at magic and dreams, then these wonders vaporize or, even worse, they never existed in the first place. If I am walking along a ridge with my mind somewhere else, then the rocks and grasses beneath my feet are just rocks and grasses. But if I am mindful, curious, and observant enough to stoop down and pick up one stone because it has an unusual shape, then it becomes magic, not just for me but for everyone around me. If I go one step further and grind up some pigments to make red ochre dye, paint the stone lovingly, and set it on the mantle as a reminder of this walk, then the magic has become a prayer for the survival of my tribe.

And I think my promise to Moolynaut goes one step further. It is a step that I started thirty-five years ago when I joined my dog on that spring day in the Colorado Rockies. At that time, I subconsciously believed that the dog and I were thinking the same thoughts, sharing the same consciousness, exchanging positive energy, but I wasn't ready to come out of the closet. Now I can say it. I believe that magic is reciprocal and interactive and passes back and forth between humans and the world we live in. Yes, I skied with Raven, just as I smelled the earth with my dog.

Bad things happen to good people. Chris died under a mountain of snow. Death is the ultimate fate of every living organism on this planet. But my friends in Siberia taught me that if I open my consciousness, a wild raven will visit me on the day I carry my wife's ashes through a storm to a mountaintop. And that is enough.

I remembered Moolynaut's words to me as we parted after our first visit, now so long ago: "Yes, please come back. It will be good for you."

She was right; it was good for me.

I had a book to write, but first I had to eat the red mushroom one more time.

I must have stood there for a long time, because when I turned toward town snow had collected between the individually coated stems and blades, forming the beginning of the white blanket that would soon tuck this landscape into its winter sleep. Absurdly, I was still wearing my porous light hiking shoes. Someday I hoped to get my act together. Or maybe I wouldn't. Maybe the giant had shaken my box so violently that all the delicate flowered teacups had broken, or maybe I never owned any such teacups in the first place, or maybe they were all in Canada when company was arriving for the tea party in Darby—it didn't matter. Here in Vyvenka, anyway, people drank tea out of sturdy, already-chipped mugs. There was a warm house close by, and my feet had been wet before.

Over the Whale's Back

The temperature plummeted to below zero overnight. Snow continued to fall, but now it was sharply crystalline, not damp and soggy. In the morning, Misha, Lydia, Oleg, Sergei, and I sat around the warm *petchka*, chatting. Moolynaut arrived after lunch with a small satchel of mushrooms. She instructed me to eat half of the largest mushroom and two smaller ones. Ritually Misha, Lydia, Sergei, and I cut the fungi into small cubes and threw a few pieces over our shoulders for Kutcha before we ate our portions. Oleg, who preferred to travel in the Real World, didn't participate.

My dose seemed like a lot to me, but Moolynaut assured me that she had instructed the mushrooms to take me to a peaceful place. I walked outside by myself, along the beach, and then over the Whale's Back, where I stopped to remember the day Angela and I knelt to pick freeze-dried cranberries. Today the delicate morsels were buried beneath the deepening white blanket. I wandered down the hill onto the tundra. The drug began to take effect and I drifted out of my body, as if I were floating above the ground, watching Jon Turk's body walking along. The snow was fluffy and light and the wind, seriously cold by now, continued from the north.

Chris had passed on. Moolynaut's healing powers had passed on. For some reason, my body had survived sixty years and too many close calls to count. It had survived long enough to watch my children grow, grandparents die, mother die, father grow old, grandchildren prepare to explore the world. Most events had occurred in the expected order. A few, like Chris's death, had not.

Still shod in those light hikers, I kicked the fluffy snow. My feet were familiar with snow: new snow, old snow, glaciers, tundra. Light hikers, ski boots, crampons, climbing shoes. My feet kicked the fluffy snow and my eyes watched the crystals poof into the wind. My right cheek warned that it was feeling the first twinge of frostbite and my feet complained that they were cold in these stupid shoes. I told my body to shut up and stop whining. Chris cuddled against me and our naked bodies intertwined beneath a fluffy down comforter. My feet grumbled that they got a raw deal in life, becoming attached to such a forgetful, disorganized, inconsiderate brain, and I told them to stop making themselves miserable, trying to change the unchangeable. Finally, realizing that there was no higher order to complain to, my feet turned uphill, back toward the top of the Whale's Back, carrying my body into the full force of the storm. My feet, my body, and I stopped by a bush, encapsulated in stellar snow crystals that balanced precariously—edge to edge, point to point—on tiny twigs. New flakes fell and clung to the ones that had already landed, holding on to one another like acrobats in a circus. Watching the snow was so much more fun than running blindly through the labyrinth. I didn't need to waste my time and energy trying to ask unanswerable questions or seeking some external bright light at the end of an imaginary tunnel. All the mystery and joy I needed was right here, wrapped in silence, in these snowflakes on this ridgetop.

My mouth blew a warm puff that lifted fallen snow off a branch, to swirl in the wind. My mind watched my body breathe; it watched the breath freeze into a tiny cloud; it watched the snow crystals scurry about when the breath got too close. Breathing wasn't something I was doing; it was something I was witnessing.

I was on my own. Without my body. Without Moolynaut or Chris. Without the wondrous and often chaotic past. Without the uncertain future. I leaned close to a branch and blew snow into the air again until it caught a vortex of wind and lifted into the void—like Chris's ashes. My body sucked in another lungful of air, and in the space between inhaling and exhaling there was only the snow and the tundra, space without form.

Suddenly I was lonely all by myself, so I slipped back into my body, accepting the battered, aging shell—cold feet, frostbitten cheeks, and all. We've had a good partnership over the past sixty years. Sometimes when my body gets tired, I encourage it to keep going until it takes me to landscapes that bring us both joy. At other times, when I'm sad or depressed, my body cheers me up by taking us skiing. We're a team, like Alexei and his deer.

I turned to face my old friend the ocean, far enough away so the waves seemed gentle, the surf inaudible, and the whitecaps like brushstrokes on a broad, green-black palette. Joy, tragedy, free will, and coincidence had all intertwined inexorably to bring me to this moment, so that I could stand in this storm. Together now, my body and I felt the wind and watched the pastel light of another evening slowly fade into darkness.

The immense expanse of tundra, stretching from the Ural Mountains to the Pacific Ocean, Vladivostok to the East Siberian Sea, was reduced to a tiny diorama consisting of me, my rapidly disappearing footprints, a few willows that oscillated in the wind, like Kutcha's wing beats—and snow. Snow that would soon blanket the land, enabling the traveler to glide across the great bogs and muskegs of the Far North. Snow that—back home—would wash into my face on a blue-sky day of powder skiing. Snow that killed.

If I remained here too long, I would freeze to death, but if I lingered just a few more moments, the snow would gently help me accept and soften the edges of my grief—present but just out of focus—shrouded in swirls of white. I stared into the tundra—the void—life without Chris. The painfully cold wind was blowing through me as if I were a skeleton, cleansing, cathartic, wonderful—so empty that it could only be a grand beginning.

Moolynaut had repeatedly summoned me to this razor-thin, storm-battered sand spit lying beneath the leviathan who was so graciously letting the people live out their lives for a while before rising from his restful sleep. She summoned me so I could be healed or so I could heal myself, so I could believe—to continue living.

The wind drove the snowflakes into my face, inflicting pain before melting into benign droplets, innocently denying now that they could ever be dangerous, just as the snow that buried Chris had eventually melted and run peacefully into its mother, the sea.

As the wind engulfed and embraced me, it gently ushered me into the void until I finally stepped over the portal into the Other World, which was now indistinguishable from the Real World, except for a feeling of consciousness without baggage, a place of infinite peace where I was always welcome, if I would only make the effort to complete the journey.

I realized now that I had become so confused and frightened three years ago when I ate the *mukhomor* and tried to step across the portal because the drug could never take me to a place where I wasn't ready to go. But that was OK; there is no shame in starting a journey, failing, and returning to complete it later. The confusion came when I panicked because I couldn't find my way back. Silly me. There is no going back. At any moment, I could cross the portal into the Other World—that void of endless contentment and knowledge—or I could fail to cross, but I could never journey backward, correct my mistakes, downshift, and try the same journey a second time.

Many mistakes lay behind and ahead of me, but now I was in this storm, listening to my body as it inhaled and exhaled its puny puffs of air, within the infinite power of that Siberian wind, certain that I would lose my way again, many times—eagerly anticipating the journey ahead.

I started down the hill but then stopped and turned into the wind one more time. Cold was a familiar acquaintance, and I welcomed it, because, like grief, it had the power to strip me of all pretense and identity, so Bear and Raven might find the space to visit. I held my arms out to embrace this blizzard, which I had come so far to feel. Then my feet told me it was time to walk down the hill, to return to My World in North America, to resume my life. At least I was a good traveler in the Real World, and I could find my way home. I turned back toward Goshe's kitchen as the sun dipped below the storm black sea.

Going Home

The next morning, the storm had passed, the air was eerily still, and the ocean was calm again. But cold had moved in, put its feet up on the table, lit a cigar, cracked a beer, and announced that it was here to stay for a while. The river was covered with a thin film of ice. I expressed concern that soon the ice would be too thick to smash through in a boat and too thin to walk across and thus we would be unable to cross and catch our flight home. Sergei waved his hand in the air, dismissing my worries wordlessly, as if they were too trivial to discuss.

Goshe drove down with the old orange bulldozer; the men hooked a chain to the bow of Oleg's speedboat and dragged it across the sand toward salt water, which wouldn't freeze until even deeper cold gripped this land.

Moolynaut assured us that she had stored enough food for the winter, but just to be sure Misha and I went to the store and bought rice, flour, sugar, and tea, as well as honey, chocolate, and a few precious jars of juice from fruit trees far away on the Caspian Sea.

Moolynaut clapped her hands in joy. She hobbled about, put another chunk of coal in the *petchka*, and boiled water for tea.

"Would you like me to tell you a story about horses?" she asked.

I nodded and she began.

"When I was very little, we didn't have any horses. Then the Americans came in their ships and brought white horses from America. I told you about this before."

I nodded.

"Beautiful horses. They were all white except for their black eyes. These horses were very smart and followed the people around without a lead rope. One day, when I was nine or ten, the horses were on the tundra, eating grass. All the people in our tribe were working with the reindeer and I was alone with the horses. Quietly, I climbed onto the broad back of the largest horse. The horse lifted its head and started to run. I was frightened and held on to the hair on the back of its neck. You know about this hair on a horse's neck?"

I nodded again.

"I held on tight and we ran across the tundra."

Moolynaut closed her eyes and rocked back and forth. She slapped her legs and started laughing until tears rolled out of the corners of her eyes and moistened the deep wrinkles that creased her cheeks.

She looked up and wiped her face with the back of her hand. "I am tired now. I must sleep."

Misha and I bid good-bye and walked into the autumn afternoon, certain that we would never see Moolynaut again.

The following day, October 23d, the dull red sun still cast little warmth across the whitened landscape. Misha and I bid Lydia and Goshe good-bye and walked down to the speedboat, now situated where the salt water mingled with the fresh. Oleg, with faithful Sergei beside him, drove Misha and me out of the lagoon, across the sandbar, and into a placid ocean. We skipped across this embracing mother-god that seemed so incapable of the chaos it had exhibited so many times in the past. After a few miles, Oleg turned toward shore and beached in the shelter of a large rock. We splashed to dry ground, getting our feet totally soaked once again. The two hunters smiled briefly, waved perfunctorily as if we would see each other tomorrow, and motored back toward town.

To the east, a mellow, gray Pacific Ocean swell broke against the sand, while inland, the snowy tundra was already churned into frozen, wind-driven *strastugi*. We walked north for a few hours until we reached the first stream. Then my body and I, as a team, stripped half-naked and forded the frigid water, breaking a path through the ice with a stick.

As Misha and I continued toward the airport, the cold Siberian wind that chilled my body also blew my grief inward, where it mingled with thoughts of Moolynaut's happy childhood on the tundra, the generation-long oppression of the Soviets, and her impending passage.

For me, the past five years had been tumultuous enough, great joy mixed with the deepest pain. Seeking my way, I had oscillated between powerful entries into the Spirit World and equally powerful—even tragic—experiences in the Real World. In the beginning, I had viewed these two worlds as sepa-rate, perhaps somewhat in conflict. But now my quest, like that of migrating deer, was moving in a circle. Northern people have taught me that the empty, treeless tundra is not a place of desolation but a bridge between real-ity and dreams. A bridge of belief that connects me to myself, grief to accep-tance.

Maybe I will make a physical mistake someday, as Chris had, and forget to listen when the snow speaks to me through a gentle warning *woomph*. I hope not. I pray that I have learned to concentrate on every snowflake that is falling every instant.

Yet my worst fear is that I will make a different kind of mistake and for-get to stand naked, on one leg, perched on a branch, with my good friend Kutcha the Raven. To be mindful, curious, and observant. Present. To be-lieve in the magic of everyday events. Maybe I will forget that Moolynaut remained happy, powerful, and peaceful through a century of Siberian winters and unimaginable political repression by believing in a great oneness of all things. But if I don't forget, I felt assured that I could find contentment in my wayward, bumbling, mistake-prone passage through life, accompanied by deep wilderness, Moolynaut's equanimity, Kutcha's unsolvable mysteries, and Chris's unconditional love.

Darby, Montana: June 2008

Eight years passed between the first time I met Moolynaut and the day I finally finished this manuscript. When I printed the last page, after uncounted edits, I walked out of my office into a wet, rainy day in early June. The bunny who lives under the kayak shed was wearing her brown summer fur, with white feet, the last remnant of her winter coat. I walked up the hill, past the aromatic serviceberry blossoms, and stopped briefly at the woodshed. The last time I cut wood, I hit a nail with my chain saw, and now it was badly in need of sharpening.

Marion and I hadn't managed to forge a life together. I lived alone for a while and then fell in love with Nina, who had been my neighbor and friend for fifteen years. Now we had been living together for almost two years, and she was an immense help and inspiration during the long, exciting, painful process of writing. Through our own brand of joy and chaos, we had become best friends, ski buddies, partners, and lovers.

When I walked in the door, Nina was baking a rhubarb pie and cooking vegetable soup for lunch. A cozy fire crackled in the woodstove. I ate a snack and then walked out to the creek, to sit in the same place where my granddaughter, Cleo, had visited with me at Chris's memorial. The peak of the spring runoff had passed, but the creek was still swollen, water bouncing over rocks and tossing droplets of white foam into the dense forest. An image came to me, as a physical memory wrapped in a dream. Moolynaut was softly, gently, holding rabbit fur against my scar. Then she rubbed me with a piece of oily seal fat. Her eyes stared intently at her hands, even as she seemed far away. Moolynaut's hand quivered from deep emotion, the energy of giving, as she rested it on my pelvis, the center of my balance, my focal point.

Now, as I look back, the physical healing seems unreal, like a metaphor, secondary to the belief she asked of me.

Moolynaut taught me to live inside a myth—not another person's myth, or that of someone who lived thousands of years ago—but my own personal tapestry of Real World and Dream World, connected by magic that hovered on black outstretched wings. My first entry into myth, forty years ago, during that spring day with my dog, gave me the power and resolve to change my life. Barriers broke down and over the decades, new input rushed in, some wonderful and some scary. At one moment, a mysterious healing energy vaulted over the lowered barrier and mended my pelvis, and that changed my life again, guiding me toward new beginnings.

I sat there for a long time and then decided to go back into the house for lunch. But there was one more thought that hadn't surfaced before, that suddenly became poignant. Moolynaut had loved me, a stranger, with a love so powerful that it brought her to the portal of the Other World. I've never known anyone else who has focused and channeled that much love.

I wasn't born in a skin tent and I'll never be able to journey, heal, or believe as Moolynaut did. But I try, guided by the human potential that I have been fortunate enough to witness and by the tundra that taught me to concentrate on the snow beneath my skis and the next step before me.

Epilogue

In December 2008, as this manuscript was moving into production, I e-mailed Misha to ask about news from Vyvenka and got the following response:

> *Large thanks for the message. I am very glad to receive it and to know that at you all very well. It is really good that you continue to do that to you it is pleasant. And health allows to do it. I called Lydia and she has said that the grandmother now feels well enough for the age. Recently has sewed a cap for Oleg. Speaks that her still early to leave this world while she has not passed all knowledge to Lydia. Fishing this year was not so good. Have caught approximately 40 % from a limit. And this year the fish could not be frozen, to sale it is more expensive. Therefore to fish distributed to the people and salted. Prepared in the basic caviar. But they have enough for family of it. They hope that the next year will be more fish and the refrigerator in Vyvenka will work. They asked to pass you hi and best regards.*

Notes

STONE AGE HUNTERS IN THE ARCTIC

1. http://archaeology.about.com/od/dterms/g/diring.htm.
2. Virginia Morell, "Did Early Humans Reach Siberia 500,000 Years Ago?" *Science* 263 (February 4, 1994): 611.
3. "Recent Finds in Archaeology," *Athena Review* 4(4) (2007): 4.
4. Pavel Pavlov et al., "A Human Presence in the European Arctic Nearly 40,000 Years Ago," *Nature* 413 (September 6, 2001): 64.
5. V. V. Pitulko et al., "The Yana RHS Site: Humans in the Arctic Before the Last Glacial Maximum," *Science* 303 (January 2, 2004): 52.
6. Igor Krupnik, *Arctic Adaptations: Native Whalers and Reindeer Herders of Northern Eurasia* (Hanover, NH: University Press of New England, 1993), pp. 107–108.
7. Stephen P. Krasheninnikov, *The History of Kamtschatka* (Richmond Publishing Company, Surrey, UK: 1973), originally published in Russian in 1755.
8. Ibid., pp. 49 and 101.

NIKOLAI

1. Leonard Shlain, *The Alphabet Versus the Goddess* (New York, Penguin/Compass, 1998), p. 2.
2. Ibid., p. 44.
3. Jill Bolte Taylor, *My Stroke of Insight* (New York, Viking/Penguin, 2008).

MUKHOMOR

1. http://botit.botany.wisc.edu/toms_fungi/dec99.html.

BACK IN THE MONTANA FOREST

1. Jim Harrison, *Returning to Earth* (New York: Grove Press, 2006).
2. Marni Jackson, *Pain: The Fifth Vital Sign* (Toronto: Random House Canada, 2002).

3. http://www.fda.gov/fdac/features/2000/100_heal.html.

4. Joseph Campbell, *The Hero with a Thousand Faces* (Princeton, NJ: Princeton University Press, 1949), p. 59.

RAVEN

1. Edwin Hall, Jr., *The Eskimo Storyteller: Folktales from Noatak, Alaska* (Fairbanks: University of Alaska Press, 1998), p. 94.

2. http://www.indigenouspeople.net/ipl_final.html.

3. Bernd Heinrich and Thomas Bugnyar. "Just How Smart Are Ravens?" *Scientific American* (April 2007): 64.

4. Candace Savage, *Crows: Encounters with the Wise Guys* (Vancouver: Greystone Books, 2005), pp. 30–31.

5. Heinrich and Bugnyar, "Just How Smart Are Ravens?" p. 71.

FOURTH JOURNEY TO VYVENKA

1. Jeremy Narby and Francis Huxley, *Shamans Through Time: 500 Years on the Path to Knowledge* (New York: Tarcher/Penguin, 2001), pp. 81–82.